KV-246-940

ACKNOWLEDGEMENTS

This volume contains a collection of papers dedicated to the field of second language acquisition and development. As will be seen, the nine contributions--by Robin Sabino (Auburn University), Terence Odlin (The Ohio State University), Frank Byrne (Shawnee State University), Elsa Lattey (University of Tübingen), Ulrich Steinmüller (Technical University of Berlin), Yoshiko Matsumato (Stanford University), Hanna Pishwa (Technical University of Berlin), Carol A. Blackshire-Belay (Temple University), and Joe Salmons (Purdue University)--represent a great multitude and variety of facts and findings, analyses and assertions with regard to the ever-growing and demanding field of second language acquisition and development. The title of this volume proved highly stimulating to the contributors asked to participate in this book project. Furthermore, the interest and need to investigate pertinent issues in second language acquisition and development is indeed a pressing and urgent one, as is evident by many of the provocative questions addressed and findings provided in this volume.

Before concluding, I would like to take this opportunity to thank those who have assisted in the preparation of this manuscript. To begin, I would like to express my appreciation to the staff at The Ohio State University Humanities Computer Center for assisting me with the final preparation of this volume. I would also like to thank colleagues and students in the Department of Germanic Languages and Literatures and the Department of Linguistics at the University of Pennsylvania from the onset of this project for providing supportive environments in which to work, and which helped to make this project possible.

But as much as any of these individuals, I would like to extend my many thanks to the contributors to this volume for their patience and cooperation, and for the range and insight of their contributions to the very fertile field of second language acquisition and development. Without their valuable contributions to this field of scientific inquiry, this volume would have gotten nowhere.

Finally, I would like to gratefully acknowledge the National Research Council and the Ford Foundation in providing the financial assistance necessary for the final preparation of this book.

Carol A. Blackshire-Belay

TABLE OF CONTENTS

CURRENT ISSUES IN SECOND LANGUAGE ACQUISITION AND DEVELOPMENT: AN INTRODUCTION

Carol A. Blackshire-Belay
Temple University

This book stems from the desire to provide students, scientists and researchers with a reference book that discusses current issues in the field of language and linguistics that rarely coalesce: aspect and transferability, spontaneity and universal simplification, second language acquisition research, variability in language contact and bilingualism, and elements of the interlanguage phenomenon. The main objective of the current work is to focus on language studies that are current and provocative. Thus, experts have been asked to deal with the various issues in these studies in order to provide a fuller understanding and appreciation of linguistic and language phenomena.

The contributors of this volume present data and information, both new and novel. They discuss previously unpublished ideas as well as hotly debate several theories and concepts in the field. A further concern was to balance the contents of the volume between theoretical and practical considerations wherever possible. As editor of this volume I have endeavored to create an effective forum for the most creative and traditional elements of language studies. However, the idea of current issues in second language acquisition and development dictated a certain sensitivity to issues of the interlanguage phenomenon and language acquisition, both areas of considerable discussion in the literature. All the papers were freshly solicited and are original contributions, and all of them balance theory with practice.

Section One entitled <u>Language Development and Transfer</u> consists of three papers. The second chapter, Sabino's "Native Language Transfer and Universal Simplification," focuses on the fact that researchers in second language acquisition (SLA) have discovered that both native language transfer and linguistic universals play roles in the acquisition of phonotactic structure; however, consensus has not been reached on the relative contribution of these factors to the acquisition process. In the discussion at hand the author is concerned with a dutch creole often referred to by many as "Negerhollands," a linguistic term that was widely used in the 19th century. Now this creole is nearly distinct. Recent research on phonotactic variability in the lexicon of this creole supports the view that native language transfer is the dominant process influencing interlanguage syllable structure. These data also show that both the frequency and permissibility of particular L1 structures play roles in shaping interlanguage phonotactics. This chapter also emphasizes the importance of considering both the extent to which the variation associated with interlanguage phonotactics is phonologically conditioned and the nature of the linguistic target concerned.

The third chapter, Odlin's "Aspect and Transferability (Or What Gets Lost in the Translation--and Why?)," thoroughly investigates the issues surrounding the distinction between the process of second language acquisition and the product that arises from that process. The claim from Odlin that the process of transfer, or rather "cross-linguistic influence" received more interest from researchers prior to the interest of the product/process distinction was brought into the discussion. Providing additional insights about the nature of the transfer process creates an impressive challenge to second language researchers. In reference to Weinreich's claim Odlin too emphasizes that "interlingual identification" occurs any time an individual judges structures in two languages to be identical or at least similar. The interlingual identification is the psychological basis not only for transfer, but for translation as well.

In chapter four, Byrne's "Creole Verb Serialization: Transfer or Spontaneity?," offers us an interesting and fruitful discussion about the direct linkage of L1 and L2 research to theoretical debates within pidginization and creolization literature. The major focus of this chapter concerns the roles of transfer and universal tendencies in both processes. With a focus on the Atlantic creole Saramaccan, Byrne discusses the viability of spontaneous generation of serial verb constructions. Based on the evidence of this study, Bryne brilliantly demonstrates that the origin of serialization in creole languages can be explained by spontaneity in the process of serialization. Syntactic, comparative, theoretical, and demographic evidence strongly support this claim.

Section Two under the heading Learner Variables in Second Language Acquisition contains three additional papers. The fifth chapter, Lattey's "Contexts for Second Language Acquisition," explores the many contexts of second language acquisition that must be considered in scientific inquiries. In a given situation many factors must be taken into consideration: linguistic, social, political, psychological, etc. Several theories of the nature of second language acquisition contexts have been propounded. Indeed, comparisons are frequently made with the way children learn their first language, as a means of providing hypotheses to guide second language acquisition research. There is as yet no single theory that can account for the diversity of second language acquisition behavior, and that is able to explain why some learners succeed in their task, whereas others fail. Lattey does an excellent job in sorting through the complexity of the task facing researchers in second language acquisition research today.

In the sixth chapter, Steinmüller's "Language Acquisition, Biography and Bilingualism," deals with the interrelationship of language acquisition, biography, and bilingualism among Turkish children in German schools. The author devotes much attention to demonstrating to the reader how the awareness process of one's own language is an essential component in achieving successful adaptation to the norms, values and systems of his/her new environment. Steinmüller takes the position that biographical aspects of language learners, such as:

1. early life-history
2. migration-history of the family
3. general schooling and a subject's progress at school
4. present situation

cannot be the only guidelines for understanding the process of second language acquisition. This claim, supported by a number of researchers, is not supported by the evidence provided in this study. This author emphasizes that factors from the different areas within the field of psychology, as well as the motivation of the person to learn the language are necessary in order to fully grasp the language learning process. These factors must also be included in any second language acquisition research. Steinmüller concludes this chapter by emphasizing the relevancy to formulate individual language acquisition biographies in order to demonstrate structures, processes, and possible correlations.

The seventh chapter, Matsumoto's "Acquisition of Japanese by American Businessmen in Tokyo: How much and why?" is most timely and appropriate with the growing interest of the United States in the economic growth and wealth of Japan. This chapter discusses the acquisition of Japanese among American businessmen in Tokyo. It examines not only the acquisition of Japanese, but also it questions the extent to which the American businessmen can be considered bilingual. As a result of questionnaire techniques by the author, evidence from this study is compared with other bilingual groups as described by Nida (1971). The author suggests that two factors must be seriously taken into consideration:

1. The attitude of Americans toward language acquisition in Japan.
2. The attitudes of native Japanese in the surrounding communities.

Section Three contains three papers as well under the heading Issues in Interlanguage Development. In the eight chapter, Pishwa's "Abrupt Restructuring Versus Gradual Acquisition," compares abrupt restructuring with gradual acquisition of the German SUBJECT-VERB AGREEMENT RULE with the objective of gaining knowledge about individual learners, the character of interlanguage, and the choice of a methodology. The data were derived from a longitudinal study of eight occasions over a period of eighteen months with fifteen Swedish school children acquiring German at the German School in Stockholm; their ages varied from seven to twelve years. The results revealed no abrupt "restructurer"; instead, the "incorrect" observable output of the selected speakers was highly systematic, as in gradual learning, where acquisition expands from one context to another. The development was dependent on and, to an amazing degree, governed by the complexity of the structures according to markedness principles. A requirement of any satisfactory method is that it meets dynamic needs--change and variability.

The eighth chapter, Blackshire-Belay's "Variability in Grammatical Analysis: On Recognizing Verbal Markers in Foreign Workers' German," focuses on selected social and linguistic aspects of the foreign worker situation in the New Germany. Blackshire-Belay expands on the characteristics of the verbal markers in Foreign Workers' German by a thorough investigation of the regular verbs with particular emphasis on the weak and strong verbs occurrences. The analysis concentrates on the person, number and tense markers in the German of sixteen speakers of different first languages.

The tenth chapter, Salmon's "Sketch of an Interlanguage Rule System: Advanced Nonnative German Gender Assignment," examines gender assignment rules in German, a topic that has received limited attention in the literature. The comparative analysis is based on evidence from a group of native speakers of German and a group of advanced nonnative speakers of German who had received a considerable amount of formal instruction in the language. Salmons clearly demonstrates that the advanced nonnative speakers use their cognitive abilities in a creative way to work out hypotheses about gender assignment in German, and these processes differ in many and varied ways from that of native speakers. In other words, the nonnative speakers construct rules, try to work them out, and alter them if these rules are proven to be inadequate. The author also pinpoints how gender assignment in the language learning process undergoes a series of transitional stages as the learners acquire more knowledge of the L2. In other words, at each stage the nonnative speakers are in control of a language system that is equivalent to neither the L1 nor the L2--an interlanguage as suggested by Selinker (1972).

It is the sincere hope of the contributors in this volume that the reader finds the contents of this volume useful as an overview of current theory and application in a variety of areas within the field of linguistics. While this work has not attempted to cover every issue in second language acquisition research and development, it has been our purpose to provide the most up-to-date discussion of the most relevant issues facing the field.

SECTION ONE:
LANGUAGE DEVELOPMENT AND TRANSFER

FIRST LANGUAGE TRANSFER AND UNIVERSAL PROCESSES
IN THE ACQUISITION OF PHONOTACTIC STRUCTURE[1]

Robin Sabino
Auburn University

1.0. INTRODUCTION

A major theme in both second language acquisition (SLA) research and research on creole languages has been the roles played by universal processes and native language transfer, as it is called in the former field, or substrate influence, as it is called in the latter.[2] In fact, this identity of research interests has been so clearly perceived that the index of a publication devoted to exploring the relationship between pidginization, creolization, and SLA cross references substrate influence as language transfer (R. Anderson 1983:331). Given this identity of research interests, it is to be expected that findings in one area will inform research in the other. A case in point is research on the acquisition of phonotactic (i.e. syllable) structure. Given findings in SLA, a recent investigation of the phonotactic variability in Negerhollands hypothesizes that this variation can be traced to native language transfer as well as to universal processes. The Negerhollands data provide support for this hypothesis. However, several details of the Negerhollands case are inconsistent with some assumptions and conclusions of the SLA studies. This paper discusses these and points out the opportunities for future research which they suggest.

2.0. REVIEW OF PREVIOUS RESEARCH

A recent publication by Ioup and Weinberger (1987) has brought together papers on the acquisition of L_2 phonology.[3] Three of these, Tarone (1980, reprinted 1987), Sato (1984, reprinted 1987), and Anderson (1987), address the acquisition of syllable structure. Tarone examines syllable errors for six non-native speakers of English: two speakers of Cantonese, two speakers of Portuguese, and two speakers of Korean. The subjects in this study 'described orally a sequence of pictures, narrating a story in the process' (1987:238). Tarone's research addresses a number of issues; her two findings vis a vis the importance of universal processes and native language transfer in the acquisition of phonotactic structure are given below. Based on a corpus of 115 syllable errors, Tarone (1987:243) reports that:

(1)   the dominant process influencing the syllable structure of the interlanguage phonology appeared to be native language transfer;

(2)   a preference for the open (CV) syllable seemed to operate as a process independent of native language transfer in influencing the syllable

structure of the interlanguage phonology[4]

Sato (1987) takes into consideration Tarone's observation that a preference for the open (consonant vowel) syllable seemed to operate independently of native language transfer. By examining the acquisition of English consonant clusters in the spontaneous speech of two native speakers of Vietnamese, Sato attempts to measure the strength of native language transfer relative to a universal preference for open syllables. Since, according to Sato, the predominant syllable type in Vietnamese is CVC, she hypothesizes that due to native language transfer, the two subjects will show a preference for closed syllables. Sato's findings are consistent with her hypothesis. She reports that both subjects show a preference for cluster simplification (i.e. deleting one of the consonants in a cluster) over deletion of the entire cluster. Like Tarone, Sato's findings indicate that although both linguistic universals and native language transfer influence the acquisition of phonotactic structure, the influence of native language transfer is the stronger of the two.

In her discussion, Sato also addresses research by Greenberg in which Greenberg argues that the structure of the native language determines whether syllable-initial (SI) or syllable-final (SF) consonant clusters are permitted in the interlanguage. Greenberg examined the interlanguage of nine native speakers: three speakers of Turkish, which allows sentence initial (SI) clusters only in borrowed words, three speakers of Greek, which allows SI but not SF clusters, and three speakers of Japanese, which allows neither SI nor SF consonant clusters. Sato reports that Greenberg's subjects performed two tasks: a picture description and a naming task involving flashcards. Greenberg found that the Turkish subjects produced the highest error rates for SI clusters while the Greek and Japanese speakers produced the highest error rates for SF clusters. Greenberg interprets these results as evidence that native language transfer occurs in terms of 'preferred cluster position' (Sato 1987:250).

Given Greenberg's findings and the admissibility of Cw SI clusters in Vietnamese, Sato predicts that her subjects will produce target-like complex onsets at a higher frequency than they will produce target-like complex codas. Her prediction is confirmed; Sato reports that both subjects had less difficulty with complex onsets than with complex codas. Thus, she concludes that her findings are consistent with Greenberg's observation that native language transfer affects the position of consonant clusters within the syllable.

Anderson (1987) also investigates the acquisition of English consonant clusters. Twenty of Anderson's subjects were native speakers of Colloquial Egyptian Arabic (CEA) which permits (C)VC(C) syllables. The remaining 20 subjects were native speakers of two Chinese dialects which permit CV(C) syllables. Ten of these subjects spoke Mandarin Chinese[5]; the remaining subjects were Amoy/Mandarin Chinese[6] bilinguals. However, in the discussion of her results Anderson combines the Chinese speakers into a single group. Anderson's subjects 'talked about a holiday in his or her native country' (1987: 284). Like Tarone and Sato mentioned above, Anderson finds that both native language transfer and linguistic universals contribute to interlanguage phonotactics.   However, unlike Tarone and Sato, Anderson sees universal factors as stronger than native transfer: based on the observation that neither Chinese nor Arabic permit SI clusters and only Arabic permits SF clusters, Anderson argues that markedness is responsible for the significant difference in the target-like production of complex onsets and codas. (See Table 1.)

Table 1
Percentage Scores and Chi Square values on SI and SF clusters for Arabic and Chinese speakers[7]

	Arabic group % correct	Chinese group % correct	Chi Square
SI	92.6	89.6	.37 ns
SF	82.6	50.2	64.6 ($\alpha < .0001$)

Chi Square   8.38 ($\alpha < .0038$) 45 2 ($\alpha < .00001$)

Table 1, which compares the percent of target-like SI and SF clusters for the Arabic and Chinese subjects, indicates that regardless of L_1, speakers produce SI clusters at the same rate. The table also shows that the Arabic-speaking subjects are significantly more successful at producing final clusters than are the Chinese speakers.   Anderson suggests that the substantial difficulty which the Chinese subjects had with final clusters is due to the marked nature of these clusters relative to initial clusters and to the absence of final clusters in the Chinese dialects investigated. She attributes the greater success of the Arabic subjects to the fact that CEA permits two consonant clusters in word-final position. Additionally, Anderson reports that for the Arabic subjects 'most of the final consonant clusters [which were] simplified (-st, -nt, -zd, -nd) [have] equivalents in CEA, indicating a preference for a more simple syllable, independent of native language transfer' (287). Anderson also reports that despite the fact that CEA permits only SF clusters, CEA speakers produce more target-like SI clusters than they did SF clusters.[8]

In summary, there are opposing claims made by SLA research on the acquisition of phonotactic structure. Tarone reports that while most phonotactic errors can be explained in terms of native language transfer, there were other errors which seem best explained by a universal preference for the CV syllable. Sato's research provides confirmation of Tarone's observation that native language transfer plays a larger role than universal tendencies in some aspects of the acquisition of phonotactic structure.   In contrast, although Anderson's data show that native language transfer was able to modify universal tendencies (i.e. SF clusters were produced significantly more frequently by her Arabic subjects than by her Chinese subjects), she argues that, because Arabic speakers produced target-like onsets more frequently than they produced target-like codas, the 'universal factor overruled the transfer factor' (1987: 290). Let us now turn to the creole case to see if this paradox can be resolved.

3.0. THE NEGERHOLLANDS CASE

During the last quarter of the 17th century a Dutch lexicon creole emerged in the Danish West Indies (now the U.S. Virgin Islands). Once the lingua franca of one of the most important commercial ports in the Caribbean, Negerhollands ceased to exist in September 1987 with the death of the last native speaker.[9] Although there are several views on the origin of the creole, Sabino (1990) presents evidence consistent with the hypothesis that Negerhollands was created on St. Thomas by enslaved L_1 speakers of Kwa languages, especially Eve, Gã, and the Akwamu, Fanti, and Twi dialects of Akan.

The data under discussion here are taken from two corpora. The first is a corpus of narrative texts transcribed in a nearly phonemic notation which was collected in 1923 by the Dutch linguist J. P. B. de Josselin de Jong. The second is a corpus of tape-recorded narratives and casual conversation provided by Mrs. Alice Stevens, the last native speaker of the language, which was collected by the author in the 1980's.[10]

The analysis is based on two important assumptions about phonological variation in creole languages. First, following Alleyne, I assume that creole languages were variable from their inception. As Alleyne writes:

> Socio-cultural factors everywhere determined the degree of
> interference, from one territory to another and also within any
> single territory. This resulted in linguistic variation and instability
> which is characteristic of any dynamic acculturative process
> (1971:182).

Second, I assume that the systematic phonological variation in the corpus reflects stages of second language acquisition in the Danish West Indies. This assumption finds support in the research of Dickerson who shows that 'sound system learning proceeds by the gradual and systematic modification of rules in a newly developed grammar in the same way that a sound change is a comparatively slow but governed alternation of rules in a first language grammar.' (1976, reprinted 1987:97). In particular, I assume that the linguistic variables which condition the alternations are those which originally conditioned acquisition. With these assumptions in mind, let us now turn to an examination of the Negerhollands data themselves.

Comparing the phonotactics of the African and European languages which were in use in the Danish West Indies at the time Negerhollands was formed, we can gain insight into the nature of the learning task which confronted the originators of this creole.[11] Table 2 shows the difference between Kwa and Germanic syllable structure.[12] This table also clearly shows the degree to which the creole has retained the syllable structure of the substrate languages.

Table 2
Words which conform to CV syllable structure[13]

	Language	% CV
	Dutch	6
Germanic	English	8
	Danish	15
	Gã	72
Kwa[14]	Eve	78
	Akwamu	44
	Fanti	50
	Negerhollands	77

3.1. Onset and Coda Complexity
Although Negerhollands is like its substrate languages (i.e. Eve, Gã, and the Akan dialects) in that its speakers show a decided preference for CV syllable structure, the situation is more complex than the table suggests. As Stolz (1986:101) indicates, while there is phonotactic adjustment in the creole towards the CV syllable, Negerhollands also preserves etymological consonants and consonant clusters. According to Stolz's figures, single consonants are preserved more frequently than CC clusters which are in turn preserved more frequently than CCC clusters. Moreover, Stolz reports a consistent increase in the modification of syllable structure from syllable onsets to syllable codas. (See Table 3.)

Table 3
Preserved etymological consonants according to Stolz 1986

	Onsets	Codas
C	95%	62%
CC	92%	22%
CCC	80%	10%

3.2. The Relative Markedness of Onsets and Codas
The differences between the retention of etymological consonants in onsets and codas are substantial.[15] Let us consider the phonotactic structure of the Kwa languages to determine if this can be attributed to native language transfer. Although as Table 2 shows, CV is the predominant syllable type in the Kwa languages listed above, other syllables types are permissible.

There are some differences among the three Kwa languages in terms of permissible onsets and codas; however, there is sufficient homogeneity for this aspect of their phonologies to warrant a single table. Table 4 is based on the dictionary entries found in Christaller (1875) for Akan, Zimmerman (1858) for Gã, and Westerman (1923) for Eve.[16] An entity is included in the table if it is permitted by at least one of these languages. Following Sprauve (1974), row (0) lists single segments which appear in word initial position. Row (1) shows segments which can precede /l/ in an initial consonant cluster, etc. Row (16) shows permissible codas. Examination of the table indicates that these languages permit a large number of complex onsets. In contrast, the Kwa languages permit far fewer codas than do either the Germanic languages or Negerhollands.

Table 4
Permissible syllable onsets and codas in the Kwa languages
Onsets

/b' - /mfr/

	b	d	ɖ	dw	dz	f	fw	ƒ	g	ɡb	r	h	hw	ɪ	k	kp	l	m	mf	coda
(0a)	b	d	ɖ	dw	dz	f		ƒ	g	ɡb	r	h		ɪ	k	kp	l			
(1a)	b					f	fw	ƒ	g	ɡb	r	h	hw	ɪ	k	kp		m		+l
(2a)	b	d			dz	f			g	ɡb		h		ɪ	k	kp		m	mf	+r
(3a)	b								g			h		ɪ	k			m		+w
(4a)		d							g			h			k					+y
(5a)																		m		+gb
(6b)																		m		+p
(7a)		d																m		+f
(8a)		d																		+š
(9a)																				+ŋ
(10a)																		m		+m
(11a)																		m		+b

Onsets Continued

/n/ - /z/

	mp	n	ns	ñ	ŋ	ŋk	ŋŋ	p	r	s	t	ty	ts	w	wv	vv	y	ỹ	z	
(0b)	mp	n		ñ	ŋ			p	r	s	t	ty	ts	w	wv	vv	y	ỹ	z	
(1b)					ŋ	ŋk		p		s	t	ty		w		v	y	ỹ	z	+l
(2b)			ns	ñ	ŋ	ŋk		p		s	t	ty	ts	w			y	ỹ	z	+r
(3b)				ñ	ŋ	ŋf	ŋŋ			s	t	ty				v	y		z	+w
							ŋŋ													+w̃
(4b)		n	nn		ŋ	ŋk				s	t		ts							+y
(5b)		n																		+t
(6b)		n																		+d
(7b)		n																		+ḍ
(8b)		n									t									+š
(9b)											t									+f
(10b)					ŋ															+k
(11b)					ŋ															+g
(12b)					ŋ															+m
(13b)		n																		+n
(14b)					ŋ															+h
(15b)					ŋ															+ŋ

Codas

(16)   m   n   ŋ   r   w

The fact that etymological word-initial single consonants and consonant clusters were preserved in Negerhollands at a higher rate than those in word-final position is readily explained given the data in Table 4. Although the basic syllable type in Akan, Eve, and Gã is CV, all three languages permit complex SI clusters, many of which are identical to complex clusters in Germanic. Thus, for Negerhollands syllable onsets, whether or not a structure was permissible in the substrate languages seems to have been of greater consequence than the predominant syllable type.

3.2.1. Modification of Negerhollands Initial Clusters
While Table 3 shows that SI etymological clusters were preserved in Negerhollands at a very high rate, there is evidence of some insecurity regarding these clusters, and it is possible to trace the source of this insecurity to both linguistic universals and native language transfer. The role of linguistic universals is demonstrated by two rules: the first inserts epenthetic vowels to create an initial CV syllable even where the initial cluster is permissible in the substrate. The second destroys CV syllables by deleting etymological schwas when deletion resulted in SI clusters that were permissible in the substrate languages. The variable rule which inserted epenthetic vowels between the initial clusters created the following alternation: Negerhollands fles, filis 'meat' < Dutch, Zeeuws[17] vleis. Since a SI fl- cluster is permissible in the substrate languages, the creation of Negerhollands filis 'meat' must be attributed to a universal preference for CV syllables.

Although 20th century Negerhollands only provides filis 'meat' as evidence for the operation of this rule, a hypercorrective rule which deleted etymological schwas suggests that this variable rule was once more widely spread. This second rule created invariant forms like Negerhollands blɔf 'promise' < Dutch beloven and Negerhollands glof 'believe' < Dutch geloven. These non-etymological clusters indicate that on the basis of their knowledge that some Negerhollands ##bəl and ##gəl were the result of an interlanguage rule of vowel insertion, Kwa speakers overgeneralized a corrective rule of schwa deletion. There is also evidence that this hypercorrective variable rule of schwa deletion affected other superstrate ##CəC sequences. This is provided by the otherwise inexplicable ##Cw clusters, which, while permissible in the substrate languages, do not exist in the superstrate languages (e.g. Negerhollands bwa 'preserve' < Dutch bewaren and Negerhollands gwɛn 'get used to' < Dutch gewennen 'habituation.' The fact that Kwa speakers encountered some difficulty acquiring superstrate initial clusters in spite of the presence of a large number of complex onsets in their native languages can be explained by appealing to a universal preference for CV syllables.

Now let us turn to consider the effect of language transfer on Negerhollands initial clusters. The first piece of evidence we must consider is the alternation between

Negerhollands sni, šini 'cut' < Dutch snijden, Zeeuws sniejen, snieën. The substrate languages do not permit initial sn- clusters. Thus, in this case, the variable rule of schwa insertion in Negerhollands reflects a native language phonotactic constraint.

We can find additional evidence of native language transfer if we consider a Negerhollands rule of variable consonant deletion. The only initial clusters in which there is deletion of a consonant, albeit variable deletion, are the sC(r) clusters--clusters (i.e., skr, str, sk, sm, sn, st, sp) which we have already seen do not occur in the substrate languages. Table 5 shows the set of words in which an initial /s/ cluster is variably deleted. The etyma and the frequency of deletion are also shown in the table. In the 20th century data, there are 34 words in Negerhollands with invariant initial /s/ clusters and eight words in which the cluster is variably modified.[18] Like the two phonological rules of schwa insertion and deletion, initial s-deletion was a minor phonological rule in 20th century Negerhollands: with the exception of Negerhollands skreu, krew 'scream,' < Dutch schreuwen, there are no words in which large numbers of tokens show initial s-deletion. Additionally, the rate of deletion is quite low (32%) compared to other alternations in the language.[19] Nevertheless, Table 5 shows that, 250 years after the arrival of the first slave ship, a substrate phonotactic constraint was still partially evident in the language of the last speakers of the language.

Table 5
Examples of initial segment deletion

NH	Etyma		Frequency of short/full forms
skrew krew	Du.	schreuwen	43/82
skrAu, krAu	Du	schraven[20]	5/7
skit, kit	Du.	schieten	2/3
stAm, tAm	Du.	stampen, Eng. stamp	1/7
sti, ti	Z.	stieren	4/50
stOm, tOmp	Du.	stompe, Eng. stomp	1/3
stOp, tOp	Du.	stoppen, Eng. stop	2/22
Total			60/186 (32%)

3.2.2. Deletion in Codas

Like the modification of initial sC(r) clusters, the substantial difference in the rate with which etymological consonants and consonant clusters are preserved in Negerhollands codas can be traced to native language transfer. Because there were only eight words affected by s-deletion in initial clusters and the rate of deletion was low, we did not explore phonetic conditioning for this alternation. Deletion in codas, however, is more frequent, both in terms of the number of words affected and in terms of the overall rate of occurrence. Therefore we will consider several factors which might condition these alternations. In the next two sections, we will examine both the deletion of single consonants and the simplification of word-final clusters.

3.2.2.1. Deletion of Word-Final Consonants

Although there are many Negerhollands words with invariant word-final consonants, there are 21 words, represented by 2038 tokens, in which a single, word-final consonant is variably deleted.[21] The rate of deletion for the variable items is 89%, which is considerably higher than the rate of 32% which Stolz reports for the entire corpus. The high rate of deletion in the variable items suggests that the overall deletion of word-final consonants was higher in the 17th century than it was in the 20th century.

In order to determine what factors originally conditioned this alternation, a binomial multivariate analysis called Variable Rule Analysis was used. Designed for linguistic analysis, Variable Rule Analysis makes it possible to measure the contribution of each of two or more independent variables to the overall probability of occurrence for one of the two forms of a dependent variable. Here we wanted to test the hypotheses that deletion of the word-final consonant was conditioned by a combination of linguistic and social factors: (1) Following Phonological Environment (i.e., whether the word was followed by a word beginning with a vowel or consonant or by a pause), (2) Speaker, (3) Lexical Item, and (4) Word Frequency. The level of significance, numbers of tokens, percent of deletion, and the probability associated with of the significant factors is shown in Appendix I.

The analysis indicated that deletion was favored when the word-final, single consonant was followed by a pause or by a consonant but that the consonant was retained when it was followed by a vowel.[22] There were two phonological strategies for eliminating word-final consonants: deletion (e.g. antut mi --> antu mi 'answer me') and resyllabification (e.g. antut an --> antu tan 'answer her'). Thus, while syllable codas were permissible in Negerhollands, we see that for the variable forms deletion was favored over resyllabification as a strategy for eliminating word-final consonants. The first factor group, therefore, reveals that the preference of Negerhollands speakers for CV structure extended beyond the word. The second group of factors indicates that speakers deleted single, word-final consonants at statistically significant different rates; however, the unfortunate absence of social information on the speakers makes it impossible to interpret the meaning of this finding. However, a cross-tabulation of the factor groups 'lexical item' and 'speaker' indicated that for cells with more than five tokens, different speakers tended to treat words in an identical fashion, thus ruling out idiosyncratic behavior, which might be due to language death, among the last speakers of the language. The third factor group, Lexical Item, was included in order, as just mentioned, to determine if all speakers treated all words in a similar fashion and to reveal any word internal constraints on deletion. The cross tabulation also indicated that the probabilities associated with the individual words were unsystematic with regard to the nature of the final segment. Thus, although it was possible to combine a number of factors in this group, this was not attempted as it could not be done on other than an ad hoc basis. The significance of this factor group indicates that the alternation has become partially lexicalized.[23] The fourth factor group, Word Frequency, did not significantly contribute to the alternation. Thus, word frequency had no effect on whether or no a word-final consonant was deleted.

3.2.2.2. Deletion in Final Consonant Clusters

Speakers also used deletion as a strategy to variably simplify word-final consonant clusters. The 13 words which were subject to variable deletion are listed below in Table 6.

Table 6
Negerhollands words in which word-final consonant clusters are variably simplified

Negerhollands word	English Gloss
wɔrt, wɔr	'word'
hart, had	'hard'
bint, bin	'tie'
lant, lan	'land'
rɔnt, rɔn	'round
hɔnt, hɔn	'dog'
mant, man	'month'
jump, jum	'jump'
plats, plas	'place'
akt, ak	'eight'
stɔmp, tɔm	'stump'
diŋg, diŋ	'think'
driŋg, driŋ	'drink'

In contrast to the words discussed in section 3.2.2.1, what is most striking about the simplification of Negerhollands word-final clusters is that many of these words behave as they do in Dutch. Let us begin with Negerhollands wɔrd 'word' and hart 'hard'. Weijnen (1952) indicates that in the Hollands dialect of Dutch there was variable assimilation in -rd clusters so that Dutch /rd/ → [r(r)]. Thus, Negerhollands wɔr and wɔrd, would have been acquired from Hollands speakers while the word-final [t] of Negerhollands wɔrt and hart could have been devoiced in either Dutch or in Negerhollands. Similarly, Weijnen (1952) reports that -nd clusters in Dutch were variably simplified to [n] and that -ts clusters were simplified to [s]. These observations allow us to account for Negerhollands bin, bint < Dutch bin(d)en[24] 'bind' ; Negerhollands lan, lant < Dutch lan(d) 'land',

Negerhollands rɔn, rɔnt < Dutch ron(d) 'round', Negerhollands hɔn, hɔnt < Dutch hon(d) 'dog', Negerhollands man, mant < Dutch maan(d) 'month', and Negerhollands plas, plats < Dutch pla(t)s 'place'. The alternation of Negerhollands ak, akt < Dutch acht 'eight' is accounted for by a rule in 17th century Dutch which deleted word-final [t]'s after non-sonorants (Den Besten 1987).

This leaves us with Negerhollands had 'hard', and the bilabial and velar-nasal-stop clusters in stɔmp, tɔm 'stomp; dɪŋg, dɪŋ 'think'; and drɪŋg, drɪŋ 'drink'. Regarding Negerhollands had, it is useful to point out that all of de Jong's consultants and Mrs. Stevens were Negerhollands/Virgin Islands English Creole bilinguals. Since Virgin Islands English Creole is r-less in post-vocalic position, I suspect Negerhollands had is a Virgin Islands English Creole borrowing.

Table 4 above suggests an explanation for deletion in the bilabial and velar nasal-stop clusters. Eve, Fanti and Gã permit /m/ and /ŋ/ in word-final position; additionally Fanti permits word-final /n/.[25] Given that nasals are permissible codas in Kwa and that /m/ and /ŋ/ occur more frequently than /n/, it is plausible that a Dutch variable rule of stop deletion in -nd clusters was generalized to become a variable rule of stop deletion which applied to all nasal clusters in Negerhollands.

We have just seen that in Negerhollands, variable deletion in word-final clusters can be at least partially attributed to target-like acquisition. As with the deletion of word-final consonants, Variable Rule Analysis was also used to determine factors which conditioned segment deletion in word-final consonant clusters. The 13 words listed in Table 5 above were represented by 236 tokens. The analysis includes all tokens in the corpus. In contrast to Anderson's subjects who simplified final clusters at a significantly higher rate than they deleted word-final, single consonants (see Table 1), the rate of deletion in Negerhollands clusters was significantly lower than the deletion rate for word-final, single consonants: 78% for word-final clusters vs 89% for word-final, single consonants.[26] The factor groups considered for this analysis were the same as those considered in the deletion of word-final consonants; however, for this alternation only factor groups (2) Speaker and (3) Word proved to be significant. The level of significance associated with each factor group, numbers of tokens, percent of deletion, and probability associated with each factor is shown in Appendix II.

Although the first factor group, Following Phonological Environment did not condition the alternation, the ranking of the probabilities associated with factor group (3), Word, suggested that the nature of the consonant cluster itself might have contributed to rates of deletion. Based on the discussions in Guy (1980) and Neu (1980), two additional factor groups were considered in a second variable rule run: factor group (4), whether or not the cluster was homorganic, and factor group (5), complexity of the cluster defined as whether or not the consonants agreed in voicing <u>and</u> place of articulation. Neither of these factor groups proved to be significant. Thus, unlike the variable deletion of word-final, single consonants, there is no demonstrable phonetic condition associated with deletion in Negerhollands word-final clusters.

As with word-final vowels, the second factor group indicated that speakers could be divided into groups. Similarly, as with the previous alternation, the third factor group showed that the variation had become lexicalized. A cross-tabulation of the factor groups (2) Speaker and (3) Word indicated that speakers tended to treat words in an identical fashion.

A comparison of these two alternations, the deletion of word-final, single consonants and deletion in word-final consonant clusters, demonstrates that, although in both cases rule output is less marked than rule input, the rules operate quite differently. In the case of a word-final, single consonants, both deletion and resyllabification to a following vowel create open syllables which, as demonstrated by Table 2, is the preferred syllable type in the substrate languages. Given that our findings for syllable onsets show that native language transfer plays a larger role than language universals in the shaping of interlanguage phonotactics, the variable deletion of single word-final consonants in Negerhollands also must be attributed primarily to native language transfer. Regarding the variable simplification of complex codas, we saw above that the majority of the Negerhollands words affected this rule were derived from Dutch words in which the word-final clusters were also simplified. In this case, it appears that speakers of Kwa languages capitalized on the variability of the superstrate to create phonotactic structure which was 1) closer to that of their native phonologies and 2) less marked. Notice, however, that although three forces converge to simplify complex codas, the fact that deletion in this instance results in a closed syllable seems be responsible for the fact that simplification of word-final clusters occurs less frequently than the deletion of word-final, single consonants. The three alternations which we have considered, simplification of SI clusters, deletion of word-final, single consonants, and simplification of word-final clusters suggest that the force driving phonotactic remodeling in Negerhollands codas was a desire for open syllables (i.e. substrate influence) not the need to simplify syllabic complexity (i.e universal principals).

4.0. Relevance of the Negerhollands Case to SLA Research

There are several points at which the Negerhollands case is relevant to the SLA research discussed in section 2.0. First, Stolz's discovery that in the lexicon as a whole, Negerhollands single consonants were preserved more frequently than CC clusters which are in turn preserved more frequently than CCC clusters is consistent with Anderson's hypothesis that target phonotactic patterns which are more marked than L_1 structure are more difficult to learn than those which are less marked. However, when we considered the rates of deletion for word-final, single consonants and for word-final CC clusters in words which were variable, we found that, in contrast to Anderson's subjects who simplified final clusters at a significantly higher rate than they deleted word-final, single consonants, the rate of deletion in Negerhollands clusters was significantly lower than the deletion rate for word-final, single consonants. Although this is counter to what markedness theory would predict, these data are consistent with Sato's prediction that her subjects, whose L_1 predominant syllable type was CVC, would simplify SF clusters at a higher rate than they would delete SF single consonants. The Negerhollands data support Tarone's and Sato's findings that native language transfer is the dominant process influencing interlanguage syllable structure.

The preceding discussion also shows that both the frequency and permissibility of particular L_1 structures played roles in shaping the phonotactics of Negerhollands. However, we also saw that the presence of a large number of complex onsets in the Negerhollands superstrates did not eliminate the difficulty which Kwa speakers had acquiring Germanic initial clusters in general and sC(r) clusters in particular. Since this finding is contrary Sato's assumption that the presence of Cw onsets in Vietnamese would predispose her subjects to acquire the complex onsets of English, the role which permissibility plays in native-language transfer needs to be more fully investigated.

The discussion of the alternations which affected Negerhollands codas raises two questions which should be considered in future research on the acquisition of phonotactic structure. In the Negerhollands case, we saw that phonological conditioning on the variable deletion of word-final consonants served to create CV syllables, but that the variable deletion in word-final clusters was unconditioned. Thus, the first of these questions is to what extent is the variation associated with interlanguage phonotactics phonologically conditioned. A related concern is that corpora be collected so that it is possible to address this issue. This was the case in the data collected by Tarone, Sato, and Anderson. Greenberg's picture description task is also likely to have provided appropriate phonological context. However, data provided by Greenberg's naming task which involved flashcards may not have done so.

The second question which must be addressed is the nature of the linguistic target. We have seen that some Dutch word-final clusters were variable while word-final, single consonants were not. The relative differences between the proportions of retention of etymological consonants for onsets and codas revealed by Stolz's analysis may be due to universal tendencies. However, it also may be the case that variation is harder to learn than invariance.[27] It may even be the case that both factors contributed to this effect. This same question is relevant to Anderson's interpretation of the data which she collected. Anderson writes that 'The standard against which the L_2 learner's performance was measured was formal, unsimplified, standard American English rather than casual speech' (1987:284).

This expedient is acceptable, and perhaps unescapable, for coding the data. However, Anderson's assumption that her Arabic subjects simplified -st, -nt, -zd, -nd word-final clusters due to a preference for a less-marked syllable type needs to be reconsidered in light of the research on t/d deletion in English word-final clusters (Labov 1966, Guy 1908, Neu 1980). Anderson's subjects may have had greater difficulty with target language codas than with target language onsets because the variation associated with word-final clusters in English is harder to learn than invariance which, for many dialects, is associated with complex onsets.

5.0. CONCLUSIONS

The Negerhollands data demonstrates that phonological variation in a creole can be traced both to native language transfer and universal processes and, thus, is broadly consistent with SLA research on the acquisition of phonotactic structure. In fact, the convergence of the Negerhollands study with those of Tarone and Sato suggest that Anderson's data may need to be reconsidered.

We also observed that for syllable onsets the variable effects of native language transfer (e.g. variable s-deletion and deletion of word-final, single consonants) persisted longer than those of linguistic universals (e.g schwa insertion in SI clusters). Like Sato's results, this fact is consistent with Tarone's findings that 1) native language transfer was the "the dominant process influencing" interlanguage phonotactics. Additionally, the existence of two rules in Negerhollands, schwa epenthesis which created structure consistent with linguistic universals and s-deletion which was attributed to native language transfer provided additional provide additional confirmation that linguistic universals and native language transfer operate independently.

The Negerhollands data also raise several important concerns which can only be addressed by future research. We have already seen 1) that what is permissible in the native language must be considered more fully, 2) that we need to explore how phonological environment conditions phonotactic acquisition, and 3) that the nature of the linguistic target must be considered before we invoke linguistic universals as an explanatory factor. Additionally, it is unlikely that any of the linguistic factors operate independently of social factors. Because de Jong provided little social information about his consultants, it was impossible to explore this issue further in the research on Negerhollands. This dearth of information about the speakers who created creole languages for many years has been a serious hinderance to researchers investigating creolization as a linguistic process. Although researching the effects of social factors on language acquisition is difficult at best, researchers in SLA are in a far better position than are creolists to make headway in this area.

There is recent interest in understanding the variation associated with SLA (Tarone 1987, Adamson 1988, and Young 1989). Researchers who consider the full range of linguistic and social factors which condition the variation associated with the acquisition of phonotactic structure will provide insight into the dynamic linguistic processes which occur in SLA. Because much of the data for earliest stages creolization can only be surmised from synchronic variation, I look forward to the day when increased insight into language acquisition in contemporary settings will enable us to better grasp the still poorly understood processes of creolization.

Appendix I
Factor groups and probabilities for the deletion of syllable codas in the final variable rule run

Factor group and factors	N	%	Pi
(1) Following Phonological Environment (α = .001)			
y (consonants and pause	1455	93	.72
v (vowel)	583	78	.19
(2) Speaker[28] (α = .001)			
A, D, K	1048	94	.89
I	78	88	.68
E, H, J	893	83	.52
B, F	19	53	.05
(3) Word (α = .001)			
AlmAl 'all'	121	99	.97
krig 'get'	216	98	.95
mAk 'make'	140	96	.91
hor 'hear'	81	96	.90
kik 'see'	264	95	.84
Alen 'only'	18	94	.82
jar 'year'	15	93	.80
kOm 'come'	536	93	.79
nem 'take'	251	93	.77
klar 'clear'	11	82	.72
drAg 'bring'	71	86	.65
sker 'tear'	10	70	.52
dor 'door'	39	87	.48
frAg 'ask'	115	65	.41
tut 'close'	32	84	.36
gEsEg 'face'	8	88	.23
sowel 'as well'	13	69	.13
altəvel 'too much'	14	64	.11
glof 'believe'	3	33	.08
antut 'answer'	12	42	.02
tit 'time'	68	1	.00

Appendix II
Factor groups and probabilities for deletion in codas
in the final variable rule run

Factor group and factors	N	%	Pi
1 speaker[29] (α =.001)			
K	81	91	.86
E, D	20	70	.48
A, J	135	71	.32
2 word (α = .001)			
bint 'tie'	36	97	.97
lant 'land'	23	96	.94
rɔnt 'round'	61	90	.92
hɔnt 'dog'	61	95	.85
jump 'jump'	17	87	.82
plats 'place'	4	75	.76
diŋg 'think'	33	82	.61
hart 'hard'	3	67	.58
stɔmp 'stump'	3	33	.27
driŋg 'drink'	30	50	.23
wɔrt 'word'	11	9	.08
akt 'eight'	3	33	.05
mant 'month'	7	14	.02
Chi- Square per cell 2.35			

NOTES

1. This paper reports research funded in part by a grant from the National Science Foundation, BNS 13415. I would like to thank Crawford Feagin, Barbara Hoekje and Gillian Sankoff for comments and suggestions on an earlier draft of this manuscript. I alone am responsible for any remaining problems.

2. In a language contact setting, substrate speakers are those who acquire a new language; the adopted language is the superstrate.

3. Although the papers by Dickerson, Tarone, and Sato were published earlier, for the convenience of the readers all page references refer to the Ioup and Weinberger volume.

4. C indicates consonant; V indicates vowel.

5. The final consonant in Mandarin Chinese may be n, ŋ, or ɹ.

6. The final consonants in Amoy Chinese may be m, n, ŋ, p, t, or k.

7. This table is based on Anderson's tables 16.3, 16.4, and 16.5.

8. Note that this interpretation is consistent with Greenberg's finding for the Japanese subjects. Japanese does not permit consonant clusters, but native speakers of Japanese found English clusters easier to acquire in SI than in SF position.

9. Although Negerhollands was moribund when the data were collected, Sabino 1990 presents evidence that language death in this case resulted in invariance, not increased variability. The alternations discussed in the present paper are not due to language decay.

10. A detailed discussion of these corpora can be found in Sabino 1990.

11. Although several dialects of the three Germanic languages were spoken in the community, Kwa speakers, especially in the earliest stages of acculturation, are not likely to have perceived these as distinct. Thus, I assume that the superstrate would have seemed to be a highly variable single language.

12. A description of the corpora on which the table is based can be found in Sabino 1990.

13. Polysyllabic words were counted as having CV structure only if all of the syllables in the word conformed to this pattern.

14. Except the Akwamu data which come from Mueller (1675), the data on which this table is based was elicited from informants. Twi is not included because no Twi informant was available at the time the data were collected.

15. Stolz (1986) does not report whether or not the differences he found were significant.

16. Because the primary dictionary entries are for the Twi dialect, I have used Twi here to represent Akan.

17. Zeeuws is a Southern Dutch dialect. In the language of the last speakers this rule only affected these two lexical items.

18. Den Besten (p.c., August 21, 1989) points out that Negerhollands lAp 'clap, slap' which Stolz (1986) derives from Dutch slappen 'to slap' can be derived from an obsolete Dutch form, lappen.

19. Given Dickerson's findings discussed above, it is likely that the frequency with which initial sC(r) clusters were modified decreased with the passage of time.

20. The Woordenboek der Nederlandsche taal gives Du. scraven as related to Dutch schrabben 'scratch.' The change of Dutch /v/ to Negerhollands /u/ can be accounted for if one posits an intermediate step of /w/. (See Sabino 1990.)

21. Negerhollands lo, lɔ, lɔp 'go' was excluded from the analysis as there were only two tokens of lɔp and 643 tokens of lo, lɔ. Additionally, Nh. antu, antut 'answer' was included for the last speaker, Mrs. Alice Stevens. However, since all of de Jong's consultants produced Nh. anturt, this word was not coded for them.

22. Similar conditioning is reported by Singler for Liberian English (ms).

23. This lexicalization is due to language death (Sabino 1990).

24. The -en, a Dutch infinitive ending, was lost to deflection.

25. Dr. Kodjo Afokpa, a native speaker of Eve, (p.c., 5/5/90) notes that native speakers of French, which has nasalized vowels in word-final position, realize word-final nasalized vowels in Eve as [n]. The presence of the nasalized vowels in word-final position in Eve and Gã may have predisposed substrate speakers to successfully acquire superstrate word-final [n].

26. The difference is significant at $\alpha < .001$; Chi Square = 22.52.

27. Payne (1980) shows that for first language acquisition, variation which has complex conditioning is more difficult to learn than that which has less complex conditioning.

28. Speaker C produced only one token. This token did not contain a word-final consonant. K represents the last speaker, Mrs. Stevens.

29. Speaker F produced four tokens, all with a reduced word-final cluster; speaker I produced one token with a full cluster.

28   Second Language Acquisition and Development

REFERENCES

Alleyne, Mervyn C. 1971. The cultural matrix of creolization. In Pidginization and creolization of languages, ed. by Dell Hymes, 169-86. Cambridge: Cambridge University Press.

Adamson, Hugh Douglas. 1988. Variation theory and second language acquisition. Washington, D.C.: Georgetown University Press.

Anderson, Janet I. 1987. The markedness differential hypothesis and syllable structure difficulty. In Ioup and Weinberger, pp. 279-291.

Anderson, Roger. 1983. Pidginization and creolization as language acquisition. Rowley, Massachusetts: Newbury House.

Christaller, Rev. J. G. 1875. Dictionary of the Asante and Fante language. Reprinted 1964. Basel: The Basel Evangelical Missionary Society.

Den Besten, Hans. 1987. Review of Einführung in Geschichte und Struktur des Afrikaans, by Edith Raidt. Journal of pidgin and creole studies. 2. 1:67-92.

Dickerson, Wayne B. 1976. The psycholinguistic unity of language learning and language change. In Ioup and Weinberger, pp. 86-100.

Guy, Gregory R. 1980. Variation in the group and the individual: The case of final stop deletion. In Locating language in time and space, ed. by William Labov, 1-36. New York: Academic Press.

Labov, William. 1966. Sociolinguistic patterns. Philadelphia: University of Pennsylvania Press.

Mueller, Wilhelm Johann. 1675. Die Africanische Landschraft Fetu. Hamburg.

Ioup, Georgette and Stephen H. Weinberger. 1987. Interlanguage phonology. Rowley, Massachusetts: Newbury House.

Neu, Helen. 1980. Ranking of constraints on /t/and /d/ deletion in American English: A statistical analysis. In Locating language in time and space, ed. by William Labov, 37-54. New York: Academic Press.

Payne, Arvella. 1980. Factors controlling the acquisition of the Philadelphia dialect by out-of-state children. In Locating language in time and space, ed. by William Labov, 37-54. New York: Academic Press.

Sabino, Robin. 1990. Towards a phonology of Negerhollands: An analysis of phonological variation. University of Pennsylvania dissertation.

Sato, Charlene. 1984. Phonological processes in second language acquisition: Another look at interlanguage syllable structure. Reprinted 1987 in Ioup and Weinberger, pp. 248-261.

Singler, John V. n. d. Phonology in the basilect: The fate of final consonants in Liberian Interior English. Forthcoming.

Sprauve, Gilbert A. 1974. Towards a reconstruction of Virgin Islands English Creole phonology. Princeton University dissertation.

Stolz, Thomas. 1986. Gibt das Kreolish Sprachwandel Model? Frankfurt am Main: Peter Lang.

Tarone, Elaine. 1980. Some influences on the syllable structure of interlanguage phonology. Reprinted 1987 in Ioup and Weinberger, pp. 232-247.

_____. 1987. Variation in interlanguage. Baltimore: Edward Arnold.

Varbrule. June 1986. Susan Pintzuk and Anthony Kroch, Department of Linguistics, University of Pennsylvania.

Weijnen, A. 1952. Zeventiende-eeuwse Taal. Zutphen: W. J. Thieme.

Westerman, Diedrich. 1923. Evefiala or Ewe-English dictionary. Reprint 1973. Liechtenstein: Kraus-Thomas.

Young, Richard. 1989. Variation in interlanguage morphology: (s) plural marking in the speech of Chinese learners of English. University of Pennsylvania dissertation.

Zimmerman, Johannes. 1858. A grammatical sketch of the Akra or Ga language. Stuttgart: Printed by J. Steinkopt for the Basel Missionary Society.

TRANSFERABILITY AND LEXICAL RESTRUCTURING
(OR: WHAT GETS LOST IN THE TRANSLATION--AND WHY?)

Terence Odlin
The Ohio State University

1.0. INTRODUCTION

The study of second language acquis tion (SLA) has increasingly emphasized the distinction between product and p~ocess.[1] As this distinction has grown in importance, investigators have changed their stance on language transfer. Transfer, also known as "cross-linguistic influence", interested researchers long before the product/process distinction became widely recognized. Contrastive analysts assumed that transfer was a process sufficiently important to justify the detailed comparisons of languages such as Moulton's (1962) study of English and German phonology. Subsequent critics of contrastive analysis (e.g., Dulay, Burt, and Krashen 1982) scored the emphasis on product in contrastive studies, but such criticism certainly did not put an end either to work in contrastive analysis or to empirical research on transfer. Discussions of cross-linguistic influence now frequently emphasize the complexity of the processes involved and often consider how transfer interacts with other factors (e.g., Meisel 1983, Kellerman 1984, Ringbom 1987, Odlin 1989).

Although the evidence for cross-linguistic influence has grown over the years, understanding the nature of the transfer process remains one of the most formidable challenges facing second language researchers. A better understanding of transfer is at least conceivable since scholars apparently agree that the most important goal of transfer research is to develop a satisfactory theory of the process underlying transfer. What Weinreich (1953/1968) termed an "interlingual identification" occurs any time an individual judges structures (in the widest sense of the term) in two languages to be identical or at least similar.[2] Such judgments may be conscious or unconscious, they may be accurate or inaccurate, and they may be made either by fully competent bilinguals or by learners still in the earlier stages of acquiring a new language. Though essentially a phenomenon promoting cross-linguistic assimilations, the interlingual identification can often lead to structures quite distinct from either the native or the target language: as the analysis in this paper will show, transfer can sometimes lead to dissimilations that would not be predicted in a simplistic contrastive analysis.

The interlingual identification is the psychological basis not only for transfer but also for translation. In view of this overlap, it seems curious that relatively few discussions of transfer have cited much of the literature on translation. There do exist real differences between studies of translation and studies of transfer in some of the questions asked. Not surprisingly, many discussions on translation focus on literary discourse, and many are concerned with translatability -- or lack thereof -- in literary texts (e.g., Steiner 1975, Frawley 1984). Some discussions of theory and practice in translation do refer specifically to issues in language teaching (e.g., Lehmann 1986). Yet of these studies, only a few directly address questions of psychological process, and most of those studies deal with translations from the language being learned back to the learner's native language (e.g., Gerloff 1987).

By the same token, work on transfer has proceeded pretty much independently of work on translation. The second language literature often does provide interesting insights about translation, as in the detailed study by Ringbom (1987) of Finnish and Swedish-speaking learners of English, and as in a briefer study by Flashner (1989) of Russian speakers' use of aspectual forms in English. However, such insights have generally arisen from concerns not directly relevant to translation theorists. The different course of SLA investigations reflects not only the different emphases in translation research but also the fact that transfer involves questions of little or no importance to translation specialists. For example, translation theorists need not be concerned with the reasons for the pronunciation of English floor by Egyptian Arabic speakers as [filoor] but by Iraqi Arabic speakers as [ifloor]. Such different pronunciations by speakers of the same language (in written form, at least) do concern transfer researchers interested in dialect differences, syllable structure, and the effects of both in transfer (e.g., Broselow 1983). Both in transfer research and in translation research, accordingly, there arise questions that may interest investigators in the one field but not the other.

Yet even with distinct areas of interest in the two fields, some common concerns exist. In his discussion of translation, Frawley (1984:168-169) makes the following observation:

> There may be identities across the two codes [involved in a translation], but that is not a crucial issue; the translation occurs regardless of them. The translation itself, as a matter of fact, is essentially a third code which arises out of the bilateral consideration of the matrix and target codes: it is, in a sense, a subcode of each of the codes involved...That is, since the translation truly has a dual lineage, it emerges as a code in its own right, setting its own standards and structural presuppositions and entailments, though they are necessarily derivative of the matrix information and the target parameters.

Most people familiar with the SLA literature will note the striking similarity between Frawley's characterization of translation and the characterizations of interlanguage as a linguistic system not entirely derivative either from the learner's native language or from the target language (cf. Selinker 1972, Bley-Vroman

1983, Eckman 1991). Emphasizing the creative nature of translation, Frawley focused on literary texts, and it is not clear whether the transfer patterns of second language learners would qualify in his analysis as "translation", as opposed to mere "transliteration". Yet even if transfer were simply transliteration, the complexity of the process would warrant investigation.

The most important reason for such complexity is the vast number of choices that an inexpert translator has. Professional translators obviously have many choices: even in the translation of prose works such as the History of Herodotus, translators find more than one way to recodify the original language. However, such recodification usually must conform to the norms of the target language, norms which are especially strict if the target code is a written standard language. In contrast to expert translators, second language learners are generally much less aware of the target norms, and their lack of knowledge will, in effect, open up many translation choices unthinkable for the expert.

The range of choices is especially wide when: 1) there is relatively little concern about the norms of the standard version of the target language; 2) there are structures in the native language that seem highly transferable. A lack of concern about target norms will surely encourage more interlanguage variants, yet transferability is just as crucial a factor. If learners do not see a close match between the native language and the target language, they may be wary about speaking or writing anything that too closely resembles a native language structure: work by Kellerman (1977, 1978, 1983), Jordens (1977), and Sjöholm (1983) provides interesting evidence of such wariness. For example, Kellerman (1978) has found that Dutch students will sometimes consider She broke his heart as acceptable English but not so often will they accept The workers broke the strike, even though both idioms are equally acceptable in Dutch (which happens to have the cognate breken). If a native language structure does seem transferable, learners may consider it a template and decide to follow it closely or loosely. Whether or not the template is followed closely, it can suggest translations that might not seem plausible otherwise.

In theory, then, cross-linguistic influence expands the number of possible translations that learners might contemplate. In practice, however, transfer does not often seem to lead to myriad translations of a native-language sentence. Some translations will indeed be non-standard, as many examples of negative transfer show. Even so, there is reason to believe that learners settle on a small number of choices--at times, perhaps just one. This article will present evidence of a case where many learners seem to have opted for a single translation choice: although many choices were available, one prevailed in the language contact situation. The discussion will focus on the reasons for the particular choice, reasons that can provide insights about interlingual identifications and the processes of transfer.

The evidence comes from Hiberno-English, a dialect arising from widespread language contact in Ireland mainly in the eighteenth and nineteenth centuries.[3] Although other influences besides transfer played a role in shaping the dialect, considerable evidence attests to the importance of cross-linguistic influence from Irish (also known as Gaelic) on the formation of Hiberno-English (cf. Henry 1957, Bliss 1976a-b, de Fréine 1977, Barry 1983, Harris 1984). Two facts about the dialect make it especially relevant to questions of interlingual identification and transferability: 1) most of the second language acquisition from 1750-1850, the period of the most intensive language contact, was naturalistic--schools probably played only a marginal role in the spread of English (Odlin 1991); 2) the target language that learners had exposure to was generally modelled by other bilinguals. Both of these circumstances no doubt encouraged cross-linguistic influence (cf. Sabban 1983, Odlin 1989, 1990).

The particular Hiberno-English structure to be considered in this paper is the use of put as a causative verb as in <u>She put him sitting at the table</u> (=She seated him at the table). The evidence suggests that this structure is indeed the result of cross-linguistic influence from Irish and that causative put is still widespread in Hiberno-English. The very robustness of this structure may have an important implication both for language contact studies and second language research: if a particular translation from the substrate language seems highly transferable, it will occur to many learners and surface in a wide geographic area. Yet while causative put had a common translation pattern, there were other choices available, some closer to the Irish substrate and some closer to the English superstrate (i.e., to the target norms). The choice that learners in the nineteenth century appear to have favored is one not entirely explainable as either a native-language or target-language form. It is a striking example of the creativity of interlanguage processes.

2.0. PUT AS A CAUSATIVE
As mentioned above, causative "put" is found in many parts of Ireland, and the following examples come from interviews by workers for the Irish Folklore Commission with speakers of Hiberno-English in four different counties.[4] The first example comes from a story told about a housewife and a beggar in County Westmeath in central Ireland:

> ...and she said what would fill eight mouths
> 'id surely fill nine and she put him sitting at the table'. (MM 1639:134)

A story from County Roscommon, farther west, shows a similar example:

> And she took him down to the fire and made him comfortable and
> put him sitting before the fire. (MM 1573:204)

A reminiscence from a speaker in County Galway, still farther west, shows comparable examples:

> There was four hundhred o' flour aboard a small little, boat, an I had a hundhred--weight o' something else aboard 'er, an' I put my daughther aboard 'er, sittin' behind the shtern an' the--meself and the three, those three young lads now, three young lads about thirteen or fourteen years. (MM 1768:108)

> ...we had a couple cattle or three here, that we couldn't couldn't rear here, we could brin them in there [an island] an' put them grazin' there until the month of October, an' brin' them out then an' sell them. (MM 1767:365)

There are yet other examples from a speaker in County Clare, to the south of County Galway, interviewed by Ó Duilearga (1962):

> The bird didn't lay any more eggs, and she [an old lady] brought the bird to the golden [sic] smith and also her daughter. The goldsmith put her daughter sitting down in the parlour. (p. 48)

> She [a king's wife] picked some herbs. She put those herbs hanging in a bag in the ceiling of the kitchen... (p. 3)

From the same speaker comes a similar construction, one without a non-finite verb:

> "I can't put you on a hide [hide you]," says the pony, "for he has sent his boy out in the stable for to watch you and me" (p. 24).

Even more than the others, this example suggests that put is a true causative and is not being used simply in a locative construction, though the locative characteristics of causative put are significant and will be discussed further on. Such uses of put do not seem to exist in other dialects of English. Neither the English Dialect Dictionary (Wright 1898) nor the Oxford English Dictionary (Murray et al. 1933, Simpson and Weiner 1989) lists put as such a causative even though both dictionaries do list many other senses. At the same time, there is a close parallel in Irish to the Hiberno-English: O Siadhail (1989:297-298) notes that cuir (put) can be used as a causative. In the case of She put him sitting at the table, the Irish parallel is :

> Chuir sí   ina   shuí   chun boird é.[5]
> put   she   in-his sitting at   table him

It is worth noting that a leading English-Irish dictionary lists this Irish construction as the normal way to translate the English verb <u>seat</u> (De Bhaldraithe 1959).[6] The predicate dominated by <u>chuir</u> (i.e., <u>shuí</u>) is a "verbal noun" rather than a non-finite verb. In Irish, verbal nouns have nominal properties not characteristic of English gerunds, infinitives, or participles: for example, verbal nouns normally have grammatical gender and they can be marked for genitive as well as nominative case. The surface category of <u>ina shuí</u> thus is not Verb Phrase but rather Prepositional Phrase.[7] By this analysis, <u>chuir</u> functions in such sentences as a three-place predicate having two noun phrases (a subject and direct object) and a prepositional phrase as its arguments:

$$\text{Chuir sí}_{NP} \quad [\text{ina shuí}]_{PP} \; ([\text{chun boird}]_{PP}) \; \text{é}_{NP}$$

While <u>chun boird</u> is an argument of <u>shuí</u>, it is optional with respect to causative <u>chuir</u>, which requires only one prepositional phrase. The progressive <u>ina shuí</u> is quite typical of the ways in which progressives are formed in Irish:

| Tá sé | ina | shuí | = He is sitting |
| Is he | in-his | sitting | |

| Tá sé | ag | teacht | = He is coming |
| Is he | at | coming | |

| Tá sé | do | mo | thóraíocht | = He is looking for me |
| Is he | to | my | searching | |

In all these cases, the progressive requires a preposition, a verbal noun, and a "substantive verb" such as <u>tá</u> (Ó Siadhail 1989). Moreover, if there is a patient affected by the action of the verbal noun, a possessive (e.g., <u>mo</u>) precedes the verbal noun. Possessives can fuse with prepositions and are obligatory for certain statives. Thus <u>ina</u>, which appears before <u>shuí</u>, is a fusion of <u>i</u> (in) and <u>a</u> (his). To summarize, there are three major ways in which Irish progressives differ from English ones: the use of a prepositional phrase instead of a verb phrase, the use of a verbal noun instead of a progressive verb, and the use of a possessive before certain verbal nouns.

The contrasts between progressives and causatives in Irish and English did not deter early speakers of Hiberno-English from viewing the Irish construction as translatable into English. As the above examples indicate, causative <u>put</u> is common in the dialect. The syntactic pattern that emerged from the translation was not inevitable, however. In the case of <u>She put him sitting at the table</u>, there are numerous other possible translations of the Irish expression, as the following examples show:

1) Put she in his sitting at table him
2) Put she in sitting at the table him
3) Put she sitting at the table him
4) Put she him sitting at the table
5) Put she him in sitting at the table
6) Her put him sitting at the table
7) She put he in his sitting at the table
8) She put him in his sitting at the table
9) She put him in sitting at the table
10) She put him in a sitting at the table
11) She put him to sit at the table
12) She put him sit at the table
13) She put him seated at the table
14) She put him in a seat at the table
15) She put him in his seat at the table
16) She made him sitting at the table
17) She had him in his sitting at the table
18) She made him to sit at the table
19) She had him to sit at the table
20) She made him sit at the table
21) She had him sitting at the table
22) She had him sit at the table
23) She seated him at the table
24) She put him sitting at the table

I have not encountered any examples in Hiberno-English of the first nineteen sentence patterns. Thus it is natural to wonder why #24 emerged as the favored translation, which has been used in Ireland along with the standard patterns seen in #20-23. Some of the other possible translations clearly violate basic constraints of English. Most striking in this regard are the first five, which mimic the verb-initial word order of Irish. If Hiberno-English were no more than an unstable pidgin, the VSO order of Irish might be used, just as Korean Bamboo English, for example, used the SOV word-order of Korean. Contrary to claims by Zobl (1986) and others, the transfer of basic word order is possible; however, such transfer seems to be restricted to very rudimentary interlanguages such as Korean Bamboo English (Odlin 1989, 1990).

Sentences #6 through 19 are not so easy to dismiss as improbable translations. Even the use of her as a subject pronoun as in #6 is attested in Hiberno-English: Him and her got married and lived happy ever after (Ó Duilearga 1962:27). Nevertheless, such uses are rare and appear to be constrained by highly special discourse factors. Space does not permit an exhaustive analysis of each of the remaining alternatives; accordingly, the focus of the paper will be on: 1) the choice of put as a causative; 2) the use of a VP in translation #24 instead of a

Prepositional Phrase (as in #8).

3.0. SEMANTIC TRANSPARENCY

Before the English translation choices are considered, the syntax and semantics of the Irish equivalent warrant discussion. Especially significant are two of the locative forms seen in Chuir sí ina shuí chun bhoird é: the prepositional phrase ina shuí noted earlier, and the causative chuir, which also co-occurs in purely locative constructions as in

> Chuir mé an pictúr os cionn an dorais.
> put I the picture above the door

As noted before, the normal way of forming progressives in Irish is to use a prepositional phrase. The choice of spatial prepositions such as i (in) and ag (at) is consonant with the close semantic relation between spatial and aspectual notions. Anderson (1973) observes that locative constructions code progressive aspect in many languages and argues that progressives in languages such as English have a locative in their deep structure (cf. Lyons 1977:719). Comrie (1976) also cites a number of languages that use locative constructions to code progressives, which in his analysis have a specialized imperfective meaning. In the same analysis, another specialized imperfective meaning is the stative. What progressives and statives have in the common is the essential characteristic of the imperfective, which by Comrie's definition "looks at the situation from inside..." (1976:4). Such a notion of interiority is useful not only to explain Irish progressive constructions such as ina shuí but also Irish statives such as i bhfolach, which may translate either as "in hiding" or "hidden", although the Irish form is not a progressive nor even a verb. While English does not rely so heavily on locatives to code progressives and statives, the non-standard progressive in He's a-going home is further support for the positions of Anderson and Comrie. According to the OED, the source of a in a-going is the preposition on.

Since Irish uses prepositional phrases to code progressive aspect, the choice of cuir as a causative seems well motivated. Other languages including English, French, and Spanish occasionally use translation equivalents of cuir in a similar way as in the English use of put in certain stative constructions such as That word really puts him in a rage. However, causative cuir is especially productive, its usual translation equivalents in English being the productive analytic forms have and make.

Such considerations suggest that the choice of cuir as a causative is semantically well motivated. In this sense, the sentence Chuir sí ina shuí chun bhoird é is highly transferable: to use Kellerman's terminology (1983), it is "transparent". Constructions such as She put him sitting at the table are good examples of the fine line which sometimes is all that distinguishes a productive idiom from a grammaticized structure.[8] The wide use of causative put seen in the various examples from different counties suggests that a transparent structure may be a more likely vestige in a substratum than "opaque" idioms such as We couldn't knock any rights of one another, idioms which exist in Hiberno-English but which may not be particularly common (Odlin 1988).[9] Future research would be useful to confirm whether there is a close relation between semantic transparency and pervasiveness in a substratum.

4.0. TRANSLATION EQUIVALENTS AND SYNTACTIC REPRESENTATION
Only three interlingual identifications seem to be necessary
to account for sentences such as She put him sitting at the table

1) chuir caus = put caus

2) $[P [(PRO) [V] N] NP]_{PP} = [V + ing]_{VP}$

3) chuir caus + PP + NPacc = put caus + NPacc + VPprog

The first identification is lexical: aside from its use as a causative, cuir frequently translates as put, and so this identification is not unusual except in preserving in Hiberno-English the causative option found in Irish. The second identification equates the surface characteristics of Irish progressives described earlier with those of English progressives. The third identification specifies the co-occurrence conditions for the distinctive Hiberno-English construction: put can function as a productive analytic causative with a progressive verb phrase.

The first identification is hardly surprising in view of the discussion of transferability in the previous section. While bilinguals in 19th century Ireland probably heard make or have used as causatives, as in translations #20-22, cuir no doubt seemed translatable as put because of the transparency of the Irish construction. Yet if this argument is sound, the second identification becomes somewhat problematic. Why did bilinguals apparently prefer sitting to in his sitting or in sitting, as in translations #8 and 9? Both of the latter translations have the typologically common locative coding of progressive aspect whereas sitting does not. There are a number of possible explanations of the choice made, but the most plausible is that learners of English usually have ample exposure to progressive verbs in their input and would therefore have little reason to believe that prepositional phrases are the normal way to code progressives in English.[10] This would also explain why learners rarely if ever coded ina shuí as an infinitive such as in translations #11 and 12.

There is another reason to consider sitting the most likely translation outcome. Specialists in Irish syntax have found reasons to argue that viewing ina shuí as a prepositional phrase is not the best formal treatment of the Irish progressive.

Stenson (1981) argues that the substantive verb (e.g., tá) functions as a main verb and that the complement of the preposition in examples such as Tá sé ina shuí and Tá sé ag teacht is not the verbal noun but rather an embedded sentence. O Siadhail (1989), on the other hand, develops an analysis in which the substantive verb is an auxiliary instead of a main verb (cf. Anderson 1973). Whatever the best formal treatment, bilinguals in 19th century Ireland must have made their interlingual identifications with at least partial recourse to surface facts. If they had not done so, there would be no basis for explaining why the Irish causative translated as put instead of as make or have. There would also be no basis for explaining the choice of a prepositional phrase for stative constructions such as I can't put you on a hide, which is based on the Irish stative i bhfolach discussed earlier. Accordingly, the resemblance between progressives, statives, and prepositional phrases makes the following explanation the most plausible:

> 1) The description of progressives in Irish may require two levels of representation, whether in a deep/surface relation or through some other representational system.

> 2) One level of representation enabled learners to see the formal similarity between ina shuí and i bhfolach: both contain the Irish preposition i (in).[11]

> 3) There may be another level of representation that allowed learners to view ina shuí as more than just a prepositional phrase. This level would designate ina shuí as a verb phrase.

Such an explanation can account for the absence of a prepositional phrase in She put him sitting at the table and the presence of one in I can't put you on a hide.

5.0. LEXICAL RESTRUCTURING

The preceding discussion indicates that there are clear explanations for the first two interlingual identifications, the choice of put for an analytic causative and the choice of a progressive verb phrase. The third identification follows from the first two in specifying a progressive verb as the complement of put. Yet this specification has intriguing consequences for the lexical representation of put in Hiberno-English since it raises the following question: Is causative put functioning as a two-place predicate?

Treatments of English syntax frequently cite put as a typical three-place predicate as in the following illustration from Radford (1981: 121):

> A. John put the book in the box.
> B. *John put the object.
> C. *John put near the table.

In most dialects of English, put requires a subject, a direct object, and a locative adverbial (typically, a prepositional phrase), and using put as a two-place predicate in examples B and C is ungrammatical. Hiberno-English, on the other hand, seems to violate this constraint in sentences such as She put him sitting at the table, which has a subject and a direct object but apparently no locative argument for put.

There are at least three possible explanations for the problematic status of put:

I. Put is still a three-place predicate because progressive forms such as sitting are treated as a locative argument.

II. Put is still a three-place predicate because it has been restructured so that the adjunct of the progressive (e.g., at the table) is the third argument.

III. Put has been restructured to be either a two- or three-place predicate.

The first explanation might seem plausible in view of the locative character of Irish ina shuí. However, there is nothing in the actual English structure to warrant this. To impute an Irish structural description to monolingual speakers of Hiberno-English is to ascribe an atavistic character to substratum effects. Another line of defense might come from a localist analysis such as that of Anderson (1973), who has advanced an interesting argument for the locative nature of the English progressive. However, it seems unlikely that there, a normal pro-form for locatives, could have an action as its anaphor:

She put him there =/= She put him sitting

Still another problem with this argument is that one of the examples does have a prepositional phrase as a complement of put: I put my daughther aboard 'er, sittin' behind the shtern, in which case put would have to be a four-place predicate. One might argue that this use of put is different from the others but it does look suspiciously like She put him sitting at the table.

Explanation II is just as implausible. At first glance, the prepositional phrase at the table might seem to be the argument of put: it is possible to delete sitting and have a nearly equivalent sentence, She put him at the table. However, to accept this explanation, one would have to claim that at the table is simultaneously a modifier of sitting and an argument of put. Such a claim will not work for set, which is sometimes a causative similar to put. One can say This set me thinking about the problem. If the prepositional phrase were an argument of set, one could conceivably delete the participle; doing so, however, results in This set me about the problem. Another problem is that behind the shtern is not the complement of put in <u>I put my daughther aboard 'er, sittin' behind the shtern</u>, as the logic of the second explanation would require.

The third explanation seems far preferable to the other two:

put has been restructured to be either a two- or three-place predicate. Thus <u>put</u> has the lexical specification of a three-place predicate found in most dialects of English, yet for Hiberno-English there is also a lexical specification for <u>put</u> similar to those for <u>set</u> and for verbs of perception (cf. Hornby 1975). Whatever formal treatment of Hiberno-English might be best, it should incorporate the co-occurrence restrictions on causative <u>put</u>:

$$\underline{\quad\quad} + [NP_{acc}] + [VP_{prog} \text{ (Adverbial)}]$$

This specification resembles the third interlingual identification given earlier but stipulates that an adjunct such as <u>at the table</u> is an optional condition. In fact, such adverbials may be obligatory in Hiberno-English since all of the examples of causative <u>put</u> cited in this paper have either prepositional phrases or adverbial <u>there</u>. On the other hand, adverbials are not obligatory in the Irish substrate, as seen in the following example cited by O Siadhail (1989: 298):

Chuir sé an churrach dhá   déanamh[12]
Put   he the coracle to-its making
He had the coracle made.

Since verbal nouns in Irish (e.g., <u>déanamh</u>) need not have adverbials, progressives in Hiberno-English may not require them either. Further research is needed to determine the exact constraints on causative <u>put</u>.

6.0. THE LIMITS OF ISOMORPHISM
The lexical restructuring of <u>put</u> is thus a likely explanation for the distinctive Hiberno-English causative: <u>put</u> has been reanalyzed as a either a two- or a three-place predicate. In one sense, such a result is paradoxical since this instance of transfer has led to a <u>dissimilation</u> between the native and target language, something that a crude contrastive analysis would not predict. Much of the time, Irish <u>cuir</u> is like <u>put</u>, functioning as a three-place predicate as in <u>Chuir mé an pictúr os cionn an dorais</u>. However, the second interlingual identification discussed earlier equates a prepositional phrase in Irish with a progressive verb phrase in English. This identification is highly accurate, but it results in the loss of isomorphism between the argument structure of causative <u>cuir</u>, having a valency of 3, and causative <u>put</u>, having a valency of 2 (cf. Lyons 1977). In this sense, Hiberno-English <u>put</u> reflects the potential of interlanguage to create new forms.

Such restructuring raises further questions. One is related specifically to causative put: was transfer in Hiberno-English restricted to physical events such as sitting? Studies focusing on prototypes in lexical semantics suggest such a possibility (e.g., Adamson 1989). On the other hand, further studies of Hiberno-English may show additional uses of causative put that involve abstract events. Another question is just how common such instances of restructuring are. In some studies of lexical transfer (e.g., Adjemian 1983) there does not seem to be a loss of isomorphism between the native and target language as in the valency change from cuir to put. On the other hand, the Hiberno-English example seems to involve transferability, which may override any principles of isomorphism in transfer. As sentences such as She put him sitting at the table are found in several parts of Ireland, the semantic transparency of Irish causatives likely accounts for the high transferability of the structure. If this conclusion is correct, one would expect to find parallels in other language contact situations.

Still one more issue warrants discussion. The focus of this paper has been on why translation #24 emerged as the favored expression of causative put, i.e., She put him in his sitting at the table. While the explanation given has much in its favor, it may seem highly deterministic. I doubt that the processes of translation in second language acquisition invariably result in one and only one outcome. What factors favor or work against multiple outcomes is yet another topic well worth investigating.

7.0. SUMMARY
In theory, cross-linguistic influence could expand the number of translations that second language learners might contemplate. In practice, however, transfer does not often seem to lead to myriad translations of a native-language sentence. Learners settle on a small number of choices--at times, perhaps just one. In this paper the evidence for a narrow range of choices comes from a structure that arose in Hiberno-English as a result of cross-linguistic influence. The widespread use of causative put no doubt reflects the high transferability of the Irish substrate pattern with cuir. Yet even a highly transferable structure does not necessarily result in the most literal translation possible as in Put she in his sitting at table him or even in She put him in his sitting at the table. The actual Hiberno-English She put him sitting at the table reflects earlier language contact when many bilinguals appear to have concurred on a particular interlingual identification sensitive to the difference between progressives in Irish and progressives in English. The very nature of this identification led to a loss of isomorphism between the argument structure of causative cuir, having a valency of 3, and causative put, having a valency of 2. Such lexical restructuring shows the potential of interlanguage to create new linguistic forms.

NOTES

1. I would like to express my appreciation to several people, especially to Jacquelyn Schachter, who encouraged me to pursue the ideas here and who provided valuable feedback on them. Thanks are also due to the Department of Irish Folklore, University College Dublin, in particular, Bo Almqvist, Séamas Ó Catháin, and Bairbre Ní Fhloinn. Dónall Ó Baoill and Diarmuid Ó Sé of the Linguistics Institute of Ireland provided helpful comments on the differences between Irish and English described in this paper. This research was supported by the College of Humanities and by the Office of Research and Graduate Studies of the Ohio State University.

2. Weinreich used the term in a somewhat narrower sense than what "interlingual identification" has in this paper.

3. The language contact situation in Ireland actually developed much earlier and it has continued up to the present. However, there is widespread agreement that the most intensive contact took place in the eighteenth and nineteenth centuries.

4. The references beginning with MM below indicate the Main Manuscripts volumes in the archive of the Department of Irish Folklore, University College Dublin.

5. There is another possible version of this sentence in Irish: Chuir sí ina shuí ag an mbord é. For the sake of consistency, I will use only the first version in discussing the substrate, i.e., Chuir sí ina shuí chun bhoird é.

6. The contrast between past and present forms in Irish is evident in the spellings of cuir (present) and chuir (past), which signal initial consonant mutations of the type found in the Celtic languages generally. Stenson (1981) provides details on the mutations specific to Irish.

7. The structural description provided here is not necessarily the best formal treatment, as discussed further on.

8. I have found that some native speakers of English consider She put him sitting at the table to be a possible English sentence, even though there appears to be no evidence of use outside of Ireland. Perhaps such intuitions are a reflection of the semantic considerations related spatial terms and aspect.

9. Without a gloss of the idiom, readers may have difficulty in understanding We couldn't knock any rights of one another (=We couldn't agree with each other). The need for a gloss is a primary indicator of opaque idioms (cf. Odlin 1988).

10. A similar explanation involving input is not so satisfactory to account for why learners sometimes preferred causative put to make or have. Even though the latter two were probably part of the input learners heard, they no doubt were less common than progressive constructions.

11. It is not clear why i bhfolach found its way into Hiberno-English as on a hide instead of as in a hide, a closer translation. One possibility is that the phonetic similarity between in and on led to innovations not related to the Irish substrate forms i (in) and ar (on). It is worth noting that i is not the only preposition that can co-occur with causative cuir.

12. For some senses not involving causative constructions, Irish cuir might be considered a two-place predicator. For example, one might consider síol a chur, which translates as to sow seed, as a two-place predicator if one used syntactic criteria since cuir need not take a prepositional phrase. On the other hand, cuir is arguably a three-place predicator by semantic criteria: seed has to be sown somewhere, even if a clause does not specify the location. Clearly, key issues of syntax and semantics are relevant to the criteria one chooses (cf. Lyons 1977). For the analysis in this paper, however, there is no need to choose between syntactic or semantic criteria since cuir as a causative normally functions as a three-place predicator having a subject, a direct object, and a prepositional phrase that codes progressive aspect.

REFERENCES

Adamson, H. Douglas. 1989. Variable rules as prototype schematas. In Variation in second language acquisition, Volume II, ed. by Susan Gass, Carolyn Madden, Dennis Preston, and Larry Selinker, 219-232. Clevedon, U.K.: Multilingual Matters.

Adjemian, Christian. 1983. The transferability of lexical properties. In Language transfer in language learning, ed. by Susan Gass and Larry Selinker, 250-268. Rowley, Massachusetts: Newbury House.

Anderson, John M. 1973. An essay concerning aspect. The Hague: Mouton.

Barry, Michael. 1983. The English language in Ireland. In R. Bailey and M. Görlach, eds., English as a World Language, Ann Arbor: University of Michigan Press, 84-133.

Bley-Vroman, Robert. 1983. The comparative fallacy in interlanguage studies: The case of systematicity. Language Learning 33. 1-17.

Bliss, Alan. 1976a. The English language in early modern Ireland. In A New History of Ireland, Vol. III., ed. by T. Moody, F. Martin, and F. Byrne, 546-560. Oxford: At the Clarendon Press.

_____ b. The English language in Ireland. Dublin: The Gaelic League.

Broselow, Ellen. 1983. Non-obvious transfer: Predicting epenthesis errors. In Language transfer in language learning, ed. by Susan Gass and Larry. Selinker, 112-34. Rowley, Massachusetts: Newbury House.

Comrie, Bernard.. 1976. Aspect. Cambridge: Cambridge University Press.

_____. 1981. Language universals and linguistic typology. Chicago: University of Chicago Press.

De Bhaldraithe, Tomás. 1959. English-Irish Dictionary. Dublin: Department of Education.

De Fréine, Sean. 1977. The dominance of the English language in the nineteenth century. In , The English language in Ireland, ed. by Diarmaid Ó Muirithe, 71-87. Dublin: Mercier Press.

Dulay, Heidi, Marina Burt, and Stephen Krashen. 1982. Language two. New York: Oxford University Press.

Eckman, Fred. 1991. The Structural Conformity Hypothesis and the acquisition of consonant clusters in the interlanguage of ESL learners. Studies in Second Language Acquisition 13. 23-41.

Flashner [Wenzell], Vanessa. 1989. Transfer of aspect in the English oral narratives of native Russian speakers. In Transfer in language production, ed. by Hans Dechert and Manfred Raupach. Norwood, N.J.: Ablex.

Frawley, William. 1984. Prolegomenon to a theory of translation. In Translation: Literary, linguistic and philosophical perspectives, ed. by William Frawley, 159-75. Newark: University of Delaware Press.

Gerloff, Pamela. 1987. Identifying the unit of analysis in translation: Some uses of think-aloud protocol data. In Introspection in second language research, ed. by Claus Faerch and Gabriele Kasper, 135-58. Clevedon, U.K.: Multilingual Matters.

Harris, John. 1984. Syntactic variation and dialect divergence. Journal of Linguistics 20.303-27.

Henry, Patrick Leo. 1957. An Anglo-Irish dialect of north Roscommon. Dublin: University College, Department of English.

Hornby, A. S. 1975. Guide to Patterns and Usage in English. London: Oxford University Press.

Jordens, Peter. 1977. Rules, grammatical intuitions, and strategies in foreign language learning. Interlanguage Studies Bulletin 2.5-76.

Kellerman, Eric. 1978. Giving learners a break: Native language intuitions about transferability. Working Papers in Bilingualism 15.59-92.

_____. 1983. Now you see it, now you don't. In Language transfer in language learning, ed. by Susan Gass and Larry Selinker, 112-34. Rowley, Massachusetts: Newbury House,

_____. 1984. The empirical evidence for the influence of L1 on interlanguage. In Interlanguage, ed. by A. Davies, C. Criper, and A.P.R. Howatt, 98-122. Edinburgh: Edinburgh University

Press.

Lehman, Volkmar. 1986. Understanding translation in foreign language teaching: Inference based on verbal and aspectual meaning. In Interlingual and intercultural communication, ed. by Juliane House and Shoshana Blum-Kulka, 139-149. Tübingen: Gunter Narr.

Lyons, John. 1977. Semantics, Vol. 2. Cambridge: Cambridge University Press.

Meisel, Jürgen. 1983. Transfer as a second-language strategy. Language and Communication 3.11-46.

Moulton, William. 1962. The sounds of English and German. Chicago: University of Chicago Press.

Murray, James, et al., eds., 1933. The Oxford English dictionary on historical principles. Oxford: At the Clarendon Press.

Odlin, Terence. 1988. Divil a lie: Semantic transparency and language transfer. Paper presented at the Second Language Research Forum, University of Hawaii at Manoa.

_____. 1989. Language Transfer. Cambridge: Cambridge University Press.

_____. 1990. Word order, metalinguistic awareness, and constraints on foreign language learning. In Second Language Acquisition/Foreign Language Learning, ed. by Bill Van Patten and James F. Lee, 95-117, Clevedon, U.K.: Multilingual Matters.

_____. 1990. A demographic perspective on the shift from Irish to English. Paper presented at the International Symposium on Germanic Languages and Literatures, Columbus, Ohio, 1991.

Ó Duilearga, Séamus. 1962. Paddy Sherlock's stories. Béaloideas 30.1-75.

Ó Siadhail, Micheál. 1989. Modern Irish: Grammatical structure and dialectal variation. Cambridge: Cambridge Univeristy Press.

Radford, Andrew. 1981. Transformational syntax. Cambridge: Cambridge University Press.

Ringbom, Hakan. 1987. The role of the first language in foreign language learning. Clevedon, U.K.: Multilingual Matters.

Sabban, Annette. 1982. Gälisch-Englischer Sprachkontakt. Heidelberg: Julius Groos.

Selinker, Larry. 1972. Interlanguage. IRAL 10.209-31.

Simpson, J.A. and Weiner, E.S.C., eds., 1989. The Oxford English dictionary, 2nd edition. Oxford: At the Clarendon Press.

Sjöholm, Kaj. 1983. Problems in "measuring" L2 learning strategies. In Psycholinguistics and foreign language learning, ed. by Hakan Ringbom, 174-94. Abo, Finland: Publications of the Research Institute of the Abo Akademi Foundation.

Sridhar, Kamal, and Sridhar, S. N. 1986. Bridging the paradigm gap: Second language acquisition theory and indigenized varieties of English. World Englishes 5.3-14.

Stenson, Nancy. 1981. Studies in Irish syntax. Tübingen: Gunter Narr.

Steiner, George. 1975. After Babel. London: Oxford University Press.

Thomason, Sarah and Terrence Kaufman, 1988. Language contact, creolization, and genetic linguistics. Berkeley: University of California Press.

Weinreich, Uriel. 1953/1968. Languages in contact. The Hague: Mouton.

Wright, Joseph, ed., 1898. English dialect dictionary. London: Oxford University Press.

Zobl, Helmut. 1986. Word order typology, lexical government, and the edition of multiple, graded effects in L2 word order. Language Learning 36. 159-83.

CREOLE VERB SERIALIZATION: TRANSFER OR SPONTANEITY?

Francis Byrne
Shawnee State University, Ohio

1.0. INTRODUCTION

Many of the research questions under discussion in L1 and especially L2 acquisition studies are inextricably linked to the theoretical debates within the pidginization and creolization literature. Of primary concern for this paper is the central issue in both second language acquisition (hereafter SLA) and creolization concerning the roles of transfer and universal tendencies in the respective processes. However, just as the relevance and/or importance of one or the other influence is unresolved in the L2 literature (see Odlin 1989 and White 1989, for example), so too is the same issue of prime importance in creole studies and is as yet still being debated. As a reflection of the theoretical diversity (and perhaps a symptom of the ongoing inconclusive discussion), a number of creolists have split into two rather contentious camps: those who espouse a substratum transfer viewpoint on the one hand, and the advocates of a universals approach to creole formation on the other.

This present paper will primarily be limited to discussing the viability of spontaneous generation of serial verb constructions (SVCs) in one Atlantic creole[1] - Saramaccan (SA), a language spoken in the central interior of Suriname, South America, by the decendants of the original African progenitors of the Saramaka tribe. The language is crucial in the argumentation on creole genesis of both the substratists and universalists and as such, any new evidence relating to one position or the other should help resolve the issue, or at least temper to some degree the perceived intractable positions. In this light, the paper will first briefly review the two divergent positions on creolization, followed by a discussion of the issue as it relates to transfer and SVCs. The following section will then present a compendium of evidence (often countering claims in the substrate literature) supporting a non-transfer position for the presence of SVCs in at least SA. The specific major concerns to be argued for and/or countered ((1) and (2a,b,c), respectively) are the following:

1)   Serialization results from an unmarked compendium of syntactic elements rather than being a highly marked strategy as intimated or claimed by Sebba (1987:213) and Joseph (1990:88). These unmarked elements directly account for the emergence of SVCs in SA (Byrne 1987: Chapter VIII).

2a)   Serialization is a rare phenomenon (Sebba 1987:213).

b)   Only those creoles whose formative substrate languages exhibit SVCs actually manifest SVCs themselves [because of transfer - my insertion] (Sebba 1987:214).

c)   The demographically strong Kwa (West Africa) substrate element in the initial stages of SA (and other Atlantic creoles) is directly responsible, through transfer, for SVCs in the language (Alleyne 1980; numerous papers in the volumes edited by Muysken & Smith (1986a) and Mufwene (to appear)).

2.0. CREOLISTICS AND ACQUISITION
2.1. The Processes and Positions

In first dealing more specifically with acquisition and creole studies, if a scholar accepts pidginization and creolization as distinct and viable operations, then they are looked upon as semiautonomous but related stages in language learning and linguistic consolidation, with pidginization being prior to creolization in the developmental continua. While no attempt will be made here to review the various views of pidginization, perhaps the less controversial of the two stages, it seems a fair generalization of the contemporary literature[2] to claim that it is extremely impoverished SLA in a multilingual[3] and strictly stratified setting; the result is that the target language is largely unavailable as a model. At the level of a community of speakers, the process in the early stages results in a highly reduced code (a non-natural language) and exhibits a very great degree of individual variation.[4] Given time, however, pidginization can "jell" (Philip Baker 1982) (i.e. gain predictability and consistency) and become a community-wide speech variety - a pidgin.

A common view of creolization, for its part (and noting that any statement on the subject will cause a nontrivial terminological debate among creolists), is that it is a subsequent development from pidginization and is typified as exhibiting at least the *minimal* attributes for the status of a natural language. From this perspective, a creole occurs when enough members of a community undergo the individual process of creolization and it consistently becomes the accepted language (as opposed to merely a speech variety) of a community (i.e. it becomes nativized - see Anderson (1983a)). It is how creolization, and hence a creole, develops natural language features that is a primary point of contention among creole scholars. Very generally speaking (and omitting many variant positions and subissues), we can classify theoretical orientations towards creolization from an acquisition perspective as being substrate or universal.[5]

2.1.1. Substrate
The first, or the substrate position, envisions a large measure of continuity from the socially subverient groups in a creole contact situation. Thus, in the case of the Atlantic creoles, there is considerable West African influence particularly from the Kwa and Mande languages, or those which substratists claim to constitute the primary African presence in the formative pidginization and creolization stages. From the standpoint of transfer and acquisition, native substrate linguistic influence (i.e. transfer) occurs in the speech of individuals in a pidgin/creole context and may then solidify in the emergent linguistic system. When and how this happens is one of the main points of disagreement in this school. That is, some substratists such as Alleyne (1980, 1986), Arends (1989, to appear), Carden & Stewart (1988) and Singler (1988), among others, do not accept creolization as an applicable concept for creole formation. For them (as a generalization but keeping in mind that they are not a theoretically homogeneous whole), all language building through grammatical expansion and complexification is done by adults during pidginization (i.e. L2) in response to an ever increasingly functional load for the incipient languages' societal interchanges. Moreover, they conclude that the process may take many generations rather than being a result of a full natural language emerging from the first native-born during L1 development (i.e. creolization) as a universals position would have it. Others such as Holm (1988, 1989), Mufwene (1986), Muysken & Smith (1986b), Sankoff & Brown (1976) and Seuren & Wekker (1986) accept the pidginization and creolization cycle, but vary in their positions as to when substrate influence primarily occurs, under what conditions, and to what degree.

2.1.2. Universals
The contending position is commonly known as either the universals or bioprogram approach (the latter coined by Bickerton (1981)). Briefly, the view as discussed in Bickerton (1981; 1984a,b; 1988), Baker (1982), Baker & Corne (1982), and Byrne (1985a; 1987; 1988b; 1989a,b) states that the grammars of the most radical creoles ("those which deviate most sharply from their original (L2) model" (Bickerton 1988:273)) come closest to approximating the unmarked state of our one innate and genetically-endowed language faculty. The depth or radicalness of a creole is a result of extremely impoverished SLA (i.e. extreme pidginization) where there is little or almost nonexistent contact with speakers of the target language. When children are born in such a situation, their primary input for L1 acquisition (i.e. creolization) will be the highly variable and linguistically deficient output of the L2 speakers. To develop the minimum attributes of a normal, natural language (which L1 acquisition ultimately produces), the children must rely on their innate linguistic knowledge as it unfolds in maturation. The process taken to its extreme, and without interference from historically longstanding or "older" languages, will eventually produce a blueprint of the human language faculty[6] and thus the most radical possible creole.

With more interference/input, however, based on more successful SLA on the part of adults, the resultant L1 will be a progressively less radical creole further away from any innate blueprint (leading to the more descriptively adequate term *differential creolization* in Byrne (1988b) to capture the disparate results). That is, since creolization is a process, there are greater or lesser degrees of application in any given creole setting depending on numerous linguistic and demographic factors. In other words, as numerous scholars have concluded (e.g., Baker 1982; Bickerton 1984a,b; Byrne 1983, 1987, 1988b; Hancock 1986; Mufwene 1987; and Carden & Stewart 1988), creolization does not apply equally in the creation of creole languages. Some of these languages are therefore "deeper" than others in that the former betray more features characteristic of the typology. (See Byrne (1987: Chapters II, VIII) as well as section 4 and associated footnotes in this paper for more references and details.) Needless to say, there is a one-to-one relationship between creolization and L1 acquisition given extremely limited and deficient input. As a result, transfer is not a primary consideration as it is with the substrate view, although there is nothing a priori excluding it if something less than the most optimum conditions for creolization exist.[7]

In the remainder of the paper, I will be primarily concerned with the question of whether a spontaneous generation analysis (based on limited but maximally unmarked categories) is a viable option to transfer to account for creole and, specifically, SA serial structures. To do so, I will first review transfer and serialization theory, and then delineate the two main creole views on serial verbs.

3.0. TRANSFER AND THE CREOLE SERIALIZATION CONTROVERSY
3.1. Transfer
The literature on transfer over the last few decades has primarily attempted to identify and define the operant constraints, conditions, and principles which are necessarily present for the process to take place during SLA. In a seminal statement on the issue, Weinreich (1953:33-44) makes a first approximation of the principle morphemic conditions which facilitate the process. These are:

1.) congruence (or the similarity between the native and target languages' forms and structures),

2.) morphemic boundedness (with free morphemes given preference),

3.) invariance (free, nonvariable morphemes), and

4.) simplicity (morphemes with perceptually simple functions).

Added to these, Larson-Freeman (1976a) found that an L2 item/structure's frequency of occurrence also aids the process. Finally, Anderson (1983a,b), in combining his own work with that of Weinreich, Larson-Freeman and others (e.g.

Zobl 1980a,b; Selinker 1969; Slcbin 1977) into a single statement, proposes the "transfer to somewhere principle," with free invariant and simple morphemes, as well as congruence again being among the foremost considerations.[8]

Finally, Odlin (1989), in the only comprehensive treatment of the subject matter to date, underscores the difficulty of definition, especially in light of the wide-ranging recent research. As a result, his "working definition" below encompasses a wider venue than previously formulated.

> Transfer is the influence resulting from similarities and differences between the target language and any other language that has been previously (and perhaps imperfectly) learned (p. 26).

The wording, especially *influence* and *similarities and differences*, permits Odlin to include expanded phenomena such as both negative and positive transfer among the scope of the topic. However, if anything, the book emphasizes that determining when *influence* has occurred is anything but easy; it is too easy to claim transfer in contact data simply due to L1-L2 congruence when other, non-transfer factors could have been the significant impetus for the emergence of particular data.

Regardless of any definitional and application difficulties with transfer, those scholars working within SLA studies also have a considerable methodological advantage over creolists in theory formation. That is, SLA specialists can empirically test their hypotheses[9] since SLA is an ongoing occurrence with no real limit to the availability of subjects, while creolists can only analyze the results of possible transfer considerably after the fact. The problem for creolists is that the primary data for their work is often 200 to 300 years removed from precisely when the languages, and possible transfer, have crystallized. Additionally, evidence of these languages' formative and/or prior states consist in large measure of amateur missionary accounts whose accuracy and integrity are usually suspect. Thus, in comparison to the direct and empirically verifiable evidence of the SLA scholars, often the only concrete and reliable data which creolists have for analysis, theory building, and a determination of possible transfer during the original pidgin/creole cycle are the indirect synchronic states of the substrate and creole languages. With regard to the transfer question, then, while the work of the SLA theorists is valuable, possibly the best and perhaps only aid their work has in determining whether transfer has taken place in creole languages is a modified version of congruence. That is, because there are no presently-existing L1 or L2 forms or structures to compare during the developmental stage of creoles, we are forced to analyze present-day versions of the contact languages which were in the original creole setting. A description of the operant principle for creolists to determine the presence or absence of transfer thus seems to reduce to something like the following statement:

3)   **Creole Congruence Condition**
        If a linguistic form and/or structure appears in a creole, and additionally
        if it is synchronically attested in one or a group of the original substrate
        contact languages, then transfer *may* be justified.

(3) should not be viewed as a license to affirm or void transfer simply because
there is or is not a morpheme-by-morpheme correspondence between selected
synchronic versions of substrate languages and present-day creoles. Just because
the most dependable and empirically sound data creolists have to work with is
synchronic, this is still not sufficient justification to uncritically apply congruence
as the final determining test (see Mufwene (1990) for extensive elaboration). Also
important is that the researcher attempt to understand the processes, structures, or
items under scrutiny through adequate analysis. That is, there should be cautious
use of superficial congruence as the first and only analytical criterion for transfer
since, in a nontrite sense, what may appear to be the same or different could
actually be quite the opposite.[10] This is exactly the point of the remainder of this
paper: Whether we have had adequate knowledge of serialization and the
demographics of the Saramaka, in both a general and creole-specific sense, to
justify transfer, or whether at least some such claims have been too hasty and
thereby do not detract from a spontaneous generation view of serial structures.

3.2. The Serial Controversy
We can generally define serialization, and by implication serial verbs, as the
phenomenon among many creole and non-creole languages in which verbs, or
verb-like formatives, function in various roles that are normally performed in
non-serializing languages by prepositions, adverbs, complementizers, or single
verbs (in the case of verbal extensions where one verb modifies another and a
serializing language's lexical repertoire is thereby expanded - see Sebba (1984)).
In adding to the definition, it is also generally assumed that SVCs have the
following characteristics:

4a)   The scope (in a semantic sense) of serial tense (TNS)[11] markers must range
        over an entire serial string regardless of the actual TNS-marking pattern
        instantiated (e.g. single, repetitive, or non-matrix marking) (Byrne, in
        press).

b)   Although two or more verbs are present, SVCs are part of a single
        proposition and retain a verbal categorical status while undertaking the
        grammatical functions or semantic extensions imposed by a central or
        matrix verb (Byrne, in press; Sebba 1987).

c)   No conjunctive (or subordination - my insertion) particle can appear in, or
        be inserted between, the serialized constituents without altering the
        meaning of the sentence (Schiller 1990:46).

d)   The second and subsequent occurrences of coindexed subjects may be
        phonologically null (i.e. are empty categories); second and subsequent
        occurrences of coindexed objects will be null (Bickerton 1989; Byrne
        1990, in press).

In relation to the above features, note first in (5a,b,c) below from SA that no
matter how the overall serial string is TNS marked,[12] the same exact reading
ensues.

5a) Kófi bi bái dí búku dá   dí muyée
     Kofi TNS buy the book give the woman
     'Kofi had bought the woman the book.'

 b) Kófi bi bái dí búku bi dá dí muyée
     'Kofi had bought the woman the book.'

 c) Kófi bái dí búku bi dá dí muyée
     'Kofi had bought the woman the book.'

Because there is but a single proposition involved in (5a-c) with the
arguments/properties determined by the matrix bái 'buy' (although two distinct
verbs are present), the temporal orientation must be the same. Thus it is
immaterial where or with which pattern TNS is overtly expressed; with matrix
verb only (5a) (the most common in and among serializing languages), repetitive
(5b), or non-matrix (5c) marking, the scopal domain (i.e. the extent of TNS
influence) encompasses the same syntactic realm.[13]

Second, there is no intrusive coordination or subordination marker between or
involved with either serial (bái 'buy' or dá 'give'). And finally, for a wide number
of reasons (see Byrne 1987), second and subsequent serials (at least in SA) have
subjects which are most commonly phonologically unexpressed (i.e. are null).
Each serial is thereby best looked at as contained within a sentential structure (see
section 4.2 for additional discussion).

3.2.1. Substratists & Serials
The substrate position is that there is a direct relationship between the presence
of SVCs in creoles and the original substrate contact languages. Arends (1989a,b),
Holm (1986, 1987, 1988), and Lefebvre (1986), among others, in a rather broad
generalization and omitting major differences, claim that there are strong lexical,
structural, and semantic links between Atlantic creoles and especially the Kwa
group of West African languages. Thus, in a simplification of the issues and
argumentation, the almost word-for-word identity in (6) and (7) below between
Kwa (e.g. Yoruba) and various creoles would loosely illustrate transfer based on
present-day congruence.

6a) Mo fí àdá   gé igi nâ   Yoruba (Nigeria)
    I take machete cut tree the   (Stahlke 1970)
    'I cut the tree with a machete.'

 b) el tuma e kuchu korta e karni   Papiamentu (Curacao creole)
    he take the knife cut the meat   (Sebba 1987)
    'He cut the meat with the knife.'

 c) mi téi fáka kóti dí páu   Saramaccan (Suriname Creole)
    I take knife cut the tree
    'I cut a tree with a knife.'

7a) mo so fún o   ...   Yoruba
    I tell give you   (Stahlke 1970)
    'I told you ...'

 b) mi e   verteri wan tori gi Meri   Sranan (Suriname creole)
    I ASPect tell   a   story give Mary   (Jansen et al. 1978)
    'I tell a story to Mary'

 c) mi táki dá i   Saramaccan
    I say give you
    'I said to you'

Included among various claims for the process, Sebba (1987:214) makes the fairly strong observation that there must be a direct causal relation between creoles and their substrate languages since "a relatively small proportion of the world's known creoles have [SVCs], and ... these are precisely the ones which have well-documented substrate input from serializing languages." And Faraclas (1989), for his part, concludes that the range and type of SVCs in Tok Pisin of Papua New Guinea and Nigerian Pidgin English duplicate what occurs in the surrounding substrate languages. This can only be explained by adducing transfer for creole serialization.

The literature on the substrate view is both extensive and impressive in its volume. The bottom line, however, seems to consistently revert back to the following syllogism: If serialization, for example, occurs in substrate languages, and they were present in the seminal contact situation, then it will appear in the creole. Taken another way, the extreme view is that **all** creole SVCs are a direct result of transfer from other languages.

3.2.2. Universalists & Serials

The contending view, in its strongest form (Bickerton 1981), states that serialization is not a product of substrate languages during creolization, but rather is a result of children having to develop a language almost ex nihilo from inadequate and deficient pidgin input. Serialization, then, is a direct reflection of our innate linguistic knowledge. In a less all-inclusive interpretation, Bickerton (1984a, b, 1988) explains that the bioprogram is best observed in the more radical creoles such as SA,[14] with others being progressively less "pure" because of more elaborated pidgin input (i.e. more successful L2 acquisition). In those cases with less than strict (i.e. deep or radical) creolization, more transfer would necessarily be expected, but in the instances of radical creolization, independent syntactic and categorical dynamics would require the emergence of a serial strategy. It is the viability of this latter position that the remainder of the paper will primarily concern itself.

4.0. Saramaccan Serialization & "Problematic" Counter-Proposals
4.1. Saramaccan Core Grammar & Serialization
In support of SVCs being a spontaneous development in at least radical creoles, Byrne (1987) found that the synchronic grammar of SA has a productive categorical repertoire consisting strictly of nouns and verbs as major categories[15] and determiners,[16] conjunctions, and TNS and aspect markers as minor categories. From the remaining normally assumed categories (taken from an Indo-European perspective), there are instances of prepositions in the language, but the only productive member of the class is the general locative *a* 'in, on, into, from, to, etc.'. The remainder such as *ku* 'with' or *fu* 'for' are functionally marginal and can generally be expressed through alternative syntactic means.[17]

In taking exception to above claims, Muysken (1987) contends that the category preposition is in fact productive in SA in that the number and frequency of prepositional instantiations are greater than implied or portrayed in Bickerton (1984b) and Bickerton & Byrne (1985) (and by extension, the expanded discussion in Byrne (1987)). However, I have some serious misgivings with his contentions. First, Muysken (personal communication) notes that the data utilized for his conclusions came from de Groot (1977), a Dutch-Saramaccan dictionary with the normal information associated with such a volume. That is, there are the usual meanings presented for each entry, assertions of categoriality, and one or two sentence examples, but there are certainly no analyses to support the categorical claims, nor does Muysken offer any analysis to add credence to his categorization of certain formatives as prepositions.

Second, the majority of items which Muysken purports to be prepositions are questionable, even without analysis. *té* 'until', for example, exhibits verbal characteristics for some speakers in the southern dialect areas.[18] All but two others (and even these are doubtful without analyses) are either wh-forms (subject to independent movement), or members of an extensive class of subordinating conjunctions (see Byrne 1988a).

Finally, Schiller (1990, personal communication) argues that the presence of the category preposition in the categorical inventory of a serializing language is immaterial to the presence of SVCs themselves. For one, in the many languages which he reviews (including creoles and West African Kwa, Papuan, and Southeast Asian languages), prepositional marking and a corresponding serial form never overlap; each has its distinct functional load and subsumes complementary semantic space (i.e. there is a specialization of SVC and prepositional strategies). Moreover, prepositions in serializing languages can be "extremely marked," but are often preferable for specific processes. For example, the focus of prepositional arguments or entire PPs are expressively simpler at the discourse level, and so a speaker would naturally select a prepositional option over serialization.

In Schiller's most important formulation for purposes of this paper (and one reminiscent of the argumentation on SA prepositions above and in Byrne (1987)), he proposes (p. 54) the *Semantic Case Instantiation Principle* which states that "semantic relations are instantiated by the most concrete possible mechanism." By this he means that if a language does not have a morphological or prepositional means of expressing certain grammatical relations, it will incorporate SVCs. However, because of functional complementarity, it is irrelevant if the category preposition exists in a language since serialization could still be needed, often overwhelmingly so, if the occurrence and selection of prepositions is minimal (as in SA). In other words, prepositions and serials can and often do coexist, with each staking out its own domain.

Given the above difficulties with Muysken's claims and the theoretical contributions from Schiller, there seems to be no reason to modify the position above and in Byrne (1987), namely that prepositions are marginal in SA and the category is neither a viable component of the most radical creolization nor significant in cases like SA in inhibiting SVCs.

In returning to the limited SA categorical repertoire, there are likewise few instances of the major category adjective in predicate contexts,[19] nor for complementizers. With very few exceptions, "complementizers" such as preclausal fu 'for, obligation' and táa/táki 'say, that' exhibit the diagnostics of a verb. Nor are adverbs a consistently productive class; their functions are often achieved through the use of SVCs.

The categorical limitations of synchronic SA, along with the primacy of one internal NP argument within a clause (i.e., there is only a limited presence of two internal argument strings with contiguous NP objects of the type *John gave THE MAN THE PEN*) and aspects of the Saramaka's chronological and demographic history (see Byrne (1987: Chapter II), Price (1976; 1983a,b), and section 4.3 in this paper), lead to the view that because early SA contained the **minimum** syntactic attributes necessary for the status of a natural language, the Saramaka had to utilize what was available to maximal possible effect to express the critical grammatical functions of language. As a result, they adopted a serial strategy in which verbs were used in place of the "missing" formative-types. Given the facts and analysis, then, serialization in at least radical creoles is not in itself a part of universal grammar per se, nor of transfer, but is a necessary by-product of such languages' phrase structure and categorical status. Hence, rather than using adverbs, prepositions, or contiguous object NPs, among other categories and configurations, the Saramaka utilized a verb serialization strategy as in (8).

8a) a féfi dí wósu kábá   Adverbial-like Serial
   he paint the house finish
   'He painted the house already.'

  b) a téí góni súti dí pingó   Preposition-replacing Serial
    he take gun shoot the pig
    'He shot the pig with a gun.'

  c) Kófi bái dí búku dá di muyée   Three Argument Intervening Serial
    Kofi buy the book give the woman
    'Kofi bought the woman the book.'

In presuming the early form of the language to generally exhibit the same categorical limitations as synchronic SA (a supposition which is supported both by the patterns of change discussed in Byrne (1987)[20] and the history of the Saramaka people),[21] the exigency of the spontaneous generation of SVCs in wide-ranging functions was and is inescapable. While serializing languages among the coterie of original African contact languages could certainly have reinforced an emerging serial system in an incipient radical creole like SA, to maintain that transfer was solely responsible for the strategy itself would be to ignore the syntactic dynamics of the language as well as the remaining evidence against such a strict view.

4.2. Markedness & Typological Rarity of Serialization
4.2.1. Markedness

A common configurational approach to SVCs among scholars such as Mark Baker (1989), Schiller (1990, to appear) Sebba (1987), Seuren (1991), and Winford (to appear), among others, is to characterize them as being within a series of VPs, or derivatives of such an analysis, as in (9a,b) below from Sebba (p. 129) and Baker (p.520), respectively.

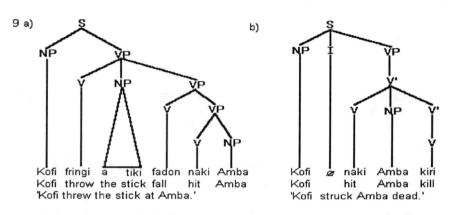

9 a)
```
Kofi fringi  a    tiki  fadon  naki  Amba
Kofi throw  the stick  fall   hit   Amba
'Kofi threw the stick at Amba.'
```

b)
```
Kofi   ø   naki  Amba  kiri
Kofi       hit   Amba  kill
'Kofi struck Amba dead.'
```

In evaluating the configurations and categorical status of serials in (9a,b), both Sebba and Baker refer to them as being somewhat exceptional. Specifically, Sebba (p. 213) observes:

> ... such a **distinctive** [emphasis added] construction type [i.e. serials]
> ... **are by no means universal** [emphasis added]: in fact they are restricted to a rather small subset of the world's languages, and to four geographical regions in particular: West Africa, the Caribbean, South East Asia and New Guinea.

Baker (p. 550), for his part, notes:

> ... there is a class of serial verb constructions that have a syntactic structure **significantly different from that of all comparable constructions** [emphasis added]: conjunctions, clausal embeddings, adpositional phrases, and "small clause" predicates. The primary difference between a language that has serialization and one that does not is that serializing languages allow V's to embed within V' **to form a double-headed construction** [emphasis added].

The implications of such statements are that SVCs constitute a particularly marked phenomenon from both a Chomskyan structural perspective and a Greenberg (1966) distributional sense.[22] In relation to creole genesis, the suggestion is that such marked structures would not naturally emerge in Bickerton's L1 universals view of creolization since it is presumed that children normally select the maximally unmarked options during L1. For SVCs to appear, then, a viable option is that they are a result of transfer, especially because, as Sebba claims (p. 214), "... a relatively small proportion of the world's known creoles have serial verbs, and ... these are precisely the ones which have well-documented substrate input from serializing languages."

If the structures in (9a,b) are in fact accurate, then to account for creole SVCs through transfer would certainly be a logical conclusion. However, additional serial evidence belies a strictly VP analysis and its associated marked status; rather, each of the serial verbs in (8), and more than likely those in (6), (7) and (9), are within separate clauses in the overall sentence complex.

Briefly, as part of the empirical evidence for a clause status is the possibility of overt nominatively-marked tense marking with most SA SVCs as in (5) in section 3.2. Such marking, where allowed, first indicates a finite status for the contiguous serial verb (those that do not allow TNS are best viewed as infinitives).[23] Second, TNS marking warrants the presence of a subject for a variety of reasons within Government and Binding (GB) theory (see Byrne 1985a, 1986). In empirical support, we find that overt subjects are variably attested for by some speakers in selected contexts, including the Instrumental serial (10) (Byrne 1984b, 1987: Chapter VI) and complements of perception verbs (11) (Byrne 1989a).

10) ai téi dí pau   (ai) náki dí dágu
     he take the stick (he) hit the dog
     'He hit the dog with the stick.'

11) a$_i$ sí en$_j$ (a$_i$) tá kó   a dí wósu
     he see him (he) ASP come to the house
     'He saw him coming to the house.'

Neither (10) nor (11) is in any way construed by the speakers as constituting parataxis or conjuncts (for empirically verifiable reasons).

A second bit of a theory-data combination for SVC clausal status involves movement phenomena. In all cases where there are serials of the type illustrated in (5), (8) and (10) (or any other non-coordinate sentence for that matter), all NPs may move through questioning or focus to sentence-initial position. The only way that this could happen, presuming multiclausal status for serials and GB theory, is for the NP to temporarily "land" in a lower preclausal slot before continuing to sentence-initial position. The configurational and categorical details for SA serials should thereby be something like (12), with each verb within a serial string dominated by a sentence node.

12) [s'[s a$_i$ téi dí pau [s'[s (a$_i$) náki dí dágu]]]]

In addition to SA, other serializing languages likewise exhibit the essential clausal diagnostics with SVCs. Consider the data below from Akan (West africa) and Seselwa (an Indian Ocean French-based creole).

13) meyɛɛ$_i$ adwuma memaa$_i$ Amma   Akan
    I-do-PRET work   I-give-PRET Amma   Schachter (1974)
    'I worked for Amma.'

14) bug$_i$ ti$_j$ pran balye koko   (i$_i$) ti$_j$ bat li   Seselwa
    guy TNS take broom coconut 3ps TNS hit him   Bickerton (1989)
    'A guy hit him with a coconut broom.'

In both Akan and Seselwa, like SA, the basic attributes for a clausal determination are present. Not only does TNS marking occur with each non-initial serial, but phonologically-overt subjects are likewise categorical (Akan) or possible (Seselwa - e.g. i's/he'), leading to a structural conclusion for (13) and (14) like that portrayed in (12).

These considerations (i.e. subject, verb, TNS marking, and movement (for SA)), along with comparisons with other attested structure types, both lead to a conclusion that each serial is within a separate clause and militate against the non-clausal analyses of Baker and Sebba (see Byrne 1986, 1987, 1991 for more details). In addition, with a clausal analysis for SVCs, there is now no reason to treat them as particularly marked and thus only plausible through transfer; with SVCs being enclosed within a basic sentence structure, there is nothing unusual in the categories or configuration since clausal constituents consistently emerge naturally in L1. From this perspective, there is no reason why clausal SVCs should not likewise appear in creolization if the conditions were felicitous.

Of course the best evidence in support of spontaneous serial generation would be data from creoles which did not have the presumably indispensable (from a transfer approach) SVC substrate presence. In fact, recent work has claimed to have uncovered just such languages. For one, Pasch (to appear) points out that Sango of the Central African Republic exhibits innovations such as SVCs which are not explicable from its substrate languages. For another, Bickerton (1989)[24] has found extensive SVCs in archival records and the synchronic speech of Seselwa as exemplified in (14) above. Critically, there was no substrate with SVCs present during or after the creole's formative years; the primary non-European input was from non-serializing Bantu languages. Such claims, if accurate, are unambiguous in advancing the likelihood of SVC creole spontaneity.

4.2.2. SVCs a Typological Rarity?

As a result of the discussion in section 4.2.1, there seems good reason not to categorize SVCs as particularly marked from a Chomskyan perspective, but still outstanding is the contention that SVCs are rare among the linguistic systems in the world and thereby marked from a Greenbergian purview. The pertinent statement, repeated from the onset of the previous section, is that "[SVCs] are restricted to a rather small subset of the world's languages ..." (Sebba 1987:213). However, based on current work, a consensus appears to be emerging which maintains that SVCs are in fact more common than anyone previously thought.

At the May 1990 Ohio State conference on SVCs, one of the main themes involved analyses of serials or serial-like forms in languages which were here-to-fore not thought to contain the structures. Of course, the danger in broadening the expanse of SVCs, as Joseph (1990:87) points out, is that it could render meaningless any restricting or qualifying definitions. Nevertheless, there are intriguing bits of data from a wide array of languages which can rationally be construed as SVCs. These are most commonly of the deictic type (Winford, to appear) in which a [+motion, +directional] verb is juxtaposed to a semantic matrix. Consider the representative data below.

15a) Come fly with me.   English

   b) Go tell it on the mountain.   (Pullum 1990)

16) viens prendre ta   lettre   French
     come take   your letter   (Schiller 1990)
     'Come take your letter.'

17a) O-ru:ʰ-O   O-ji:b-O   ʔaxu-uk   min l-ja:m'a   Arabic
      imp-go-2sg imp-get-2sg brother-your from the-university
      'Go get your brother from the university.'   (Hussein 1990)

   b) ca:d-O   ʔal-O-l-i   ʔiʔnu ʔistara-O   sayya:ra
       came-back-3sg told-3sg-to-me that brought-3sg car
       'He told me again that he bought a car.'

18a) Tom-i   cip-uro ttwi-a ka-ɛss-ta   Korean
      NOM house-to run   go-PAST-DEC   (Jo 1990)
      'Tom ran to the house.'

   b) Tom-i   kong-lul kaci-a ka-ass-ta

NOM ball-ACC have   go-PAST-DEC
'Tom took the ball away.'

As Pullum (1990) describes such potential SVCs, they are typically found in imperative sentences (but not always - e.g. (17b; 18a,b), and are preposed to a matrix (but not in (18a,b)). In addition, Winford (to appear) notes that if a language minimally exhibits a serial strategy, it will at least include the deictic types as exemplified above (i.e. with go, come or their equivalents). Thus Korean, for example, but not the other languages, includes deictics and additional types such as the causative in (19) (again from Jo).

19)   Tom-i   Mary-lul ttayli-a cuki-ass-ta
      NOM   -ACC strike   kill-PAST-DEC
      'Tom struck Mary dead.'

The purport of such data is that what was previously thought to be a limited phenomenon is actually wider-ranging and includes more languages and geographical areas than claimed by Sebba. The implications are, first, that SVCs are not the rare marked structures which a more restricted distribution would warrant and, second, that they can apparently appear spontaneously and/or as part of normal diachrony (unless someone wants to argue transfer for the languages above as well as others discussed in Joseph & Zwicky (1990)).

4.3. Demographics of SA Briefly Revisited
In returning to strictly a discussion of SA and the Saramaka, the conventional wisdom as found in Price (1976; 1983a,b) and Byrne (1987: Chapter II) in relation to the development of Suriname and the tribe and language in question is that one-third of all African slaves were always from the non-serializing Benue-Congo languages. The remainder spoke serializing languages primarily from the Kwa group (64% before 1700 and 50% after until 1723). Since SA is generally thought to date from roughly 1680, and in taking the percentages at face value while presuming that the provenience of the original and subsequent members of the Saramaka tribe reflected the overall slave population, then it follows that the tribe should have been dominated by speakers of the Kwa serializing languages. It is this presumption which is open to question here.

Before discussing possible Kwa influence in SA, we should first backtrack a bit to put the tribe and its formation into perspective. Suriname was initially colonized in 1651 by English settlers from Barbados. It was not until 1667, however, when the Dutch captured the colony and commenced the importation of massive numbers of slaves for plantation labor that radical creolization began. The circumstances fostering the creation of deep creoles, perhaps unique in degree during the era of Western expansion and colonization, were in large measure due to the Dutch philosophy towards slavery and the treatment of slaves. They were the acknowledged masters of large-scale plantation development in the Caribbean, and as such, they felt there had to be a continual influx of disposable slaves for maximum efficiency in agricultural production. The statistics in Suriname from 1671 to 1700 and, in a wider view, from 1671 to 1750 reflect the inhuman treatment. During the 29 years of the first period, 13,180 slaves were imported and approximately 6,000 perished (or almost one in two). The second period is even grimmer; 145,980 slaves arrived during this 79 year time span and roughly 91,000 died (or almost two out of every three). Overall, the chance of death for an African slave in Suriname within ten years of arrival was 50%.

For our purposes here, the gruesome statistics had two major implications. First, while many who died were more than likely the earlier arrivals who were literally worked to death, they were also the ones who had become most fluent with pidgin. There must have been constant repidginization (i.e. ever more deficient SLA from continually more marginal models) on the part of the new slaves who doubled or tripled the slave population every ten years until 1730. With such a scenario, there was no possibility for pidgin stabilization and complexification because the new imports acquired the speech of slaves who themselves had little time in the colony. That is, there was no generational continuity over normal life spans which would foster the syncretism of early pidgin's widespread variation and the development of natural language features.

Second, the horrendous slave conditions in Suriname along with the simple desire to be free motivated the slaves to escape into the rain forest at the first opportunity. This led directly to the formation of the independent bush maroon communities, of which the Saramaka were the earliest to coalesce. The process by which this happened is what is at issue; the claim is that pidginized SA developed on the Portuguese Jews' plantations with the serializing Kwa languages not being as significant in the genesis of SA as the gross percentages above would suggest.

The Portuguese Jews arrived in Suriname from Brazil around 1665. With the onset of the Inquisition in the Iberian Peninsula, many Jews left and settled in more harmonious areas, one of these being "the rich sugar-producing region of Pernambuco in Brazil" (Rawley 1981:82) which the Dutch briefly controlled. When the Dutch were ejected, the Portuguese and some of their slaves also departed, many to Suriname to again establish plantations around Joden Savannah, an area contiguous to the first villages of the Saramaka. On these plantations, unlike the others in the colony on which English pidgin was spoken, the slaves developed a strictly Portuguese pidgin (Morris Goodman, personal communication). Since the first contingents of the Saramaka largely escaped from the Portuguese plantations (Goodman 1987), it is a reasonable assumption to think that early SA primarily emanated from this pidgin (thus explaining the strong Portuguese lexical presence in SA). Moreover, there is also good reason to believe that many of the original Saramaka natively spoke non-serializing Bantu languages. In support of the somewhat unorthodox claim to the provenience of the Saramaka, Postma (1975) notes that the Dutch, the exclusive supplier of slaves to both Suriname and the Pernambuco region of Brazil before their ejection, maintained extensive trading with Bantu-speaking Angola because many planters, especially the Portuguese sugar growers in Brazil (Rawley, p. 83), preferred these Africans over Kwa-speaking slaves. Now it is not unreasonable to presume that the Portuguese Jews in Brazil also preferred Angolan slaves. When they moved to Suriname, their preferences undoubtedly did not change. Since at least one-third of all slaves introduced into Suriname were from Angola,[25] I suggest that the Portuguese Jews, whose plantations in the colony appear to have grown and expanded much faster than those of the Dutch (and others) (Byrne 1987:23), primarily populated their holdings with Angolan slaves. The significance of the claim to the genesis of SA is that the language developed the most extensive serializing system that we know of among the creole languages in the Western Hemisphere (Winford 1990) from a deficient Portuguese pidgin whose substrate largely consisted of non-serializing input. Overall, the compilation of the intriguing facts in this section would seem to therefore suggest that the origin of SVCs in SA could have been a result of the particular combination of categorical and configurational properties discussed in section 4.1, and not transfer. Once more, then, the evidence indicates that a spontaneous generation of SVCs is certainly possible in at least SA.

5.0. CONCLUSIONS

In relation to the positions iterated in section 1 concerning the origin of serialization in creole languages (i.e., whether due to substrate transfer or spontaneous generation), given the facts and discussion, the obvious conclusion would seem to be that spontaneity is possible in creolization. A combination of syntactic, comparative, theoretical, and demographic evidence posed in this paper strongly points in this direction. However, to completely dismiss SVC transfer is another matter. There undoubtedly are close similarities in the semantics of particular serial-types in Atlantic creoles and West African languages. And the syntax of the structures is for all intents and purposes apparently the same (based on imperfect knowledge of the phenomenon from ongoing and somewhat contentious research and claims). From a congruence standpoint, then, there would seem to be a causal relationship between the substrate languages in the contact situation and the evolution of serialization in a resultant creole. The positions of Faraclas (1989) and Sebba (1987) (see section 2.1) would therefore appear to have merit.

However, to ascribe transfer to all creole serialization is jumping the gun a bit. For one, Byrne (1987) has shown that a serial strategy is a perfectly natural consequence of certain categorical and phrase structure features (see section 4.1). Arguments to the contrary have not proved effective (e.g. Muysken 1987). Even though there were undoubtedly some serializing languages in the original SA contact situation, the demographics of the people's early history most probably rendered transfer ineffective. At the least (and this is my contention), any serializing substrate languages could have contributed serial reinforcement to a naturally spontaneous process and grammatical stratagem.

It would seem, then, that the only viable approach to serialization in these languages is to leave open the possibility of both transfer and universal processes operating within creolization. In support, L2 scholars such as White (1989) and Odlin (1989) conclude in quite different books with quite divergent themes that both universals and transfer processes are operant in SLA. Moreover, studies by numerous creole scholars (see sections 2 & 3 and associated footnotes) have concluded, contrary to previous thinking, that creolization does not apply equally in the creation of creole languages. Rather, due to extralinguistic factors, these languages may emerge with a greater or lesser degree of input from both the superstrate and substrate languages and will consequently be variably creole from the onset. The implications of such thinking could mean that serialization develops in creoles either as a result of the syntactic dynamics of the emergent system (e.g. SA), or, given possibly less radical creolization, a product of some level of transfer. When and in what degree one process contributes to serialization over the other should be the center of investigative efforts, not whether one or the other is exclusively the cause of serialization in creole languages.

NOTES

1. These are creoles found in the Atlantic basin, or those of West Africa, the Caribbean,   and eastern North and South America (Hancock 1971).

2. See, for example, Baker (1982), Bickerton (1981), Bickerton & Odo (1976), Blackshire-Belay (1993), Holm (1988, 1989), and Mühlhäusler (1986). The following definition is based on Byrne (1987), although there will be no attempt here at defending it since this is not the main purpose of the paper.

3. But Philip Baker (personal communication) counters this statement by noting that "multilingual communities are not a necessary precondition - pidgin English developed in Canton, Australia, and many essentially monolingual Pacific islands as a result of their contact with Anglophones."

4. However, Givón (1984) has found significant rule-governed behavior in early pidgin settings. See that reference for details.

5. A third view, or the superstrate approach, is commonly attributed to the French School and especially Chaudenson (1977, 1986, 1991), Hazaël-Massieux (1988), and Valdman (1977, 1983). It views creolization primarily as developing from a linguistic approximation of the socially dominant and most powerful language group (the superstrate) in a pidgin/creole setting. In the case of the French creoles, which is the school's primary interest, their elaboration originated largely from 17th century substandard French dialects through a process of overgeneralization on the part of non-French-speaking slaves/workers. The superstrate view thus represents fairly normal dialect transmission, but mediated somewhat in the French creole varieties by the demographics and multilingual setting of plantation society. The differences among the superstratists reside in the degree of superstrate influence allowed.

6. The view is that "older" languages can change in many different directions, but within prescribed boundaries. By so changing, they inevitably take on features/characteristics, at least in part, that move away from our linguistic bedrock. For an incipient creole to have contact with an "older" target (i.e. superstrate) language during its formative stage will cause the creole to deviate from our basic language faculty by acquiring differing levels of the target.

7. An ever-increasingly larger group of scholars allows for a combination of both positions. See, for example, Huttar (1991), Mufwene (1986) and Muysken & Smith (1986b), among others.

8. The actual statement of the 'transfer to somewhere principle' is found in Anderson (1983c:182). This states:
A grammatical form or structure will occur consistently and to a significant extent in the interlanguage as a result of transfer if (1) natural acquisitional principles are consistent with the L1 structure or (2) there already exists within the L2 input the potential for (mis)generalization from the input to produce the same form or structure. Furthermore, in such transfer preference is given in the resulting interlanguage to free, invariant, functionally simple morphemes which are congruent with the L1 and L2 (or there is congruence between the L1 and natural acquisitional processes) and the morphemes occur frequently in the L1 and/or the L2.

9. As examples of such empirical SLA analyses, see Meisel (1983) and Slobin (1985), among many others.

10. See endnote 13 for an example of rather hasty conclusions dealing with both transfer and a universals presumptions.

11. This is a metaphorical use of the term *tense* to save unnecessary discussion. As extensively elaborated in Byrne (1987, 1989a) and the theoretical literature in this paper, "tense" markers exemplified here may actually range somewhere between tense and aspectual readings (a characteristic common to creoles and many West African languages), but all function, as far as is known, in the same way as tense operators in scopal considerations.

12. The only nonrepresentative aspect of the data in (6) is that sentences like (b) and (c) often are variably grammatical among the informants - see Byrne (in press) for an elaboration and explanation of the variable TNS patterning in SA and other serializing languages.

13. A recent discussion over the significance of the data in (5), and especially (5c) repeated below, nicely exemplifies the type of misunderstandings which led to the original formulation of the Creole Congruence Condition.

i)   Kófi bái dí búku bi dá dí muyée
        Kofi buy the book TNS give the woman
        'Kofi had bought the woman the book.'

Briefly, Boretzky (to appear) took issue with my claim in Byrne (1987) that the TNS marking in SA serials like (i) apparently had no counterpart, as far as was known, among the Benue-Kwa group of West African languages and thus could not have resulted from transfer. He responded that in fact Fante does indeed exhibit similar marking as in (ii) and thereby could have served as the source for transfer to SA.

ii)   o- fi   dan no mu a-   ba
        he leave house the in perfective-come
        'He has arrived from the house.'
                        (Balmer & Grant 1929:120)

However, as it has turned out, both sides were incorrect. First, (ii) is quite different from (i) (see Byrne, to appear), and second, the combined processes of scope and spreading determine the TNS patterning in a serializing language (see Byrne, in press, for an extensive discussion of the processes). That is, transfer has nothing to do with TNS instantiations since they are a characteristic of the entire typology of serialization.

14. This view has been expressed by a theoretical cross section of creolists, but not for the same reasons. See Alleyne (1979), Bickerton (1984a, b), Byrne (1987; 1988a, b), and Washabaugh (1981) for the details and reasoning behind the various positions.

15. The other major categories postulated in the theoretical literature are prepositions and adjectives. See Chomsky (1981, 1982) for more details on both major and minor categories.

16. From a non-theoretical viewpoint, determiner forms are usually looked upon as articles and demonstratives in many languages, but in others such as creoles, a wider distribution of functions is clearly evident. In SA, for example, not only do determiners and determiner-like formatives function as articles and demonstratives, but also as relative clause markers, subordinating conjunctions, and as markers of syntactic focus. See Byrne (1988a) for more details.

17. For example, the Instrumental role can either be expressed prepositionally (i) or serially (ii).

i)   a kóti dí beée ku   wan fáka
          he cut the bread with a   knife
          'He cut the bread with a knife.'

ii)   a téi wan fáka kóti dí beée
          he take a   knife cut the bread
          'He cut the bread with a knife.'

Of the two, (ii) seems to be the older, original SA structure primarily because the prepositional
pattern in (i) seems to be currently supplanting the serial strategy in terms of its ever increasing
functional load.

Possession also has alternatives of expression: through a postnominal prepositionally fu (iii), or
positionally in a possessor-possessed juxtaposition (iv).

iii)   koósu fu Johánesi tene bigá a bi tá   féti
          clothes of Johánesi torn because he Tense Aspect fight
          'Johanesi's clothes are torn because he was fighting.'

iv)   Johánesi koósu   tene bigá a bi tá féti
          Johánesi clothes...
          'Johanesi's clothes are torn because he was fighting.'

For more details on the Instrumental role and fu in SA, see Byrne (1984a, b; 1985b).

18. See Byrne (1987: 237f, 1990) for a discussion of SA dialects and dialect areas.

19. What we might call predicate adjectives in many languages exhibit the full range of verb
diagnostics in SA and other creole languages. For example, like unambiguously verbal forms, tense
and modality markers can precede these forms (i), and they can copy in sentence-initial position
for emphasis (ii).

i)   dí wómi bi   sa   wísíwási
          the man Tense Modal worthless
          'The man would have been worthless.'

ii)   wisiwási dí wómi wísíwási
          'The man is really WORTHLESS.'

See Sebba (1986) and Seuren (1986) for many more details along these lines.

20. The patterns of change deal with fully finite SVCs passing through numerous diachronic stages
before ultimate reanalysis to other non-verbal categories. See Byrne (1987) for in-depth
discussions.

21. What primarily distinguishes SA from other creoles around the world is that the progenitors of the language escaped from plantations into the jungle interior of Suriname, usually only after a short time in the country as a slave. This scenario guaranteed two things: first, there was little time for any slave to acquire pidgin before escape and so the communal speech should have been maximally marginal and thereby linguistically distant from the basic attributes of a natural language. With pidgins being the primary input to creolization, the children born under these conditions would consequently have had minimally developed input for their L1 acquisition, thus presumably producing a particularly deep (i.e. radical) creole. Second, the incipient Saramaka (the tribe formed around 1680) excluded themselves from significant contact with the socially dominant Europeans and their languages until the 1950s and '60s. SA thereby did not undergo contact-induced influence as did virtually all other Atlantic creoles. This ensured that the language primarily sustained only internal change over the centuries and maintained, as near as possible, its original creole structures and categories.

22. See Mufwene (1991) for a detailed discussion on markedness and creoles.

23. For a detailed analysis of the process of clause change from a finite to infinitive status, see Byrne (1987: Chapters VI, VII). Also see Joseph (1983) and Mufwene & Dijkhoff (1989) for additional comments, particularly on the nature of *finiteness*.

24. Also see Bickerton (1990) and Seuren (1990) for a debate on the details of Seselwa SVCs in Bickerton (1989).

25. The one-third figure is somewhat in doubt. Postma (1975:37) reports that "owing to the relative independence of the D[utch] W[est] I[ndia] C[ompany] Angola trade, comparatively little data has been preserved for this area." The actual figures could therefore be a some percentage points higher or lower. See Postma for more discussion on the issue.

REFERENCES

Alleyne, Mervyn. 1979. On the genesis of languages. The genesis of language, ed. by Kenneth C. Hill, 89-107. Ann Arbor, MI: Karoma.

Alleyne, Mervyn. 1980. Comparative Afro-American: An historical-comparative study of English-based Afro-American dialects of the New World. Ann Arbor, MI: Karoma.

Alleyne, Mervyn. 1986. Substratum influences: Guilty until proven innocent. In Pieter Muysken & Norval Smith, eds, 301-315.

Anderson, Roger W., ed. 1983a. Pidginization and creolization as language acquisition. Rowley, MA: Newbury House.

Anderson, Roger W. 1983b. Introduction: A language acquisition interpretation of pidginization and creolization. In Roger W. Anderson, ed., 1-56.

Anderson, Roger W. 1983c. Transfer to somewhere. Language transfer in language learning, ed. by Susan Gass & Larry Selinker, 177-201. Rowley, MA: Newbury House.

Arends, Jacques. 1989. Syntactic developments in Sranan. Doctoral dissertation, Katholieke Universiteit, Nijmegen, Holland.

Arends, Jacques. To appear. Towards a gradualist model of creolization. In Francis Byrne & John Holm, eds.

Baker, Mark. 1989. Object sharing and projection in serial verb constructions. Linguistic Inquiry 20:513-553.

Baker, Philip. 1982. The contribution of non-Francophone immigrants to the lexicon of Mauritian Creole. Doctoral thesis, University of London.

Baker, Philip & Chris Corne. 1982. Isle de France Creole: Affinities and origins. Ann Arbor, MI: Karoma.

Balmer, W.T. & F.C.F. Grant. 1929. A grammar of the Fante-Akan language. London: Atlantis Press.

Bickerton, Derek. 1981. Roots of language. Ann Arbor, MI: Karoma.

Bickerton, Derek. 1984a. The language bioprogram hypothesis and second language acquisition. In William E. Rutherford, ed., 141-161.

Bickerton, Derek. 1984b. The language bioprogram hypothesis. The Behavioral and Brain Sciences 7.173-188.

Bickerton, Derek. 1988. Creole languages and the bioprogram. Linguistics: The Cambridge survey. Vol. 2, Linguistic theory: Explanations and implications, ed. by Frederick J. Newmeyer, 268-284. Cambridge: Cambridge University Press.

Bickerton, Derek. 1989. Seselwa serialization and its significance. Journal of Pidgin and Creole Languages 4.155-183.

Bickerton, Derek. 1990. If it quacks like a duck ... A reply to Seuren. Journal of Pidgin and Creole Languages 5.293-303.

Bickerton, Derek & Carol Odo. 1976. General phonology and pidgin syntax. Vol. 1 of Final Report on NSF Grant No. GS-39748. University of Hawaii, ms.

Bickerton, Derek & Francis Byrne. 1985. Syntactic markedness and parametric variation. University of Hawaii, ms.

Blackshire-Belay, Carol A. 1993. Foreign Workers' German: Is it a Pidgin?. In Francis Byrne & John Holm, eds.

Boretzky, Norbert. To appear. The concept of rule, rule borrowing and substrate influence in creole languages. In Salikoko Mufwene, ed.

Byrne, Francis. 1983. Algunos aspectos del Saramacán. Cumaná, Venezuela: Publication of the Universidad de Oriente.

Byrne, Francis. 1984a. Fi and fu: Origins and functions in some Caribbean English-based creoles. Lingua 62.97-120.

Byrne, Francis. 1984b. Instrumental in Saramaccan. York Papers in Linguistics 11.39-50.

Byrne, Francis. 1985a. Proprox in Saramaccan. Linguistic Inquiry 16.313-20.

Byrne, Francis. 1985b. Some aspects of the syntax of fu in Saramaccan. Amsterdam Creole Studies VIII.1-25.

Byrne, Francis. 1986. Evidence against grammars without empty categories. Linguistic Inquiry 17.754-759.

Byrne, Francis. 1987. Grammatical relations in a radical creole. Amsterdam/Philadelphia: Benjamins.

Byrne, Francis. 1988a. Deixis as a noncomplementizer strategy for creole subordination marking. Linguistics 26.335-364.

Byrne, Francis. 1988b. Towards a theory of theta-marking and creole depth. Language change and contact: NWAVE-XVI, ed. by Kathleen Ferrara et al. Texas Linguistics Forum 30.66-72.

Byrne, Francis. 1989a. Determining finite/nonfinite complement and serial structures in Saramaccan and other languages. Paper presented at the Round Table on Finite and Infinitival Clauses in Creole Languages, University of Chicago, April 18.

Byrne, Francis. 1989b. Some consequences of exceptionally deprived L2 input in first language acquisition. Interlingual processes, ed. by Hans Dechert & Manfred Raupach, 17-32. Tübingen: Gunter Narr Verlag.

Byrne, Francis. 1990. Review of Studies in Saramaccan language structure, ed. by Mervyn Alleyne. Journal of Pidgin and Creole Languages 5.131-138.

Byrne, Francis. 1991. Approaches to "missing" internal (and external) arguments in serial structure: Some presumed difficulties. In Francis Byrne & Thom Huebner, eds., 207-222.

Byrne, Francis. In press. Tense scope and spreading in Saramaccan. Journal of Pidgin and Creole Languages 7.

Byrne, Francis. To appear. Rules, language contact, substrate and what not: A reply to Boretzky. In Salikoko Mufwene, ed.

Byrne, Francis & Thom Huebner, eds. 1991. Development and structures in creole languages: Essays in honor of Derek Bickerton. Amsterdam/Philadelphia: Benjamins.

Byrne, Francis & John Holm, eds. 1993. The Atlantic meets the Pacific: Papers from the Society for Pidgin and Creole Linguistics. Amsterdam/Philadelphia: Benjamins.

Carden, Guy & William A. Stewart. 1988. Binding theory, bioprogram, and creolization: Evidence from Haitian Creole. Journal of Pidgin and Creole Languages 3.1-67.

Chaudenson, Robert. 1977. Toward the reconstruction of the social matrix of creole languages. Pidgin and creole linguistics, ed. by Albert Valdman, 259-276. Bloomington/IN: Indiana University Press.

Chaudenson, Robert. 1986. And they had to speak any way...: Acquisition and creolization of French. The Fergusonian impact. Vol. 1: From phonology to society, ed. by Joshua A. Fishman et al., 69-82. Berlin: Mouton de Gruyter.

Chaudenson, Robert. 1991. From botany to creolistics: The contribution of the lexicon on the flora to the debate on Indian Ocean creole genesis. In Francis Byrne & Thom Huebner, eds., 91-100.

Chomsky, Noam. 1981. Lectures on government and binding. Dordrecht: Foris.

Chomsky, Noam. 1982. Some concepts and consequences of the theory of government and binding. Cambridge, MA: MIT Press.

Faraclas, Nicholas. 1989. From old Guinea to Papua New Guinea II: Tracing Niger-Congo influence in the development of Nigerian Pidgin. Paper presented at the 20th African Linguistics Conference, University of Illinois, 19-21 April.

Givón, Talmy. 1984. Universals of discourse structure and second language acquisition. In William E. Rutherford, ed., 109-139.

Goodman, Morris. 1987. The Portuguese impact on the New World creoles. Pidgin and creole languages: Essays in memory of John E. Reinecke, ed. by Glenn Gilbert. Honolulu: University of Hawaii Press.

Greenberg, Joseph H. 1966. Some universals of grammar with particular reference to the order of meaningful elements. Universals of language, 2nd edn., ed. by Joseph H. Greenberg, 73-113. Cambridge, MA: MIT Press.

de Groot, A.H.P. 1977. Woordregister Nederlands-Saramakans: Met context en idioom. Paramaribo, Suriname: Vaco.

Hazaël-Massieux, Guy. To appear. Le filtre africain dans la genèse du créole de la Guadeloupe: Au confluent de la génétique et de la typologie. In Salikoko Mufwene, ed.

Hancock, Ian. 1971. A provisional comparison of the English-derived Atlantic creoles. Pidginization and creolization of languages, ed. by Dell Hymes, 287-291. Cambridge: Cambridge University Press.

Hancock, Ian. 1986. The domestic hypothesis, diffusion and componentiality: An account of Atlantic Anglophone creole origins. In Pieter Muysken & Norval Smith, eds., 71-102.

Holm, John. 1986. Substrate diffusion. In Pieter Muysken & Norval Smith, eds., 259-278.

Holm, John. 1987. African substratal influence on the Atlantic creole languages. Varia Creolica. Bochum-Essener Beiträge zur Sprachwandelforschung, vol. 3., ed. by Philip Maurer & Thomas Stolz, 11-26. Bochum: Brockmeyer.

Holm, John. 1988. Pidgins and creoles. Vol. I: Theory and structure. Cambridge: Cambridge University Press.

Holm, John. 1989. Pidgins and creoles. Vol. II: Reference survey. Cambridge: Cambridge University Press.

Hussein, Lutfi. 1990. Serial verbs in colloquial Arabic. In Brian D. Joseph & Arnold M. Zwicky, eds., 340-354.

Huttar, George. 1991. Ndjuká organization of experience: African or universal? In Francis Byrne & Thom Huebner, eds., 101-110.

Jansen, Bert, Hilda Koopman & Pieter Muysken. 1978. Serial verbs in the creole languages. Amsterdam Creole Studies II.125-159.

Jo, In-hee. 1990. Multi-verb constructions in Korean. In Brian D. Joseph & Arnold M. Zwicky, eds., 265-287.

Joseph, Brian D. 1983. The synchrony and diachrony of the Balkan infinitive: A study in areal, general, and historical linguistics. Cambridge Studies in Linguistics, Supplementary Series, vol. 1. Cambridge: Cambridge University Press.

Joseph, Brian D. 1990. On arguing for serial verbs (with special reference to modern Greek). In Brian D. Joseph & Arnold M. Zwicky, eds., 77-90.

Joseph, Brian D. & Arnold M. Zwicky, eds. 1990. When verbs collide: Papers from the 1990 Ohio State mini-conference on serial verbs. The Ohio State University Working Papers in Linguistics 39.

Larson-Freeman, D. 1976. An explanation for the morpheme acquisition order of second language learners. Language Learning 26.125-134.

Lefebvre, Claire. 1986. Relexification in creole genesis revisited: The case of Haitian Creole. In Pieter Muysken & Norval Smith, eds., 279-300.

Meisel, Jürgen M. 1983. Strategies of second language acquisition: More than one kind of simplification. In Roger W. Anderson, ed., 120-157.

Mufwene, Salikoko. 1986. The universalist and substrate hypotheses complement one another. In Pieter Muysken & Norval Smith, eds., 129-162.

Mufwene, Salikoko. 1987. Pidginization/creolization: An evolutionary biology analogue. Lecture presented at Northwestern University, 5 May 1987.

Mufwene, Salikoko. 1990. Transfer and the substrate hypothesis in creolistics. Studies in Second Language Acquisition 12.

Mufwene, Salikoko. 1991. Pidgins, creoles, typology, and markedness. In Francis Byrne & Thom Huebner, eds., 123-143.

Mufwene, Salikoko, ed. To appear. Africanisms in Afro-American language varieties. Chicago: University of Chicago Press.

Mufwene, Salikoko & Marta Dijkhoff. 1989. On the so-called infinitive in creoles. Lingua 77.319-352.

Mühlhäusler, Peter. 1986. Pidgin & creole linguistics. Oxford: Basil Blackwell.

Muysken, Pieter. 1987. Prepositions and postpositions in Saramaccan. Studies in Saramaccan language structures. Amsterdam/Philadelphia: Benjamins.

Mervyn, Alleyne, 89-102. Amsterdam: Instituut voor Algemene Taalwetenschaft, Universiteit van Amsterdam; Mona, Jamaica: Folklore Studies Project, University of the West Indies.

Muysken, Pieter & Norval Smith, eds. 1986a. Substrata versus universals in creole genesis. Amsterdam/Philadelphia: Benjamins.

Muysken, Pieter & Norval Smith. 1986b. Problems in the identification of substratum features in the creole languages. In Pieter Muysken & Norval Smith, eds., 1-13.

Odlin, Terence. 1989. Language transfer: Cross-linguistic influence in language learning. Cambridge: Cambridge University Press.

Pasch, Helma. To appear. Pidginization and creolization processes in Sango. In Francis Byrne & John Holm, eds.

Postma, Johannes. 1975. The origin of African slaves: The Dutch activities on the Guinea coast, 1675-1795. Race and slavery in the Estern Hemisphere: Quantitative studies, ed. by Stanley L. Engerman & Eugene D. Genovese, 33-49. Princeton: Princeton University Press.

Price, Richard. 1976. The Guiana maroons: A historical and bibliographical introduction. Baltimore: Johns Hopkins University Press.

Price, Richard 1983a. First time: The historical vision of an Afro-American people. Baltimore: Johns Hopkins University Press.

Price, Richard. 1983b. To slay the hydra: Dutch colonial perspectives on the Saramaka wars. Ann Arbor, MI: Karoma.

Pullum, Geoffrey K. 1990. Constraints on intransitive quasi-serial verb constructions in modern colloquial English. In Brian D. Joseph & Arnold M. Zwicky, eds., 218-239.

Rawley, James A. 1981. The transatlantic slave trade: A history. New York: Norton.

Rutherford, William E., ed. 1984. Language universals and second language acquisition. Amsterdam/Philadelphia: Benjamins.

Sankoff, Gillian & Penelope Brown. 1976. The origins of syntax in discourse: A case study of Tok Pisin relatives. Language 52 631-666.

Schachter, Paul. 1974. A non-transformational account of serial verbs. Studies in African Linguistics 5.253-270.

Schilr, Eric. 1990. On the definition and distribution of serial verb constructions. In Brian D. Joseph & Arnold M. Zwicky, eds., 34-64.

Schiller, Eric. To appear. Why serial verb constructions? Neither bioprogram nor substrate! In Francis Byrne & John Holm, eds.

Sebba, Mark. 1984. Serial verbs Something new out of Africa. York Papers in Linguistics 11.271-278.

Sebba, Mark. 1986. Adjectives and copulas in Sranan Tongo. Journal of Pidgin and Creole Languages 1.109-121.

Sebba, Mark. 1987. The syntax of serial verbs: An investigation into serialization in Sranan and other languages. Amsterdam/Philadelphia: Benjamins.

Selinker, Larry. 1969. Language transfer. General Linguistics 9.67-92.

Seuren, Pieter. 1986. Adjectives as adjectives in Sranan: A reply to Sebba. Journal of Pidgin and Creole Languages 1.123-134.

Seuren, Pieter. 1990. Still no serials in Seselwa. A reply to "Seselwa serialization and its significance" by Derek Bickerton. Journal of Pidgin and Creole Languages 5.271-292.

Seuren, Pieter. 1991. The definition of serial verbs. In Francis Byrne & Thom Huebner, eds., 193-205.

Seuren, Pieter & Herman Wekker. 1986. Semantic transparency as a factor in creole genesis. In Pieter Muysken & Norval Smith, eds., 57-70.

Singler, John Victor. 1988. The homogeneity of the substrate as a factor in pidgin-creole genesis. Language 64.27-51.

Slobin, Dan. 1977. Language change in childhood and history. Language learning and thought, ed. by J. Macnamara, 185-214. New York: Academic Press.

Slobin, Dan (ed.) 1985. The crosslinguistic study of language acquisition. Vol. 1: The data. Hillsdale, NJ: Erlbaum.

Stahlke, Herbert. 1970. Serial verbs. Studies in African Linguistics 1.60-99.

Valdman, Albert. 1977. Creolization: Elaboration in the development of creole French dialects. Pidgin and creole linguistics, ed. by Albert Valdman, 155-189. Bloomington: Indiana University Press.

Valdman, Albert. 1983. Creolization and second language acquisition. In Roger W. Anderson, ed., 212-234.

Washabaugh, William. 1981. Pursuing creole roots. Generative studies on creole languages, ed. by Pieter Muysken, 85-102. Dordrecht: Foris.

Weinreich Uriel. 1953. Languages in contact. New York: Linguistic Circle of New York.

White, Lydia. 1989. Universal grammar and second language acquisition. Amsterdam/Philadelphia: Benjamins.

Winford, Donald. 1990. Serial verb constructions and motion events in Caribbean English Creoles. In Brian D. Joseph & Arnold M. Zwicky, eds., 109-148.

Winford, Donald. 1993. Serial verb constructions in Caribbean English creoles. In Francis Byrne & John Holm, eds.

Zobl, H. 1980a. The formal and developmental selectivity of L1 influence on L2 acquisition. Language Learning 30.43-57.

Zobl, H. 1980b. Developmental and transfer errors: Their common bases and possibly differential effects on subsequent learning. TESOL Quarterly 14.469-479.

SECTION TWO:
LEARNER VARIABLES IN SECOND LANGUAGE ACQUISITION

CONTEXTS FOR SECOND LANGUAGE ACQUISITION

Elsa Lattey
University of Tübingen (Germany)

1.0. INTRODUCTION

Although virtually everyone learns at least **one language** in the course of cognitive development, fewer people manage to acquire more than one. The number of those who do, however, is much greater than we might at first think. As a matter of fact, we can say, with Howard Giles (1985:iv), that "the monolingual mortal is in actuality a somewhat scarce commodity" or, with Peter Hornby (1977:1): "For a large percentage of the peoples of the world, speaking more than one language is a natural way of life." This, then, would suggest that the group of individuals who command a second (or additional) language is quite large. It is, however, not a uniform group and consequently quite difficult to define.

Another reason for the difficulty is that there is no widespread agreement on what it means to learn or know a language when we are talking about a language or languages beyond the first. Do I as a native speaker of English "know French" if I can successfully read my way through an article in an academic journal written in that language? Do I "know Tok Pisin"[1] if I can sketch for my students how it varies from British or American English? Do I "know Spanish" if I can successfully communicate with people in Spain or Latin America about the necessities of everyday life when traveling?

In certain respects - and in certain communicative contexts --the answer to all of the above questions would have to be yes. And yet, if those individual functions were all we could do with our **first** language -- our so-called **mother tongue or native language** -- we'd be in a sorry state indeed. So we must accept, as a given or understood basis for discussing our topic at all that knowing a language is a gradable phenomenon, that we always know a language in some relative way and that, especially for language(s) beyond the first, we can say of an individual such things as "She speaks English rather well" or "He has a reading knowledge of Japanese" or "They are fluent in Spanish, German and Tagalog[2]."

Gradability is a feature of a person's native linguistic skills as well, of course. We can consider someone to be a good speaker or an excellent writer, someone "gifted" with respect to his or her use of language, but that doesn't mean that the remaining members of a speech community don't **know** their native tongue.

We can put these difficulties of definition aside, however, for we all have **some** idea of what is meant when we say that someone knows a particular language (though you and I and the next person may have only partial overlap in our ideas). That this is fine and within the necessary limits of vagueness ascribable to language use can be seen from the fact that each one of us would use our statement "X knows L" (where X is a person and L some language) in different contexts and of different individuals whose skills in L may vary greatly.

So, for example, if your child were trying to decipher instructions in French on how to change the lightbulb in a slide projector and you couldn't help, you might say "Go ask Grandma. She knows French" even if Grandma couldn't carry on a basic conversation in that language. All that matters in the situation described is that she is likely to be able to decode the instructions that she knows enough French to do that. And yet we use the expression "knows French" both of Grandma in the above situation and of most people who are natives of Paris, France.

We can deduce from the applicability of the statement "X knows L" in diverse situations that the contexts of learning L are likely to be quite different and varied as well. And this is indeed the case. It will not be possible in an introductory chapter such as this to detail the many possible contexts and combinations of factors contributing to second language learning, but I would like to sketch for you the major distinctions that linguists and educators have made. In doing so, I will proceed from a discussion of three main oppositions:

1)   that between **simultaneous and successive** language acquisition,

2)   that between X **as a foreign language and** X **as a second language,** and

3)   that between language **acquisition** and language learning (although this last will turn out not to be very useful).

2.0. FACTORS CONTRIBUTING TO SECOND LANGUAGE LEARNING
2.1. Simultaneous vs. successive (or sequential) acquisition of two languages
The distinction between **simultaneous** acquisition of two languages (reference here is to speakers' first and second languages, though it is possible in certain contexts that an additional language or languages play a role as well) and **successive** acquisition of those two languages entails all of the arguments involved in the discussion of first vs. second language acquisition as well.

That is, in order to appreciate the issue one has to ask: how is acquiring an additional language different from acquiring the first one? And the answer will include - at least the following observations:

i)   that the first language was acquired in the course of the child's cognitive development,

ii)   that a subsequent language is acquired in a context where the speaker has already successfully learned a language (with all that that implies), and

iii)   that second or subsequent language "learners are confronted with the dynamic interplay of two (or more) linguistic systems" (Gass/Schachter 1989:6).

2.1.1. Simultaneous

That first language acquisition and cognitive development go hand in hand is something most researchers will agree on, even if they disagree about what the trade off relationship is between the two, or on what precisely the child is equipped with at birth: just a general cognitive learning ability, a language acquisition device with certain linguistic basics, or a set of parameters which will be set in certain ways in the course of experience with the language of the environment[3]). The implication of this is that the child is developing cognitive skills so, for example, the making and rejecting of hypotheses about the world, e.g. "all four legged creatures bark" - at the same time as linguistic data are coming in, e.g. "four-legged creatures are called *dogs*" Children are expected to be able to apply learning that takes place in the one area to decision-making in the other. When children are exposed to two languages simultaneously at this early stage in life, we have an interaction between the developing cognition and the acquisition of each language including learning that there are **two** languages involved.

2.1.2. Successive

This is a different context in that first language acquisition has taken place, and cognitive development reached a more-advanced point before the second language is introduced. In this case the child has certain questions already answered, or the linguistic parameters for the first language (L1) already set before beginning to cope with L2. Part of the research in this area must then be concerned with:

> understanding how the language acquisition skills interact with other cognitive skills in the unique situation where the learner already has the advantage (or disadvantage) of a relative degree of conceptual maturity, and a fully implemented realization of Universal Grammar in his first language. (Pankhurst and Sharwood Smith 1985:editorial)

Let us sketch typical situational contexts for A and B above to make this clear:

Situation A: the child acquires both L1 and L2 in the home. Let us say the mother is a native speaker of German, the father a native speaker of English, and each parent speaks his or her native language with the child.

Situation B: the child acquires L1 at home and L2 in school. The parents are native speakers of German and speak German to the child. Schooling proceeds in English from kindergarten on; consequently the child is exposed to and must learn to function in English from age 5 or 6 onwards.

Even in these relatively simple sketches, we can see that there are questions to be raised. In Situation B it seems clear that the parents speak German not only to the child but also to each other, but what about Situation A? What language do the parents use with each other? English? German? Each his own? All of these are conceivable and all occur in bilingual homes around the world.

The second question that looms large is: what is the language of the speech community? **Speech community** is again a relatively vague concept -- it could be applied to the home or to the school or both, but it is most often applied to a larger unit such as a village or town. We will want to know for both Situation A and Situation B what language is spoken outside the home, for it will have distinct bearing on the linguistic context in which the child grows up. In both situations, we can imagine either English or German as the language of the wider speech community. Household A may be located in the United States (in which case the mother could be an immigrant) or in Germany (in which case it might be the father who immigrated).[4]

Both of these questions -- what language do the parents speak with each other and what is the language of the speech community -- are crucial to defining the linguistic input to the child's language acquisition. For as developing speakers we are not only active participants in first- and second-person exchanges (the *I - you* of two-person conversations), we are also third persons (the *he, she* and *they* of ordinary pronoun reference in conversations). As such we hear and react to language that is not directly addressed to us as well as language that is. In both of our sketched situations this can mean further exposure to L1 or L2 or both.

Depending on the answers to these questions, the child will have additional linguistic facts to deal with, which means he or she will have to fit them into the total picture of language understanding being developed.

Example 1: If both parents (in Situation A) speak their own native language even when conversing with each other, the child will have to rely on clues in the one to-one conversations with each parent to determine what is an acceptable response for him or her in L1 and what in L2. After all, Father in Situation A is responding to German utterances by Mother with English utterances of his own and yet the child is probably expected to respond to Mother's German with German.

Example 2: If the parents speak German to each other, the child will have to learn that although Mother may speak German to Father, the child is expected to speak to Father in English.

Example 3 : If the parents speak English to each other, the child will have to learn that although Father may speak English to Mother, the child is expected to speak German to her.

It is amazing how well children manage to sort out linguistic facts such as the above and at what an early age. This is perhaps less surprising when we make it clear to ourselves that even monolingual speakers can be faced with similar tasks.

Example 4: Max was a little German boy just 6 years old. He lived in Munich with his father, who was a native of Munich, and his mother, who was born and raised in Stuttgart. Now, Munich is in Bavaria (one of the states of Germany), an area where the local dialect is Bavarian. And Stuttgart is in the state of Baden-Württemberg and people who are born and live in Stuttgart generally speak the local dialect there, namely Swabian. In addition, most people learn to speak some variant of the standard language in the course of their education. Often the language of the school is not the local dialect, but a version of the standard (colored slightly by some local phonological features, but much closer to the written language than the local dialects are). So, little Max was exposed to -- at least -- three different language varieties: his mother's Swabian, his father's Bavarian and his teacher's standard German. Max had mastered these three varieties and was so skilled in their use that he could switch from one to the other at the drop of a hat - or better, at a change in interlocutor. The standard was also the variety he spoke with adult strangers until they could be sorted into the Bavarian-speaking or Swabian speaking category.

How aware children are of linguistic context and the linguistic capabilities of speakers they meet can be seen from Examples 5 and 6:

Example 5: 3 1/2-year-old Mirjam refuses to speak English to her parents although they speak only English to her and with each other. (The family lives in Germany and the parents speak German to Germans.) Yet, when her U.S. grandparents come to visit, she'll use English with them after a while (having become aware that they are not competent in German). Fantini (1978) reports that children clearly make their own choices as to what language is appropriate in a given context, by citing the following example.

Example 6: When Mario (a Spanish/English bilingual, with some knowledge of Italian) was seven years and five months, his mother invited several students of

Spanish for a Bolivian meal and Spanish conversation. She consequently coached her son to speak only Spanish to the students. "When the first guest arrived, however, Mario looked him over and after only a few words of Spanish, decided that English was the only choice which made sense" (Fantini 1A78:289,294):

Mario to Student:	Do you speak Spanish? (in disbelief)
Student to Mario:	Well...not very well.
Mama to Mario:	(from the kitchen)
	Háblale en español, Mario. (Speak to him in Spanish, Mario.)
Mario to Mama:	Tú me mentiste, mamá! (You lied to me, Mama!)

Let me add another case history to the contexts we are considering. Actually this is a subset of Situation A in that both L1 and L2 are being learned simultaneously in the home. And the family situation is a one-parent-one language one as in A above.

Example 7: The difference in the current case is that both parents are native speakers of English and the family lives in Australia, an English-speaking country, and yet the father, who is a German teacher, decided to teach his children German and to use that language as the vehicle of communication between himself and his children (Saunders, no date). Although this is a somewhat artificial situation, as far as languages in the home go, there is intrinsically nothing unusual about the scenario. As long as the father feels comfortable using German with his children, this situation does not differ for them from any Situation A context.

And as far as this father's relationship with his children is concerned, it is hardly different from many cases (we might call these Situation C contexts -- one home language, not native to either parent) in which the parents speak two different languages natively, while they have a second language, let's say Tok Pisin, in common, and have made this jointly spoken (but non-native) language the language of the home and consequently the language in which they communicate with their children. (In Example 7, the non-native German is used only by the father, while the mother speaks her native English with the children.) If both parents (in our Situation C context) exclusively use Tok Pisin with their children, these children will end up as monolingual Tok Pisin speakers as long as they are still at home. They may add English[5] in school and thus be Situation B (i.e., successive) learners of Tok Pisin and English. If one parent does use a local language with the children in the home, however, they will be Situation A speakers (i.e., simultaneously acquiring Tok Pisin and the local language) until English is added in school, and they will become trilingual speakers by successively adding English to an already bilingual situation.

The Papua New Guinea example is not unusual, neither in terms of the home experience nor in terms of that in school. There are many countries in the world where the language of the school is not the language of the home or where at least part of the schooling takes place in a language that has not been learned natively. This brings us to the second major distinction mentioned above.

2.2. X as a foreign language vs. X as a second language

In principle, these contexts are relatively simple to distinguish. You learn X as a foreign language if you study X in a country whose normal language is something other than X. So, if you are learning English in a Greek school in Greece, or in a Spanish school in Spain, you are learning English as a **foreign** language. If, on the other hand, you are Greek or Spanish and you emigrate to the United States and go to school in the U.S. to learn English, you are learning English as a **second** language.[6] This seems simple enough.

But now what about the Pilipino child who speaks Tagalog at home and begins to learn English in school, where all of the instruction is given in English from the third grade on?[7] Technically English is a foreign language in the Philippines or in Papua New Guinea and yet it is the (or a) language of instruction in the schools and in some cases the language of a certain segment or class in society. So, for example, an Afrikaans-speaking child in South Africa may have his or her schooling entirely in English from a certain grade on, this education enabling that child to function in certain prestige governmental positions in a nation that is officially bilingual (Afrikaans - English) but in fact has many local native languages spoken as well. (Lanham 1982)

Multilingual nations pose a problem for the simple foreign language vs. second language dichotomy. Here we need to revert to the idea behind the distinction: is one learning the language in the absence of its cultural, social, political and economic context (= foreign) or not (= second)? Each unclear case will be gradable in some way (in terms of some features) in between. (Cf. discussion of "additional languages" below.)

We can see from the above discussion of this second context distinction that it has primarily to do with where a language is **taught.** That is, we are discussing tutored language acquisition, which brings us to the third opposition mentioned earlier.

2.3. Language Acquisition vs. Language Learning

This opposition distinguishes between **acquiring** a language by being exposed to it and trying it out (much as a child learns the first language) and **learning** a language by being taught (or teaching oneself). A. Krashen (1985:1) and Krashen & Terrell (1988:18) claim that these are two independent ways of developing ability in a second language, acquisition being "picking it up," "a subconscious process identical in all important ways to the process children utilize in acquiring their first language," while learning is different in that it is a conscious process that results in 'knowing about' language, "having a conscious knowledge about grammar," "knowing the rules."

Originally this distinction was equated with simple exposure to a language vs. being taught a language. There are, of course, many different ways of teaching a language.[8] It can be taught in an essentially communicative way, or in any of several other approaches, including some which focus on the rules of the grammar and their use. This obscures the simple equation between untutored and tutored[9] on the one hand and "picking it up" vs. "learning the rules" on the other.

That is, acquisition and learning are not restricted in time and space, nor in terms of formality. Krashen & Seliger (1975) suggest that although rule isolation and feedback--the two factors they see as common to all language teaching systems-- are not present in informal environments, motivated second language students can provide themselves with the essential ingredients of formal instruction without going to class. And, given different teaching techniques, "it seems plausible that the classroom can accomplish both learning and acquisition simultaneously." (Krashen 1985:47)

As a matter of fact, Krashen & Terrell (1988) seem to agree with those they cite when they say that "many researchers now believe that language **acquisition** is responsible for the ability to understand and speak second languages easily and well", thus reducing language **learning** to an editing function (what Krashen calls a Monitor of language production) that operates **"only as a kind of after-thought to make alterations and corrections"** (Krashen & Terrell 1988:18) [emphasis mine]. In describing this acquisition, however, Krashen distinguished between **intake** and simple **exposure,** pointing out that simply hearing the target language is not enough. The acquirer must also utilize the primary linguistic data[10] (Krashen 1981:46). In Krashen (1985:4) he details this further and claims: "people acquire second languages only if they obtain comprehensible input [i.e., if they understand messages] and if their affective filters are low enough to allow the input 'in'" [that is, if they are sufficiently motivated and are not mentally blocked e.g. by anxiety about linguistic performance].

Butzkamm takes this a step further, focussing on the "double nature of comprehension": "In order for acquisition to take place," he says, "mere situational or context-bound comprehension is not enough. We must also get transparent syntactic data to work on" (Butzkamm 1990:270).

While the conceptual distinction outlined above between a) making and rejecting hypotheses about a language's structures and functions and b) learning explicit rules and applying them would seem to be a useful one (for these are, indeed, different processes), that distinction has been obscured in the discussion of subconscious vs. conscious or untutored vs. tutored acquisition or learning. This may well be why some researchers are in favor of rejecting the terminological distinction of acquisition vs. learning altogether.[11] McLaughlin, while acknowledging that Krashen's Monitor Model is "the most ambitious theory of second language learning process" (McLaughlin 1987:19) ultimately rejects Krashen's theory as "counterproductive" because he feels that "more limited and more specific theories are needed at this stage" (McLaughlin 1987:58).

One finds **acquisition and learning** used interchangeably by many researchers in the field. Spolsky (1989:9) terms their distinction "confusing and unnecessary" and puts forward the hypothesis that second language learning (and acquisition) can be accounted for by a set of 74 conditions for learning, some "necessary" (such as Condition 1: A second language learner's knowledge of a second language forms a systematic whole) and others "typical" (e.g. Condition 26: The social situation faced by a child in a second language environment favours second language learning).

Bley-Vroman (1989:43) goes so far as to use "foreign language learning" and "second language acquisition" interchangeably, thus blurring both distinctions 2) and 3) above. Because the term **development** "connotes internally driven growth", Bley-Vroman prefers to contrast **adult foreign language learning** and **child language development** and argues for the position that these "are in fact fundamentally different" (1989:42).[12]

We have, then, in our discussion so far addressed three fundamental distinctions that have been made by researchers and theorists in the contexts of second language acquisition:

1) simultaneous vs. successive
2) foreign vs. second
3) tutored vs. untutored

whereby 2) and 3) sometimes coincide. That is, if we make the distinctions mentioned above, foreign language learning will almost always be tutored, simply because the classroom provides the only context of contact with the foreign language in many cases. (This does not, however, exclude the possibility of your learning a foreign language from a friend in tutored or untutored fashion in a situation in which that friend is your only access to the foreign language.)

It can be seen from the above **discussion** that the contexts of second language acquisition are many and varied. In principle there are as many contexts for learning a second language as there are people who do. This variety is no doubt responsible in part for a great deal of uncertainty and vagueness that still exists in the field. In addition to these varied contexts there are also varied goals, ranging from near native fluency, through being able to participate in academic conferences, or being able to get by on vacation, to having a reading knowledge only or to being able to explain the etymology of the words extant in a language today.

This multivaried picture led B. Spolsky to call for a **general** theory of second language learning distinct from "theories of formal classroom learning, or of informal natural learning, or the learning of one part of a language" (Spolsky 1989:2). He has explored the possibility of developing such a theory in terms of a preference model[13] based on conditions relating to a) the complexity of learning outcomes, b) the effects of some aspects of ability, c) the nature of attitude and motivation and d) learning opportunity (Spolsky 1989:211) --all features that contribute to individual contexts of second language acquisition. His general theory "consists of a set of preference conditions which ... might go together somewhat as the rules of an expert system do" (1989:223) and is intended to show which pieces of information are relevant to understanding the likelihood of a learner's learning.

3.0. ADDITIONAL LANGUAGES

When I first made the distinction between a second and a foreign language above, you may have assumed that such language-learning contexts tend to be monolingual. If you live in a place where only one language is the language of the land, or in a country with a single official language, you may readily think that this is the norm. If this were so, then indeed second language learning would be either foreign language learning (where we learn the language of some other country) or second language learning (where we learn the language of the country we have emigrated to). However, even among the few context examples I cited above, there were those that suggested a more complicated picture (e.g. the Philippines) and we have acknowledged in our introductory paragraph how widespread multilingualism is.

If we cast our eyes around the world, we see that there are many and varied multilingual societies. The perspective for language learning is very different in these countries. Learning another language (and yet a third or fourth) is a commonplace, nothing unusual, nothing reserved for some educated elite. In many cases the language of the home is not the language of the immediate community. The language of the local community may not be one of the official languages of the country. The language of education may just be one among several national languages. It may not be a national language at all, but one that is nevertheless necessary if one wishes to advance in terms of one's career, and so on. Many possible combinations can be imagined and many of those that are imaginable exist. Precisely what combination is available in any particular context is determined in part by language planning decisions made by politicians, educators and linguists, in part by the historical development of the country or region.

When describing such contexts of language acquisition, the term **additional language** is a useful one.[14] An additional language is any language beyond the native language(s) that an individual finds the need or desire to learn in order to function in his/her society -- or in order to interact with other societies where different languages prevail. This additional language may be an official language (e.g. French for Anglophone students in Quebec or English for Afrikaans speakers in South Africa).

It may be a language of wider communication, that is, a useful additional language learned by people who live in a country where a language is spoken that does not have extensive communicative implementation outside the borders of that country (e.g. the learning of English by speakers of Danish or even Dutch today -- despite the fact that the Netherlands had a substantial colonial empire at one time).

It may also be what Larry E. Smith calls an **auxiliary** language: "a language, other than the first language, which is used by nationals of a country for internal communication.' (Smith 1976, reprinted in Smith 1983:1), which he contrasts with an **international language,** used "by people of different nations to communicate with one another" (Smith 1983:1). Quirk (1985) makes the same distinction in terms of use for "internal" and "external" purposes. In Japan, for example, English is important as an international language, but not as an auxiliary language. In the Philippines, on the other hand, it is of near equal importance as an international and as an auxiliary language.

What these latter terms have in common that distinguishes them from the **foreign or second** language concepts is the extent to which they refer to the use of a language between non-native speakers. Intranationally, an additional language that is an auxiliary language will not have many native speakers around by definition. Internationally, communication could be between non natives and natives, let's say communication in French between an African statesman and a French delegate to his country, but it might just as well be from non-native to non native: the Italian businesswoman who negotiates a contract with a German firm in English because it is their only common language Campbell et. al. (1982) include both aspects in their definition of English as an International Language (EIL) as "that English in all its linguistic and sociolinguistic aspects which is used as a vehicle for communication between non-native speakers ... as well as between any combination of native and non-native speakers." They go on to point out that:

> a major principle of EIL is that when speakers of more than one country or culture interact, more than one set of social and cultural assumptions will be in operation. Each culture has its own ways of speaking, patterns of discourse and argument, rules for turn taking, choice of topic in conversation, methods of thanking, apologizing, interrupting, giving advice and permission, in short, communication

devices and repertoire types. A knowledge of these ways, patterns, and rules has to be developed by speakers of EIL if they are going to be concerned with *effective* cross-cultural communication. (Campbell et. al. 1982:66)

It follows from this that "(1) native speakers of English need training in the use of their own language in international settings, and (2) non-native speakers of English need training in the use of English not just with native speakers, but with non-native speakers as well" (Campbell et al 1982:66). The intranational use of an additional language leads in many cases to a **nativization** of that language -- so, for example, "the Africanization of English" (Bokamba 1982) -- where it takes on local characteristics not to be found in the varieties in use elsewhere. As a matter of fact, such a nonnative variety of a world language can go through a life cycle all its own, developing from foreign language (FL) status to a second language (SL) and back to FL status, as described by Rodney F. Moag (1982) for Fijian English. Of course, what is said here for English applies to any other additional language in international and auxiliary functions as well, and we must bear in mind that each new situation and each new language will provide a new context of second language acquisition.

As communication between and among people speaking different native languages continues to spread, the contexts of second or additional language acquisition will become more varied still. I have said nothing about the role of the particular native and additional languages involved, a very interesting linguistic question: How closely related are they? What does this relationship imply for ease or difficulty of acquisition? What is the role of interference (from L1 or L2)? These and other questions must be considered in a study of language acquisition beyond the first language, but they are beyond the scope of this chapter.

4.0. LANGUAGES FOR SPECIFIC PURPOSES

We should take a brief look at a subdiscipline known as LSP (languages for specific purposes) or, when specifically addressed to English, ESP (English for specific purposes). Here, we can see the functioning of language planning perhaps more clearly than in other areas. "Whatever the administrative level at which [the] decision is made or [the] policy formulated, the context out of which it arises is usually either a dissatisfaction with the status quo or an awareness of the emergence of a new need" (Mackay & Bosquet 1981:4). One example cited by Mackay & Bosquet is the establishment of occupational and professional French language courses by educational institutions in Quebec to enable English-speaking employees to be able to work in the French language as decreed by the Quebec government.[15] Or we might consider special courses in English for people in medicine conducted at a university in Germany to enable those in the medical profession to read medical publications in English or to attend medical conferences in English-speaking countries.

However, LSP need not be viewed only from educational contexts. There are many fields where a working knowledge of a particular language is mandatory to carry out one's job. I mention only the situation of air travel and air traffic control and its reliance upon English as a language of international communication. Ability in the English language may be quite restricted for the air traffic controllers at many airports around the world, and they may not be able to carry on a casual conversation in the language. Yet within the domain of exercising their profession, they function adequately and appropriately in this -- for them -- additional language.

5.0. REDUCED FORMS OF LANGUAGE

One final note to contexts of second language acquisition: Sometimes language learners are in the process of acquiring a language and for some socially determined reasons stop short of reaching their goal. There can, of course, be many personal reasons for not attaining the level of proficiency one desires to attain. But I would like here to address some sociolinguistic factors that may contribute to this state of affairs, namely those having to do with contexts of acquisition. I am thinking here of contexts in which the model provided for the learner is something less than a full-fledged version of the target language.

In one way, the special purpose example of the air traffic controllers' English is a reduced form of that language. But there are other reduced forms that constitute simplified versions of a language without being reduced to a specific semantic or functional domain such as getting planes onto and off the ground safely.

One such simplified form of a language can be the **foreigner talk** of native speakers of that language, i.e., the variety they use to speak with foreigners to whom they do not attribute full competence in the language in question. Many speakers tend to reduce the complexity of their linguistic output when speaking with people who do not know the language well. Sometimes what develops is a rather stigmatized, easily recognized stereotype of the "me Tarzan, you Jane" type. When language learners are exposed only to this variant of the target language, that of course affects their acquisition as well.[16]

Reduced forms also occur where the linguistic input on a larger social scale has led to the mixing of languages, to the creation of a **pidginized** variant of some language, in contexts in which that language has a certain political, economic or cultural status but not sufficient implementation to be learned in its entirety.

Let me be a bit more specific by way of illustration. If we return to a language mentioned earlier in this chapter, Tok Pisin, spoken in Papua New Guinea as a lingua franca and as a native language, I can illustrate my point. Tok Pisin is spoken in a country where there are many local languages[17] and where the inhabitants of the local regions typically practiced exogamy, that is marrying outside their immediate community. This led to marriages among people who did not speak the same language. Yet there was -- because of Papua New Guinea's colonial history -- another language on the scene, namely English. There developed a pidginized variant of English, originally called Melanesian Pidgin English and various other names, that eventually evolved into a relatively uniform, now official language known as Tok Pisin.[18] Tok Pisin has developed as a language and expanded, since it is now the first language of a significant percentage of the population, into a creole (a less reduced, more fully developed type of language) to fulfill the needs of its speakers. Yet in its early days, when it was a pidgin, it served restricted communicative functions for people, all of whom had some other native language at their disposal. In the context of Papua New Guinea at that time, speakers were faced with this reduced regional form of English as a target, one that served for communication in situations where other languages failed (the speakers involved did not have a language in common other than this reduced variety of English). Because the original English source was in most cases far removed from the speakers I am talking about, it was not available as a target. The target was, and continued to be, the local form of English, which developed into this Tok Pisin spoken in Papua New Guinea today.

Whereas the Tok Pisin example describes a reduced, pidginized form of a language expanding into a creole to fulfill the needs of its speakers, we saw in our discussion of additional languages that in other contexts a process of nativization can serve to alter the shape of a world language when its primary use is as an auxiliary language within some country where it is not spoken natively. Raja Ram Mehrotra, writing of Indian English and the substantial differences between varieties in the south and north of India, ventures the generalized prediction: "The inevitable fact seems to be that the more widely English spreads in a country, the more internationally incomprehensible it becomes" (Mehrotra 1982:78).

These, too, are facts we must consider when we study the contexts of second language acquisition. Which brings me back to the statement I made earlier: There are about as many contexts of second language acquisition as there are individuals learning a second (or additional) language. In describing and analyzing any particular situation we must bear in mind all of the many factors (linguistic, social, political, psychological etc.) that go into constituting that situational context, drawing in our study on the wealth of knowledge that research has already provided and will continue to provide in a varied and extremely challenging -- both descriptively and theoretically -- field of linguistic inquiry.

NOTES

1. An English-based creole language spoken as a lingua franca and as a first language in Papua New Guinea.

2. A language of the Philippines.

3. Parameters such as whether the language typically has phrases in which the head (X in XP) comes first or phrases in which the head comes last have recently been discussed within the framework of government-binding theory.

4. I have used the conditional in the clauses referring to immigration because it is, of course, in principle possible to grow up speaking a language other than the "national" language.

5. Standard English, as opposed to Tok Pisin, which is an English-based creole. Tok Pisin: *Yupela go long Rabaul*? (English: Are you going to Rabaul?)

6. Bley-Vroman (1989:43) points out that "second" is an unfortunate term, since it suggests that third, fourth, etc. languages are not included.

7. This was the case from 1957 to 1974 in the Philippines. In 1974 a bilingual education policy was implemented there, whereby some academic subjects are taught in English (e.g. science and math), others (e.g. history and geography) in Pilipino, which is based on Tagalog. For many students neither English nor Pilipino is their mother tongue, but one of 9 major regional vernaculars, were used in grades 1 and 2 as transitional languages. The goal of educational policy is to produce English-Pilipino bilinguals (Tucker 1988).

8. Cf. Larsen-Freeman, Diane. *Techniques and Principles in Language Teaching*. (1986. Oxford University Press.), where eight approaches to language teaching are described and analysed.

9. Cf. research on the language of foreign workers in Germany, where the terms *ungesteuerter* and *gesteuerter Zweitspracherwerb* distinguish **untutored** and **tutored** language acquisition.

10. This distinction between utilized linguistic data [intake] and heard language [exposure] derives from B. Friedlander et. al. (1972), where the authors cite a situation in which a child heard only 4% Spanish all told, but this amounted to 25% of the language addressed to the child, thus making it a significant percentage of the language data the child was actively involved with, with consequent impact on acquisition.

11. In effect, Krashen appears to be coming closer to the theoretical if not the terminological conviction as well. In Krashen (1985:3) he states that "...deep down, the 'mental organ' for language produces one basic product, or human language, in one fundamental way."

12. We are here, however, faced basically with the distinction made in 1) above, that between learning a language at the same time as cognitive development is taking place and learning a language after cognitive development has progressed apace.

13. A preference model "presented informally as a competence model": "the preference conditions ... model the underlying system and account for it without making particular claims as to how it works." (Spolsky 1989:222)

14. Cf. for example, Fishman 1982.

15. Another example is the ESP program set up at the University of Kuala Lumpur, Malaysia, "to ensure adequate English reading standards" for university students after the national language, Bahasa Malaysia was introduced as the medium of education (replacing English) in the public school system.

16. Some foreigner talk is more pronounced than others, this being in part a function of the structure of the language and the processes of simplification employed by the speakers. Cf. Lattey 1981, 1989.

17. Loreto Todd (1984:158) claims that it is "one of the most multilingual countries on earth. Its three million inhabitants use approximately seven hundred different mother tongues."

18. Tok Pisin is not the only lingua franca in Papua New Guinea. Hiri motu, which was used as a trade language in Papua, spread rapidly in the 20th century because of trade with Australia and its use (under the name of Police Motu) by the multilingual police force in Papua New Guinea (Todd 1984:158).

REFERENCES

Bailey, R.W. & M. Görlach, eds. 1982. *English as a World Language*. Ann Arbor: University of Michigan Press.

Bley-Vroman, Robert. 1989. "What is the logical problem of foreign language learning?" In: Gass & Schachter (1989): 44-68.

Bokamba, Eyamba G. 1988. "The Africanization of English." In: Kachru (1982), 77-98 .

Butzkamm, Wolfgang 1990. Five hypotheses about language learning and teaching. Die neueren Sprachen 89:264-278.

Campbell, Donald, Peansiri Ekniyom, Anjum Haque & Larry Smith. 1982. English in international settings: problems and their causes. English World-Wide 3.1:66-76. Reprinted in Smith (1983), 35-48 .

Fantini, Alvino E. 1978. Bilingual behavior and social cues: case studies of two bilingual children. In: Paradis, Michel, ed. Apects of Bilingualism. Columbia, S. Carolina: Hornbeam Press, 283-301.

Fishman, Joshua A. 1982. Sociology of English as an additional language. In: Kachru (1982), 15-22.

Friedlander, B., A. Jacobs, B. Davis & H. Wetstone. 1972. Time-sampling analysis of infants' natural language environment in the home. Child Development 43:730-740.

Gass, Susan M. & Jacquelyn Schachter, eds. 1989. Linguistic Perspectives on Second Language Acquisition. Cambridge, etc. Cambridge University Press.

Giles, Howard A. 1985. General preface to Gardner, R. C. Social Psychology and Second Language Learning. The Role of Attitudes and Motivation. London: Edward Arnold.

Hornby, Peter A., ed. 1977. Bilingualism. Psychological, Social and Educational Implications. New York, etc.: Academic Press.

Kachru, Braj B., ed. 1982. The Other Tongue. Urbana: University of Illinois Press.

Krashen, Stephen D. & Herbert W. Seliger. 1975. The essential contributions of formal instruction in adult second language acquisition. TESOL Quarterly 9:173-183.

Krashen, Stephen D. & Tracy D. Terrell. 1988. The Natural Approach. Language Acquisition in the Classroom. New York, etc.: Prentice Hall.

Krashen, Stephen D. 1981. Second Language Acquisition and Second Language Learning. Oxford: Pergamon Press.

Krashen, Stephen D. 1985. The Input Hypothesis. Issues and Implications. London /N.Y.: Longman.

Lanham, L. W. 1982. English in South Africa. In: Bailey & Görlach (1982), 324-352.

Lattey, Elsa. 1981. Foreigner talk in the U.S.A. and Germany: contrast and comparison. Washington, D.C.: ERIC Clearinghouse on Languages and Linguistics. AED 221 064).

Lattey, Elsa. 1989. Interlinguistic variation and similarity in foreigner talk. Illustrated with respect to English speaking and German-speaking contexts. In: Eisenstein, Miriam R., ed. The Dynamic Interlanguage. Empirical Studies in Second Language Variation. New York A London: Plenum Press, 87-100.

Mackay, Ronald & Maryse Bosquet. 1981. LSP curriculum development from policy to practice. In: Mackay, Ronald & Abe Darwin Palmer 7 eds . (1981). Language for Specific Purposes. Program design and evaluation. Rowley, Mass.: Newbury House Publ., Inc., 1 28.

McLaughlin, Barry. 1987. Theories of Second-Language Learning. London: Edward Arnold.

Mehrotra, R. R. A. 1982. International communication through nonnative varieties of English: the case of Indian English. In Brumfit, C.J., ed. (1982). English for International Communication. Oxford, etc.: Pergamon Press, 73-80.

Moag, Rodney F. 1982. The life cycle of non-native Englishes: A case study. In: Kachru (1982), 270-288.

Pankhurst, J ., & M. Sharwood Smith. 1985. Editorial. Second Language Research 1.1.

Quirk, Randolph. 1985. The English language in a global context. In: Quirk, R. & H.G. Widdowson, eds. English in the World. Teaching and learning the language and literatures. Cambridge, etc.: Cambridge University Press, 1-6.

Saunders, George. No date. Bilingual Children: Guidance for the family. Clevedon, Avon, England: Multilingual Matters, Ltd.

Smith, Larry E. 1976. English as an international auxiliary language. RELC Journal 7.2. Reprinted in: Smith (1983), 5.

Smith, Larry E. 1983. Readings in English as an International Language. Oxford, etc.: Pergamon Press.

Spolsky, Bernard. 1989. Conditions for Second Language Learning. Oxford, etc. Oxford University Press.

Todd, Loreto. 1984. Modern Englishes Pidgins & Creoles. Oxford: Basil Blackwell in association with André Deutsch.

Tucker, G. Richard. 1988. Educational language policy in the Philippines: a case study. In: Lowenberg, Peter H. A. ed.

Tucker, G. Richard. 1988. GURT '87. Language Spread and Language Policy: Issues, Implications, and Case Studies. Washington, D.C.: Georgetown University Press, 331-341

LANGUAGE ACQUISITION, BIOGRAPHY AND BILINGUALISM[1]

Ulrich Steinmüller
Technical University of Berlin[2]

1.0. LANGUAGE ACQUISITION AND BILINGUALISM OF TURKISH SCHOOLCHILDREN

The individual and social development of immigrant children in our society takes place under the influence of two or often, as in the case of Kurdish children e. g., even three languages, cultural contexts and systems of norms and values. Both the individual families and the German educational institutions often fail to relate divergent aspects of immigrant life to each other; inconsistencies as such are often not taken into account at all.

M. Hartig points out that the process of becoming aware of one's language is an essential prerequisite for an awareness of the interpretation of social acts and therefore is of great importance for the development of a person's identity as well as their ability to act socially. (Hartig, p 76)

For foreign children and young people this process of developing an awareness of their own language takes place under the additional task of acquiring at least partial bilingualism. The necessary adaptation to given norms, values, and systems of evaluation, essentially the process of forming both an awareness and an image of the self is made considerably more difficult by the need to orientate oneself within two or more languages. With regard to the individual's ability to act within German society the mastering of the German language as the most vital means of communication in this context is of outstanding importance. Much the same goes for the mastery of German as a means both of imparting knowledge and of cognition with regard to one's progress at school and professional qualification; the latter two are vital factors in the development of an individual's future prospects and therefore hold great responsibility for a successful integration into German society. In the early phases of socialization within the family these processes and stages of development are naturally linked with a child's first language, i.e. his or her mother tongue.

Their specific migrant situation given, foreign children and young people are, however, forced to become bilingual. Forming a minority as far as at least their language and cultural background are concerned it is neither for them or their parents to decide, but circumstances admit no option but bilingualism.

When immigrant children are introduced into German educational institutions, namely the German school system, German accordingly becomes the medium that determines the most fundamental processes of socialization. Even at the moment of acquisition, German already serves as the vehicle for conveying norms and values and determines the educational process.

The development of the personality and a person's individual identity, the formulation of one's role and position in society, and the negotiation of one's position within a group of peers all take place within a framework of communicative activities for which the mastery of German is of central importance. Despite or because of the said functional qualities of German with regard to the process of socialization of foreign children, bilingualism presents a burden for those children.

In the case of immigrant children we are not dealing with 'natural' bilingualism; their bilingualism does not originate in a family context as would be the case in families in which the parents have different mother tongues, but develops from the pressure of circumstances. It is characterized by a compartmentalization into different domains: certain areas of life are associated with one language, while others belong to the second language. The child's mother tongue, for example, is used in the affective-emotional area, e.g. in the family, with friends and relatives. German, on the other hand, is the public language and is associated with school, shopping, and dealing with the authorities. A connection between the two is at best only basically established. This division is even more strained by the fact that with regard to social prestige there is a difference between the two languages of immigrant children: The surrounding German speaking majority has a higher regard for German than for Turkish so that the mastery of one, namely the German language is more prestigious than the mastery of the other, i.e. Turkish language.

This results in 'conflict bilingualism', because the child is forced to learn the language of the majority despite the conflicting values, norms, and expectations it conveys. Therefore we can, possibly though in an exaggerated fashion, state that because of the sole use of German in class, the alienation from the parental home has essentially become a part of the general objective German schools pursue. In this context, Haas states that "institutionalized pressure forces" the concerned children and young people to "break with their parental home" without German society really answering for the consequences of the pressure it exerts. In contrast to the so called 'elite bilingualism', i.e. English or French as a second language, the bilingualism of immigrant children is socially not regarded as a valuable addition to our culture; pressure is put on immigrant children to assimilate with the objective to become monolingual in their second language.

Second language acquisition research, basically concerned with the linguistic aspects of migration, has, especially since it established itself in Germany, paid particular attention to the description of the outcome of the process of acquiring a second language. Of particular importance are, above all, the works of Meisel, Pienemann and Clahsen as well as Wode and Felix's research. While in an early phase mainly questions on the formation of set linguistic structures deviating from the accepted German norm were discussed (cf. the research of the "Heidelberger Forschungsprojekt 'Pidgin-Deutsch'", Meisel 1975, Steinmüller 1979), the German of different nationalities became a central issue of research in the period following (e.g. Meyer-Ingwersen, Pienemann, Meisel, Stölting for Turkish, Spanish, Italian, and Serbo Croatian).

From a psycholinguistic point of view, the explanation of the process of second language acquisition as well as the reasons for the strikingly varied results of this process became central questions. In this context, the so called 'three great hypotheses' were widely discussed (e.g. Bausch and Kasper 1979, Felix 1977, Steinmüller 1981b): the Hypothesis of Interference that implies that the patterns, structures, and elements of one's first language serve as a basis for acquiring a second language; the Hypothesis of Identity that interprets the acquisition of a second language as determined by the succession of fixed steps of learning; and lastly the Interlanguage Approach that regards the concept of individual learning varieties and interim grammars as a central aspect of second language acquisition.

All three hypotheses have not yet succeeded in developing a wholly provable and convincing model of explanation; recently though, the number of papers supporting the Interlanguage Approach has increased. In most recent times the hypothesis assuming a proficient and sophisticated mastery of one's first language as an essential prerequisite for a sophisticated and discriminative mastery of one's second language is being discussed with increasing interest. (e.g. Cummins, Skutnabb-Kangas, Steinmüller 1981a, c, Swain).

Interpreting foreign children's language faculties as a result of the process of language acquisition under the specific conditions of their migrant situation it is this paper's aim to relate Turkish schoolchildren's proficiency in their two languages, that is German and Turkish, to their previous life-history at that time in their lives that, according not only to the accepted opinion of psycholinguists but also according to developmental psychology, marks the end of the process of language acquisition. By way of analyzing the children's biographies this paper attempts to discern those elements and factors of influence that contribute to or impede the process of language acquisition. Boos-Nünning, among others, points out that it is necessary to include the "interrelation between language and culture, between the process of learning a language and one's cultural and social situation" (Boos-Nünning, p 63) in the analysis. Finally it has to be examined in what way the mastery of German and Turkish and the children's self-assessment of their linguistic skills influences the children's schooling and professional training as well as the degree to which they make use of their chances, their orientation and assessment of their future prospects and their ethnical identification. An examination of this kind has to be based on the conclusion that a proficient and sophisticated mastery of one's first language is an essential prerequisite for a proficient and sophisticated mastery of one's second language. (cf. for example Cummins, Steinmüller 1987) The linking of data concerning language acquisition and language skills on the one hand with the social and cultural situation on the other hand (as, for example, postulated by Boos-Nünning and Damanakis (cf. Damanakis 1983)) can be seen as a consequence of the so far unsatisfactory state of research.

2.0. GERMAN LANGUAGE SKILLS OF TURKISH SCHOOLCHILDREN
Data regarding the level of linguistic development of Turkish as well as of a comparable group of German schoolchildren was collected at two Berlin schools. (This survey was part of a far more comprehensive research on the level and development of language skills of Turkish schoolchildren; cf. Steinmüller 1987). A total of 320 Turkish and 60 German students took part in the survey, which recorded the children's language skills in the seventh grade, i.e. the point in time where pupils have just changed from elementary school to the first level of secondary school. The survey was carried out with the aid of the "Soziolinguistisches Erhebungsinstrument zur Sprachentwicklung (SES)" (cf. Portz, R. and C. Pfaff 1981, Steinmüller 1984).

The results of the survey substantiate the assumption that as far as linguistic skills are concerned the mere subdivision into German and Turkish students represents a distorting simplification. It is rather within the group of Turkish students that a more subtle differentiation is necessary to record the different levels of their linguistic faculties.

The Turkish schoolchildren of this survey can be subdivided into five groups:

-        one group whose language skills do not at all or only marginally differ from those of German pupils
-        one group whose language skills in all areas are so little developed that they are hardly able to participate in class discussion and for whom lessons, for the most part, go by not understood
-        three groups that show gaps and deficits to a varied extent

This extraordinary disparity in language skills has not yet been sufficiently accounted for by any of the hypotheses that form the basis of any one relevant linguistic and psycholinguistic research.

Even at the very early stages of language acquisition, German as a second language - unlike a foreign language - serves children of foreign workers in Germany as an important means of communication and as the language of socialization and cognition. It is therefore not possible to postpone communicative activities to a time when controlled second language acquisition has lead to the internalization of grammatically 'correct' forms and structures. As a result, children are forced to develop as quickly and as efficient as possible a however 'ungrammatical' interlanguage with its own rules and norms. Their extraordinary skill and success in doing so becomes apparent in the analyses of immigrant children's linguistic faculties, which show that despite the sometimes serious deficiencies in the knowledge of German - compared to the standard usage of a native speaker of German - they often possess an impressive communicative fluency. This very often leads to a misjudgement of a child's actual knowledge of German and in turn is often responsible for the fact that, in many cases, the need for further language instruction fails to be recognized.

Second language acquisition - just as any other form of mental activity - is based on a process of selection The limitedness of human perception, that is our ability to simultaneously perceive, distinguish and assimilate signals and information, causes a child to filter out single elements and structural features of the set of linguistic data he or she is confronted with in every communicational situation. The nature of this filter, that is the specific criteria that cause certain elements to stuck, others, however, to fall through, is still uncertain. In some research papers an important role is attributed to interference phenomena. Comparative analyses of the language faculties of Turkish and German schoolchildren, however, show that the assumption that the influence of interference really is of such an outstanding importance has to be modified.

The following table outlines the results of the aforementioned survey on the level of linguistic development in the 7th grade of both schools with specific emphasis on results in the areas of morphology and syntax, which are regarded as linguistic prerequisites for learning. The number of Turkish students and their German counterparts that had difficulties in mastering the various categories listed below is expressed in per cent.

	GERMAN STUDENTS	TURKISH STUDENTS
Sentence construction	53,3%	69,0%
Conjunctions	8,3%	13,4%
Negations	5,0%	8,2%
Verb Inflection	10,0%	32,2%
Prepositions	28,3%	77,3%
Adjective Comparison	6,7%	8,3%
Pronouns	14,3%	36,9%

Declension	47,2%	88,0%
Use of the Article	58,3%	89,1%

This table shows that in the area of the morphologic-syntactical categories examined - for the sake of clarity here combined in nine generic terms - there is no single element that exclusively Turkish children have difficulty with. Against the background of one part of the linguistic discussion about second language acquisition these results are of considerable importance in so far as they qualify the assumption that there are 'typical Turkish mistakes' in second language acquisition. This assumption is based on the hypothesis of interference within the theory of second language acquisition, which implies that the acquisition of a second language is mainly orientated towards the already known categories and structures of a person's first language. From this an argumentation follows that tries to explain deviances and mistakes in immigrant children's German by tracing them back to structures of the child's first language.

If this hypothesis were correct, German and Turkish children should not make mistakes in the same areas. This is, however, quite obviously the case. The assumed 'typical Turkish mistakes' are therefore not so very Turkish after all. This observation (the consequences of which for linguistic theory shall not be discussed further at this point) will have to cause teachers to rethink the approach that in the past years was principally conveyed to them as explaining idiosyncratic features in the language acquisition of their foreign students and which was supported by a number of research papers based on the Hypothesis of Interference. By introducing this observation we do not mean to imply that from our point of view interferences do not play a part in second language acquisition at all; the said observations, however, considerably qualify the importance of interferences as the principal cause of mistakes and irregularities. (cf. Thomé among others).

3.0. TURKISH SCHOOLCHILDREN'S PROFICIENCY IN THE TURKISH LANGUAGE

The survey on Turkish schoolchildren's proficiency in their first language we refer to in this context (cf. Steinmüller 1987) is the first of its sort that tried to systematically examine and describe Turkish schoolchildren's knowledge of Turkish in adequate detail. A total of 130 Turkish students of the 7th grade were surveyed for their mastery of their first language. The instrument used for ascertaining and analyzing the linguistic data was specially developed for this purpose in the academic part of the experiment "Integration türkischer Schüler in Gesamtschulen (Integration of Turkish students in comprehensive schools)". (cf. Thomas)

The survey on the knowledge of Turkish consists of an oral and a written part; the written part is subdivided into one part related and another part unrelated to a text. The observed linguistic elements and categories range from oral and written articulateness to the use of idiomatic expressions, findings concerning vocabulary, morphology and syntax and the mastery of the Turkish alphabet and orthography. A total of 35 elements and categories on all levels of linguistic structures and usage were ascertained and analyzed. The resulting overall picture portrays the results of the development of Turkish children's first language under the conditions of migration. Their knowledge of their first language is so heterogeneous and deficient that it is impossible to draw up a unified picture of Turkish children's proficiency in the Turkish language. The variations and degrees of proficiency differ so greatly between individual students and present themselves as so complex that we have to ask on what grounds it should still be possible to speak of these children's 'own' or 'common' language.

In the field of both language psychology and developmental psychology it has, for years, been an undisputable fact that a person's first language acquisition is, under normal conditions, come to an end around the twelfth to fourteenth year of the person's life: morphology, syntax, communicative skills and strategies, conceptualization, etc. are used more or less confidently and are at least mastered adequate to an adult's use of the language; merely the lexical areas are capable of continuous development through the whole of a person's lifetime.

The level of proficiency the children surveyed have reached in 'their' language under the specific conditions of life and personal development imposed on them is anything but adequate to an adult's use of the language. Even if only their oral proficiency were to serve as a yardstick, most serious deficits would be discovered: more than two thirds show deficiencies in their vocabulary and understanding of the meaning of words, while the oral articulateness is underdeveloped with almost half of the children surveyed; less than a third are able to express facts and details in an adequate and intelligible manner. If, in addition to that, we also consider their skills in mastering the written language, the results are even more depressing: sometimes more than two thirds of the Turkish students were not able to carry out the most elementary linguistic-grammatical operations in order to describe connections between facts, facts as such or a course of events in an adequate manner or appropriate to their age.

A large majority of the children surveyed show serious deficits in the knowledge and use of their first language. To prevent my being misunderstood I would like to state that I am by no means talking of quasi-refined additional language skills or of a stylistically sophisticated and elegant way of expressing oneself, but of a deficit in the most elementary and basic qualifications. May I also emphasize that the mere number of words, phrases or syntactical structures unknown is not my point. The deficits detected belong to areas that are indispensable for linguistic reception and the penetration and intellectualization of knowledge and experiences. On the linguistic level they were able to reach under the specific circumstances of migration, the majority of Turkish schoolchildren living in Germany are not able to master 'their' language in a way appropriate to their age and the requirements of, for example, school.

When these results are related to the results of the survey on the children's knowledge of German the full extent of the dilemma becomes apparent. There, too, the most elementary areas of the language, necessary for the ordering, linking, and decoding of information, knowledge, and experiences as well as for the linguistic and intellectual learning of the world, are seriously underdeveloped and do not meet the requirements of school.

While it is true that deficits in the second language do not admit of the conclusion that a person's general intellectual processes and his or her cognitive faculties are also underdeveloped, it is often, particularly when this argument turns up in politico-educational debates, implied that these processes could be completed in another, for example the first language. In the light of our observations, this implication, i.e. Turkish children's ability to fall back upon their first language, seems more than questionable.

For processes of learning, in fact for all forms of education of Turkish children, this realization is of utmost importance: neither the development of the first language nor that of the second language meets the requirements and standards that would be appropriate to the young people's general level of development. Which other medium can then possibly serve as a means to acquire knowledge, form concepts, and to assimilate and convey essential contents?

While the children do possess the cognitive abilities appropriate to their age they - in two languages - lack the means to make intellectual and communicative use of their abilities by way of employing linguistic symbols.

The degree of psychological strain, uncertainty, confusion, discontentment and disorientation must be extremely difficult to assess for a person not affected; the young people affected are, however, well aware of this as remarks on deficiencies, possible choices of profession, plans for the future and comments on prospects and failures show.

4.0. THE BIOGRAPHICAL METHOD AS A MEANS OF COMPILING LANGUAGE ACQUISITION BIOGRAPHIES

Since the categories 'biography' and 'life' have received increased attention in social science, the theoretical and methodological approaches that try to disclose circumstances of real life by way of abstraction and objectivation are confronted with other approaches that use biographical data to gain an insight into the social reality and circumstances. From a sociological point of view, Kohli formulates the necessity for a biographical sociology as an established part of social science. Via biographical sociology the whole of life is to be brought to the researcher's attention, and because of that the relation between a person's present situation and their biographical past and future becomes a central subject of consideration. This approach is mainly aimed against the preoccupation with a particular age or a particular situation. This way, the subjectivity of biographical approaches gains its legitimate scientific status. By the inclusion of subjectivity we can, on the one hand, mean the scientific perception of knowledge structures and patterns of interpretation of the objects surveyed; on the other hand, the concept of subjectivity includes the discernment of individual features or peculiarities of a person's circumstances as well as the attempt to determine a subject's individual and active contribution to the shaping of his or her conditions of life.

Elsewhere, Kohli describes the expectations regarding the biographical method as follows: the biographical approach is to facilitate a methodical access to social life, which should firstly be as comprehensive as possible, secondly enable us to discuss the active subject's own perspective, and thirdly take the historic dimension into account. So far, the biographical method has not lived up to these high expectations since, on the one hand, we have comparatively little experience in the use of the biographical method, and, on the other hand, there is hardly a common understanding of the term in all the research papers that claim it as their basis; moreover, the biographical approach has not yet been clearly delimited from other methods, above all the interpretative social research.

In the development of the biographical method Polish sociologists held an exemplary position during the Twenties and Thirties up to around the middle of the 20th century. Only in Polish sociology has the biographical method developed a continuing tradition, and in turn, Polish sociology is closely connected with this method. It is in this context that Markiewicz-Lagneau speaks of the 'methode polonaise'. The research papers are, however, for the most part published in Polish and have therefore remained practically unknown to Western sociologists. Exceptions are, for example, Znaniecki's English books and Szcepanski's essays and papers.

The unchallenged classic of the biographical method is the work by Thomas/Znaniecki, The polish Peasant in Europe and America (1918 - 1921; revised edition 1927). This study attends to the subject of social organization and disorganization in rural Poland and among Polish immigrants in the USA. The report is substantiated through personal letters, letters to the editors of newspapers, letters to associations protecting Polish immigrants interests, court records and suchlike as well as a 300 pages long autobiography of a young Polish emigrant.

In Germany, the use of the biographical method was mainly limited to psychology and educational theory, although numerous autobiographies of laborers appeared as early as 1903, and we consequently have to ask why similar studies did not emerge in this country. After 1945, the biographical approach disappeared from the general methodological and theoretical debate; only in the field of deviance research an interest in this method was kept up.

Halfway through the 1960s, American sociologists tried to revive an interest in the biographical approach but failed to present any significant innovations or further development. In Germany, the discussion of the biographical method only began as late as the 1970s.

Today, qualitative social research is increasingly preoccupied with biographical research. Beside an interest in the biography of certain age groups within society, most research concentrates on two main points: on the one hand, emphasis is laid on surveys on workers, while, on the other hand, research mainly focusses on socially deviant groups. (cf. Kieper, Lebenswelten verwahrloster Mädchen (The life and world of neglected girls), 1980).

The research on language acquisition and language acquisition biographies of Turkish schoolchildren belongs to the latter field of study. Its aim is to show correlations between Turkish children's language acquisition by way of analyzing linguistic data compiled over years of research on language faculties and their biographical data ascertained in interviews and through questionnaires. Although our data as well as the actual group of experimentees is not as extensive and large as that of surveys based on quantitative social research, biographical research presents, with regard to our objectives, a possible methodical approach.

The analysis of the biographical data on hand is based on a method that Schütze suggests in his essay "Biographieforschung und narratives Interview (Biographical research and the narrative interview)" and that served as a basis for his own research.

Right from the start of our analysis it will be important to bear the chronological, i.e. sequential structure of a person's life-history in mind. A person's life-history is a sequentially ordered accumulation of larger or smaller self-contained process-structures. The first step of the analysis presents a structural description of the contents of a life-history and elaborates single, time-wise limited process-structures. When determining the so called 'framework-switch elements', i.e. the points that mark a change in the framework of a biography, formal inner indicators like linking elements between individual accounts of events, e.g. subjective times, can be particularly informative.

In a second step, namely the analytical abstraction, the result of this description is detached from details of the described individual areas of life; subjective elements are filtered out in order to deduce a general biographical framework and to elaborate the succession of experience-dominating process-structures up to the presently dominant process-structure.

In the following step, namely the knowledge analysis, the subject's own theoretical and argumentative testimony on his or her life-history and identity are explicated. In the context of our research, this includes, above all, the Turkish students' self-assessment of their linguistic skills as well as their comments on their future prospects.

The next step of the analysis of biographical data consists in the detachment of the individual case study and an emphasis on contrastive comparisons. For this, we firstly pursued the strategy of minimal comparison in which very similar life-histories are compared to each other. Our aim was to examine in how far similar factors or phenomena in the life-histories of individual subjects had similar effects on their language acquisition. After the strategy of minimal comparison it is necessary to bring in the strategy of maximal comparison and compare biographical data of maximal dissimilarity in order to scrutinize hypotheses and assumptions regarding Turkish students' language acquisition that were put forward in the context of our research-project. As I have mentioned before, this method of Schütze constitutes the basis of our analysis of the biographical data on hand.

The first step of our analysis of biographical data consisted in detecting the decisive common elements relating to the 'framework-switch elements', that is the points that mark a change in the framework of a person's biography. In the course of this, the following 'framework-switch elements' were revealed, which, at the same time, represent the dominant process-structures:

a) early life-history
b) migration-history of the family
c) general schooling and a subject's progress at school
d) present situation

Factors like a person's circumstances of life, language habits, his or her fields of interest as well as the subject's personal assessment of future prospects and his or her language skills belong to the areas that determine a person's present situation. The homogeneity of the dominant process structures detected with a great number of people interviewed resulted from the underlying academic interest in the course Turkish children's language acquisition takes and the ensuing specific questions which, in turn, were directed at a specific group of people with common social features.

In the following step of our analysis, the biographical data on hand were structured in a way that for every student a short biography was drawn up in which the individual details were assigned to the so called 'framework - switch elements'. This way, a certain clarity was to be gained for subsequent contrastive comparisons. It turned out, however, that this method did not suffice to facilitate optimal comparisons. A tabular form of representation provided a solution. The table is subdivided into the following areas:

1. Biographical framework-elements
2. Course of migration
3. The child's schooling and progress at school
4. Socialization within and outside the family
5. Linguistic situation and usage
6. The students future perspectives

Point 1 combines details regarding personal data, country of birth, place of residence, and time of migration as well as details regarding the rest of the person's family.

Point 2 deals with the course of migration, which includes the child's as well as the parents migration-history and the domestic and family situation in Berlin. The fact that the student's statements often lack connecting elements makes it necessary to draw our own conclusions. One statement, for example, reads as follows: My father went to Germany in 1974, I only followed in 1980. We can conclude that, for a period of six years, the child most probably knew the father only from his visits, and we may consequently assume a certain alienation on both sides. For such or similar interpretations an extra column headed 'Assumptions and Interpretations' was included in point 2 of our table, while possible more far reaching interpretations, particularly with regard to connections between migration - history and language acquisition, are to be dealt with elsewhere.

Because of the general data on schooling, a great number of details were available for point 3 of our subdivision. This includes elementary school recommendations as well as information on a child's secondary education.

Point 4 of our table records data that gives information about 'socialization within and outside the family'; this includes, on the one hand, the consideration of the parental conduct of the upbringing of their children together with a child's domestic chores as well as the parents attitude towards German school and their child's social contacts and friends, while, on the other hand, information on leisure time activities and holidays in Turkey is gathered. This data sequence gives, among other things, information about the degree to which a person is orientated towards his or her country of origin, i.e. Turkey, and is therefore of considerable importance for any interpretation in regard to the course of second language acquisition of the Turkish students surveyed. Point 5 directly relates to the details on language skills, usage and the language situation within the family; because of the analysis of the children's linguistic faculties, information on their actual knowledge of the language is available in addition to their own assessment of their linguistic skills.

Point 5 also includes details regarding reading habits and the consumption of audio-visual media since both areas can be equally important for the linguistic development in the German language if we look at them from the point of view 'Does the student read? Does he or she watch television or video? If so, how often and what does he or she read or watch?'.

For the last point in our table, which contains details on the student's future prospects and perspectives, it seemed useful to differentiate between a child's own future perspective and that of his or her parents, since experience shows that there usually is a big difference between the two.

5.0. DISCUSSION OF THE RESULTS
5.1. General assessment
The results and insights that where gained and filtered out contain a deeply pedagogical tendency: it was clearly proved that no single biographical factor which, in a positive or negative sense, determines the success or failure in acquiring German as a second language could be detected. The assumption that certain single linguistic-biographically relevant factors were decisive for a successful second language acquisition in the sense of a conditio sine qua non proved to be definitely wrong.

For an example of this kind of basic assumption that enjoys great popularity in the argumentations on the subject of educational integration of Turkish migrant children in the academic and, to an even greater extent, in the discussion of educational politicians, may I refer to the much flogged criterion of the age at which immigration takes place.
Opinions that are based on this kind of assumption are clearly refuted by our results; they are empirically as well as theoretically untenable.

5.2. No correspondence between the actual knowledge of the language and the school marks for German
This is a very early result that emerged long before the systematical analysis of all our data. This amazing result already became apparent in the first test-phase of minimal and maximal comparison.

To this end, a first grading of all the individual biographies according to their fitting into a five-stage scale of proficiency in German was carried out. This gradation showed that there are, on the one hand, students with a good knowledge of German that got low marks for English and German, a recommendation for junior high school and ended up without any completed secondary education, while, on the other hand, there are students that, with, at the most, a mediocre or poor knowledge of German, completed a high school education. The systematical analysis of our data verified the findings of a missing correlation between the proficiency in German and the school marks for German.

A comparison between the mark in German on the final report of the 6th grade and the result of the survey on the proficiency in German at the beginning of the 7th grade proved very informative with regard to the question in how far the actual knowledge of German correlates with the school mark for German since both evaluations date from the same period of a student's life, and it can be assumed that the mark in German mirrors what, in the context of our educational system, is assessed and evaluated as a knowledge of German. To this end, the average school marks for German were ascertained for the five groups the students were subdivided into in the course of our analysis:

actual knowledge of German	average mark for German
good	2,80
good-medium	3,30
medium	3,45
medium-poor	3,09
poor	3,41

The very marginal difference of, at the most, 0,6 per cent in the marks for German of students with, on the one hand, a good and, on the other hand, a poor knowledge of German is striking; the students of the medium-group even got poorer marks than those of the weakest group and students regarded as having a medium to poor knowledge of German got better marks than students with a good to medium knowledge of the language. Moreover, almost only the marks 2-4 are used in the marking for German, and the mark 5 only appears within the weakest group that is three times in a total of 132 students surveyed. The scale of marks, ranging from 1-6, is therefore not fully exhausted.

Even though we can note a slightly falling tendency in the marks for German following the actual knowledge of the language, the differentiations are so slight and, what is more, too conflicting as to enable us to speak of a correspondence between the actual knowledge of and the school mark for German as a measurement for a person's success at school. It might possibly be justified to divide the students into two groups - a good group, slightly above the average mark 3, and a group of medium to poor students whose marks for German are slightly below average. The standard of work in the German language that is demanded and assessed in school obviously relates mostly to other linguistic areas than to the area of oral communication in German. Our survey did not, however, examine in how far this qualification (i.e. a student's oral articulateness) has a part to play in the assessment of work in other subjects - such implicit influence ought to be considerable. The success at school in the area of the German language as acknowledged in the school mark for German has obviously little to do with the actual knowledge of the language.

5.3. No correspondence between the actual knowledge of German and the prognosis on a person's success at school

Based on the widely stressed importance of the knowledge of German for one's success at school we may assume that a student with a better knowledge of German will accordingly be more successful at school. The prognoses on an individual student's expected success at school are expressed in the recommendations on the type of secondary school student ought to attend after leaving elementary school. These recommendations are drawn up by the teachers of a student's elementary school.

The elementary school's recommendations were compared to the student's actual knowledge of German in order to scrutinize the importance of language skills for the prognoses on a student's success at school.

Comparing the five groups of students with regard to their knowledge of German at the beginning of the 7th grade and the prognosis on their success at school, the usual gradation of elementary school recommendations into grammar school, high school or junior high school was retained. The possible additional recommendation "comprehensive school" can be ignored, since all the students surveyed attended comprehensive schools. The number of students is given in absolute figures - occasional differences to the total number of experimentees have their roots in a partial lack of details about individual students.

Actual knowledge of German	number of students	elementary school's recommendation	
I. good	17	grammar	3
		high	6
		junior high	8
II. good-medium	22	grammar	1
		high	7
		junior high	14
III. medium	11	grammar	0
		high	6
		junior high	5
IV. medium-poor	29	grammar	2
		high	10
		junior high	17
V. poor	31	grammar	0
		high	13
		junior high	28

This comparison, too, shows that there is no clear relation between a student's actual knowledge of German and the prognosis on his or her expected success at school. This also means that the young people concerned can see no connection between the prognoses on their success at school and the resulting further prospects on the one hand, and the actual mastery of the language on the other hand. This lack of connection has a negative influence on the motivation for a correct linguistic self-assessment and a conscious reduction of linguistic deficits.

5.4. Biographical factors and level of linguistic development
The attempt to draw up standardizable language acquisition biographies for the students surveyed and to correlate these with the actual level of linguistic development was just as little successful as the attempt to isolate single elements or a set of factors from the objective course of biographies and to identify those as causally related to the actual knowledge of the language. We cannot rule out the possibility that the nature of the underlying data-basis is partly responsible for this failure. It seems more likely, however, that the great disparity and heterogeneity of the biographies do not admit of such standardizations. Moreover, while we may make the justified assumption that a certain biographical factor - by itself or in combination and/or confrontation with other factors - influences language acquisition, it remains open how a certain factor affects this process.

Whether a child immigrated together with his or her parents and brothers and sisters, whether it followed together with his or her father or mother after sometimes years of separation from the other parent, whether a child was separated from both parents and was left with relatives in Turkey, whether it lives together with his or her brothers and sisters or found a number of "new" brothers and sisters in Germany, whether there are older brothers or sisters that may already have learned German, whether a child is first born, or whether a child has been sent back and forth between Turkey and Germany a couple of times (there are a number of girls that were only fetched to join their family when they were old enough to mind their younger brothers and sisters while their mother was at work) - from the point of view of developmental psychology, all this must have a considerable influence on second language acquisition. In this survey, though, it was not possible to obtain clear evidence on the nature and results of those influences. The same goes for the connection between schooling and a person's progress at school and his or her language acquisition.

There is an amazing variety of the individual school-situations immigrant children often go through because of their parents' work situation and the regulations applying to foreign students in the German educational system. Repeated changes between different types of classes within the German school system are not unusual, and the change from a Turkish school to a school in Germany often adds to this experience. Moreover pre-school institutions were attended only in exceptional cases. Stable, clear, and, in the long term, effective learning is almost impossible; it is obvious that there is no single variable which alone significantly influences a child's language acquisition - whether, for example, a child at first attended a special preparatory class, then changed to an ordinary class for immigrant children and finally completed his or her education in an ordinary German class, or whether the child might have missed out or was moved down into a class for immigrant children, etc. cannot be proved as the significant factor.

It seems reasonable to suppose that there would be considerably more students with a high or at least sufficient level of linguistic development, if the children's educational history, the first six years of their schooldays in particular, were not as tangled up as our data shows them to be.

It was, however, not possible to gain clear evidence on questions like whether teaching in a bi-national, that is German-Turkish class is more successful than in a multi-national class. While it can be proved that systematical and continuous encouragement and fostering of a child's linguistic faculties has a positive effect on language acquisition, we cannot clearly determine the influence of such factors as atmosphere, the personality of a teacher, the teaching methods, etc., beyond their influentiality as such. Unlike suggested in the research by Röhr-Sendelmeier this holds also true of a child's leisure time habits. All details concerning extracurricula activities and contacts to Germans and Turks, particularly to people of one's own age, were combined under this heading. It includes statements on friends of different nationalities, informal playgroups, and spontaneous or organized leisure time activities like, for example, club membership (for which only Turkish boys' membership of football clubs seemed significant), visits of youth clubs and Koran school.

Even rather frequent contacts to German playmates do not result in a better knowledge of German, which, by the way, also allows insights into the level of the mastery and usage of German that suffices in informal playing situations.

It has been shown that even students with a poor knowledge of German are able to master simple everyday communications in the German language. Organized leisure time activities that would require and train more complicated forms of expression (such as the participation in a drama group, a political youth organization, etc.) are not known of. All statements on the kind and extent of a child's domestic chores, jobs within the family, minding of younger brothers and sisters, etc. indirectly hint at the child's opportunities to do his or her homework or to find time for activities and occupations that would in some way encourage and support the acquisition of the German language. As could be expected, girls were significantly more involved in domestic duties than boys. The equally significant result that the girls surveyed had a better knowledge of German than the boys can be compared to this. It would, however, certainly be inappropriate to infer one's linguistic proficiency from one's sex or to construe a causality between domestic chores and the knowledge of German. This result again shows what has already been emphasized before - namely that it is neither possible nor useful to isolate a single factor or a set of individual factors and to declare them a determinant.

The reasons for the few and rather imprecise findings on a connection between actual biographical factors and the actual level of linguistic development lie, above all, in the specific features and circumstances of language acquisition as such. First as well as second language acquisition are creative processes that involve the entire personality with its intellectual, psychic, and social characteristics.

Unlike processes that follow a stimulus - response pattern, learning a language is an acquisition process for which selection and interpretation are of outstanding importance. The individual range of variations of selection and interpretation is amplified by the extremely various possibilities of individual reactions to an objective condition and external influences. The same biographical factor can therefore have different effects on different children, since its assimilation in the processes of selection and interpretation varies from one individual to the other.

Generalizing and standardizing analyses can only marginally do justice to this individuality and subjectivity; the individual analysis, which can pay due attention to individuality and subjectivity, is more informative. Generalizations that are based on such individual analyses will inevitably be vague or demonstrate tendencies rather than facts. The analysis of our category "future perspectives" makes this clear. It combined all details on possible choices of profession and future laces of residence and included both the plans and wishes of the parents and of the children. Most parents have a clear but time-wise indeterminable perspective of their future: they want to spend their old age, financially provided for, in Turkey. Their children's wishes concerning the country they want to live in vary greatly; unambiguous statements are relatively rare, while most children hope for ways to realize both possibilities. A few students express the wish to live in other countries than Turkey or Germany. The children's possible choices of profession include an assorted range of dream jobs just as could be expected of thirteen to fourteen years old. They do, however, show a striking tendency regarding their general attainability. If we compare the choice of profession and the level of school education that is required for the respective vocational training with the level of school education the students later actually reach, false estimations are relatively rare. The professional careers that the parents wish their children to enter on are completely unrealistic in this context. Yet again a clear correlation to the actual knowledge of German is missing. This situation is being aggravated by the fact that our schools fail to elucidate the connection between one's future perspective and one's success at school on the one hand and the knowledge of German on the other hand. (cf. our remarks on the actual knowledge of German and the mark for German as well as on the knowledge of the language and the prognoses on a student's success at school.)

Another result of the analysis of language acquisition biographies concerns the Turkish students' own assessment of their knowledge of German. This self-assessment represents an important and fundamental element of the concept of the self, which, in the context of personality development and the forming of an identity, greatly influences the individual and affects the various levels of socialization and the shaping of the consciousness. Self-assessment also influences a student's motivation and eagerness to learn.

In this context, it seems important that all students surveyed regarded their knowledge of German as good to satisfactory. While 53% of those students that had already gone to school in Turkey assessed themselves correctly, this only holds for 27% of the students that have only attended school in Germany. Almost 60% of the latter group decidedly overrate their knowledge of German. Particularly students with a poor knowledge of German show this tendency. This overestimation is also expressed in the fact that in almost 80% of these cases the families enlist the child as an interpreter in contacts with the German surroundings because of the child's supposed proficiency in the language; despite their actually better knowledge of German only 59% of the children that previously attended school in Turkey fulfill similar tasks within their families. The overestimation of one's linguistic abilities that was observed among students with a highly deficient knowledge of German can possibly be seen in relation to a stagnation and fossilization of language acquisition (i.e. the linguistic development stops at a yet highly deficient level) which was observed for the same group of people: the false assessment of one's own linguistic abilities stands in the way of further acquisition and development, since the student is not aware of the necessity of further development because of his or her supposed good knowledge of German. A student's motivation and eagerness to learn are consequently considerably diminished and have to be aroused again by the teacher. As our examination of linguistic abilities in experimental schools shows, this is not nearly as successful as one would wish (cf. Steinmüller 1987).

Another of the students' self-assessments elucidates the problem of subtractive bilingualism, that is the inadequate mastery of the two languages which can be observed particularly among students that have only ever attended German schools. Just 30% of those children state that their Turkish is better than their German, while approximately 46% think their German better than their Turkish; they do, however, for the most part regard their knowledge of German as, at best, mediocre to sufficient and their knowledge of Turkish therefore as even poorer. Hence it is particularly necessary to foster and encourage these students with the aim to attain a sophisticated and differentiating mastery of the language.

The potential psychological conflict that lies in the assessment of one's own inadequacy, particularly in those areas which are, at least socially, attributed to one's own identity, has so far not been sufficiently ascertained and analyzed. We can only assume the consequences of such self-assessment and the potential conflicts involved on the forming of an identity and an individual's chances to plan for the future.

5.5. The family's orientation and the child's level of linguistic development

With a level of significance that is clearly and doubtlessly significant, there is a correlation between a child's actual level of linguistic development and the family's orientation towards either the country of migration or the country of origin: an orientation towards the country of origin clearly goes along with the child's poor knowledge of German, while children of families that are orientated towards the country of migration have a distinctly better knowledge of German. The category "Orientation of the family" as a biographically relevant feature is very complex and, similar to the category "Future Perspective", highly subjective and individual.

An overall-picture of a family's orientation was compiled from very ramified individual data, details on the parents' language habits and the conduct of the up-bringing of their children, the formulation of future perspectives, opinions on the German and/or the Turkish school system, the participation in class trips, parents' evenings, school events, parents' accounts of their experiences at work, and suchlike as well as from the pedagogical experience of teaching foreign students. This orientation subdivides into five characteristic features:

- strong orientation towards the country of origin
- balanced, with a tendency towards the country of origin
- balanced
- balanced, with a tendency towards the country of migration
- strong orientation towards the country of migration

This category draws our attention to the motivational background and the atmosphere in which a child that is confronted with the task of second language acquisition grows up. This category can indicate whether a child lives in a situation which makes the learning of German actually seem desirable and useful, and it is therefore instructive from a qualitative-educational point of view.

A strong orientation towards the country of origin implies a value system that maintains and emphasizes traditional norms and ways of life which are based on a rural-islamic milieu, and which we often tend to simply call "Turkish". It turns backwards and is often orientated towards a nostalgically transfigured past of an ostensibly intact village live of parents and grandparents; rules are often obeyed far more rigidly than is and was the case in the reality of the emigrants' native village. At the same time, they rather anxiously cut themselves off from the present demands of the country of migration, and everything unfamiliar is stamped as "German", the dealing with which is avoided where possible. Such an orientation has a certain stabilizing effect on the identy and can often be found in connection with processes of emigration.

A child that grows up in such an atmosphere can only develop an intrinsic motivation to learn the second language if he or she consciously dissociates him- or herself from the rest of the family.

A balanced orientation takes into account that one originally comes from a different country, but that one is also capable and willing to find one's way in the country of migration. A certain degree of conformity is regarded as both natural and necessary. Tolerance of different value systems, open-mindedness about conditions in the country of migration, and the wish to tackle the situation without denying one's own origin characterize this kind of orientation. A marriage to a German partner, for example, is regarded as normal and acceptable.

A strong orientation towards the country of migration mostly goes along with the wish to stay long-term or to settle permanently. Occasionally, over-assimilation takes place; values that are classified as "German" are adopted uncritically. The orientation towards the majority, the avoidance of being noticed at any price, and great efforts to adapt and conform characterize such orientation. The acquisition of the German language is greatly encouraged, but too heavy a pressure to adapt can have an inhibiting effect on one's language acquisition.

This list of a family's possible orientations towards the country of either origin or migration is a classification into ideal types whose transitions are, in reality fluid. The pure balance in particular is a theoretical construct; the more data we have on a family, the sooner will we ascribe them a "tendency towards....".

Orientations mirror processes of the development and assimilation of experiences; children as members of a family do contribute to the change or stabilization of norms and value systems. While the assumption of a simple cause - consequence relation between a family's orientation and a child's language acquisition is certainly false, interaction and feedback-effects are highly probable.

6.0. CONCLUSIONS
It has become clear that certain combinations of biographical features which can be assumed to influence second language acquisition in a positive or negative way do by no means guarantee a good or poor knowledge of the language. We might conclude that second language acquisition research should, in future, increasingly take factors from the areas of psychology and a person's motivation to learn into consideration. However, it remains to be examined whether this really enables us

to compare biographical data more successfully with regard to the drawing up of standardized language acquisition biographies.

Judging from our previous findings and because of the target group's heterogeneity it should be extremely difficult to make general statements about Turkish children's second language acquisition. The reasons for failure or success in the second language are extremely various. Every student develops different and individual interrelations. These different structures are to be discerned and formulated by way of individual case studies. An application or rather a generalization in the sense of statistically significant statements would again dismiss the individuality of language acquisition.

In the future, it will rather be necessary to draw up individual language acquisition biographies in order to demonstrate structures, processes, and possible correlations. Results thus obtained can be significant for second language acquisition research as well as for practical counselling and all sorts of help and support.

As I have mentioned above, these results cannot just be applied to any student at all, since the individual varieties of the process of language acquisition remain, in the end, the decisive factor.

NOTES

1. The original manuscript was written in German entitled Spracherwerbsbiographie und Zweisprachigkeit. The english translation was done by Alexa Alfer.

2. This chapter was written in cooperation with Britta Bock, Claudia Niermann, Maria Steinmetz, Günther Thomé.

REFERENCES

Betel, Peter; Schübo, Werner. 1983. SPSS9. Statistik-Programm-System für die Sozialwissenschaften. Eine Beschreibung der Programmversionen 8 und 9. 4. ed. Stuttgart, New York: Gustav Fischer.

Clahsen, Günther; Jürgen Meisel and Manfred Pienemann. 1983. Deutsch als Zweitsprache. Der Spracherwerb ausländischer Arbeiter. Narr Verlag Tübingen.

Clauss, Günther; Heinz Ebner. 1979. Grundlagen der Statistik für Psychologen, Pädagogen und Soziologen. 3rd revised ed tion. Frankfurt/M.: Thun.

Cummins, Jim. 1979. "Linguistic Interdependence and the Educational Development of Bilingual Children." In: Review of Educational Research. vol. 49, C29.

Damanakis, M. 1983. "Muttersprachlicher Unterricht für ausländische Schüler." In: Deutsch Lernen 4.

Felix, Sascha. 1977. "Natürlicher Zweitsprachenerwerb: Ein Überblick." In: Studium Linguistik 4.

Friedrichs, Jürgen. 1977. Methoden empirischer Sozialforschung. 6th ed., Reinbeck: Rowohlt.

Haas, Peter. 1981. "Türkisch - Gedanken zu einem Modellversuch in Berlin-Kreuzberg." In: Gesamtschulinformationen, No. 2/3.

Hartig, Matthias. 1981. Anwendungsorientierter Sprachunterricht. Düsseldorf:

Kaspar, G.; K. Bausch. 1979. "Der Zweitspracherwerb. Möglichkeiten und Grenzen der 'großen' Hypothesen." In: Linguistische Berichte, No. 64.

Kellerer, Hans. 1972. Statistik im modernen Wirtschafts- und Sozialleben. 14th rev. edition. Reinbeck: Rowohlt.

Kieper, Marianne. 1980. Lebenswelten verwahrloster Mädchen - Autobiografische Berichte und ihre Interpretationen. Frankfurt/M.: Juventa Verlag.

Kohli, Martin (ed.). 1978. Soziologie des Lebenslaufs; Neue Folge - Soziologische Texte 109. Darmstadt: Luchterhand Verlag.

Maurenbrecher, Thomas. 1985. Die Erfahrung der externen Migration. Eine biografie- und interaktionsanalytische Untersuchung über Türken in der Bundesrepublik Deutschland. Vol. 2 of Interaktion und Lebenslauf. Frankfurt/M.: Verlag Peter Lang.

Meisel, Jürgen. 1975. "Ausländerdeutsch und Deutsch ausländische Arbeiter. Zur möglichen Entstehung eines Pidgin in der BRD." In: Zeitschrift für Literaturwissenschaft und Linguistik 18, 9-53.

Meisel, Jürgen; Harald Clahsen and Manfred Pienemann. 1979. "On Determining Development Stages in Natural Language Acquisition." In: Wuppertaler Arbeitshefte für Sprachwissenschaft 2.

Meyer-Ingwersen, Johannes; Rosemarie Neumann and Matthias Kummer. 1977. Zur Sprachentwicklung türkischer Schüler in der Bundesrepublik. Kronberg/Ts.: Scriptor Verlag.

Portz, Renate; Carol Pfaff. 1981. SES - Soziolinguistisches Erhebungsinstrument zur Sprachentwicklung. Ein Instrument zur Beschreibung der Sprach- und Kommunikationsfähigkeit ausländischer Schüler in deutschen Schulen. Pädagogisches Zentrum Berlin.

Röhr-Sendelmeier, Una-Maria. 1985. Zweitspracherwerbs- und Sozialisationsbedingungen. Frankfurt/M., Bern, New York Lang, (= Europäische Hochschulschriften Reihe XI Pädagogik, Vl. 256).

Schütze, Fritz. 1983. "Biographieforschung und narratives Interview." In: Neue Praxis 3.

Schütze, Fritz. 1981. "Prozeßstrukturen des Lebenslaufs." In: Biographie in handlungswissenschaftlicher Perspektive. ed. by Matthes; Stoßberg; Pfeiffenberger. Nürnberg.

Selg, Herbert; Werner Bauer. 1973. Forschungsmethoden der Psychologie. Eine Einführung. 2nd ed., Stuttgart: Kohlhammer.

Skutnabb-Kangas, Tove; P. Toukoumaa. 1977. The Intensive Teaching of the Mother Tongue to Migrant Children at Pre School Age. Tampere.

Stoelting, Wilfried. 1980. "Die Entwicklung der Zweisprachigkeit bei ausländischen Schülern." In: Praxis Deutsch, Sonderheft "Deutsch als Zweitsprache".

Stoelting, Wilfried and Franz Januschek. 1982. (ed.). Handlungsorientierung im Zweitspracherwerb von Arbeitsmigranten. Verein zur Förderung der Sprachwissenschaft in Forschung und Ausbildung. Osnabrück.

Steinmüller, Ulrich. 1981a. "Ein Argument für den muttersprachlichen Unterricht." In: Ausländische Kinder in Berliner Schulen. Materialien des Kongresses vom 11./12.12.1981, ed. by GEW Berlin.

Steinmüller, Ulrich. 1981b. "Asumans Grammatik. Zum Problem von Normverstoß und Regularität im Zweitspracherwerb." In: Diskussion Deutsch 60.

Steinmüller, Ulrich. 1981c. "Begriffsbildung und Zweitspracherwerb." In: H. Essinger; A. Hellmich and G. Hoff (ed.), Ausländerkinder im Konflikt. Königstein/Berlin: Athenäum.

Steimüller, Ulrich. 1984. "Sprachstandserhebung und Sprachförderung bei ausländischen Schülern der Sekundarstufe I." In: Diskussion Deutsch 75.

Steinmüller, Ulrich. 1987. "Sprachentwicklung und Sprachunterricht türkischer Schüler." In: Gesamtschulinformationen, Sonderheft 1.

Steinmüller, Ulrich. 1979. "Sprachunterricht für ausländische Arbeiter? Überlegungen zu Kommunikationsfähigkeit und Sprachvermittlung." In: Linguistische Berichte, LB-Papier 56.

Thomas, Helga. 1987. "Modellversuch 'Integration ausländischer Schüler in Gesamtschulen'". In: Gesamtschulinformationen, Sonderheft 1 + 2.

Thomas/Znaniecki. 1927. The Polish Peasant in Europe und America. 1918 - 1921. revised ed.

Thomé, Günther. 1987. Rechtschreibfehler türkischer und deutscher Schüler. Heidelberg: Julius Groos.

Yletinen, Riita. 1978. Probleme der Zweisprachigkeit bei Migrantenkindern. Schweden als bildungspolitisches Beispiel. Berlin: Technische Universität Berlin.

ACQUISITION OF JAPANESE AMONG AMERICAN BUSINESSMEN IN TOKYO: HOW MUCH AND WHY?

Yoshiko Matsumoto
Stanford University

1. 0. INTRODUCTION
1.1 Preface
This chapter is based on research conducted in 1978 as part of a project on bilingualism in Japan that was supported by the Japanese Ministry of Education.[1] As such, the focus is not simply of second language acquisition but on the degree to which American businessmen in Tokyo can be described as bilingual, and on comparisons with other bilingual groups. The data and analysis are presented in the form in which they were originally reported; only the exposition has been revised.

It is quite possible that the thirteen years that have elapsed since the original study was carried out have brought changes to the situation described in this paper. In that case, the data here will, I hope, furnish a bench mark for newer and broader investigations of the degree and kind of bilingualism among American businessmen stationed in Japan. Regrettably, it is also quite possible that very little has changed. Indeed, in a recent interview reported in the New York Times[2], an American businessman, Bill Totten, says:

> But most Americans trying to do business in Japan cannot speak the language at all. These Americans live in Tokyo in the equivalent of the Trump Tower and even though they are middle-level managers, they'll be chauffeured to and from their offices. These Americans will also spend all their time at the American Club or at the Foreign Press Club. They don't associate with the Japanese and they don't live in the Japanese consumer culture.

If these comments are an accurate assessment, then very little has changed since the data for this study were gathered.

1.2 Introduction to the Study
This study examines the linguistic behavior of American businessmen stationed in Tokyo. The focus of the study is not the (presumably negligible) influence of this group on the language of the rest of the country, but the interactions of American businessmen with the Japanese with whom they come into daily contact.

The number of American businessmen in Tokyo can be gauged from the figures in the publication Za ryuu Gaikokujin Tookei (Statistics on Resident Aliens) of the

Japanese Ministry of Justice, which, in 1974, listed 1,100 businessmen out of a total of 10,000 American residents in Tokyo. A corroborating source, which I was fortunate in obtaining from the American Chamber of Commerce in Japan (ACCJ), is the unpublished directory of the membership of the ACCJ; in November 1978 they listed 1069 individual members, of whom 970 were based in the Kanto district (centered on Tokyo).

From many interviews I have had with American businessmen in Tokyo and with Japanese people who come in everyday contact with them, I would describe in outline as follows what could be called the typical American businessmen in Japan. First, he is in Japan because he was sent there, rather than by choice or from a particular personal interest in the country. He has, perhaps, obtained some knowledge about Japan before his arrival, but will work mainly through English-speaking secretaries and assistants. He is likely to live in the relatively affluent area of Tokyo where there are American social clubs, as well as American schools that cater to the families of Americans.

An interesting question to study is how people's language is affected by a radical change of environment. In this paper, I examine three aspects of that question. I look first at the extent and success of American businessmen's attempts to learn Japanese in Japan, secondly, at what sort of person actually conducts his business in Japanese, and thirdly, at the extent of the interference between the Japanese that the person has picked up and his native English. By considering the inter-relationship between linguistic behavior and social and psychological factors, I attempt to give an accurate portrait of some aspects of the life of the American businessmen and, at the same time, to lay foundations for future studies on bilingualism in Japan.

2.0. LITERATURE RELATED TO THIS STUDY
In spite of the increasing number of Americans in Japan, there have not been many studies devoted to their experiences. Aside from the numerous first-hand accounts that one finds in popular books, and aside from the survey on foreign-affiliated business conducted by the Ministry of International Trade and Industry, there have been just small-scale in-house studies at businesses and institutions that deal with foreign trainees and students. The linguistic behavior of American businessmen in Japan has not been a topic examined by the Research Institute of the National Language.[3] In the absence of directly related studies, I will describe below material on language contact, bilingualism and on the lives of Americans in Japan. This material, though not immediately related to this study, will still give us some background on the issues that have arisen in this general area. In section 4, I will discuss in detail the comparisons and contrasts between the literature cited and this study.

Bilingualism has been defined variously: Bloomfield (1933) defines it as 'native-like control of two languages,' while Haugen (1953) claims that to be bilingual one has to be at least able 'to produce complete meaningful utterances in the other language.' In contrast to these relatively strict definitions, Diebold (1964) defines minimal bilingual skill as 'contact with possible models in a second language' (his illustrations of such models are mainly lexical items of the second language used either by native or non-native speakers of the language) and 'the ability to use these in the environment of the native language.' The last definition is quite broad since it was designed to describe a situation of incipient bilingualism. If this definition is employed, almost any Japanese or American businessmen in Japan can be considered as bilingual.

One aspect of language contact between the United States and Japan was studied by Higa (1974,'75,'76) and others. Higa examined the sociolinguistics of what he called 'Hawaiian Japanese': that is, the Japanese used by Japanese immigrants in Hawaii, which has been influenced by the surrounding (and socially prestigious) language and culture. While our present study does not deal with the situation of permanent immigrants assimilating to the host country, Higa's description of how Japanese in one case interacts with a foreign language, and his classification of loan-words will be helpful for our study.

Jorden, in her article 'Linguistic fraternization' (1977) comments on a language spoken by foreigners in Japan that is a mixture of English and Japanese. An example she gives of the mixed language is: 'It started out as just a <u>sko-she</u> (<u>sukosi</u> 'a little') problem, but in the end there was a terrible <u>yacha-ma-she</u> (<u>yakamasii</u> 'noisy').' She claims that the mixed language spoken by resident foreigners reflects their position as the 'out-group' in a society where to be 'in' one must be Japanese.

In his popular book <u>Tozasareta Gengo: Nihongo no Sekai</u> (The Closed Language: The World of the Japanese Language) (1975), Suzuki discusses the attitude of Japanese people towards accepting foreigners in their society. From the opinions given by foreigners in Japan, he points out two characteristics of the Japanese attitude: first, a persistent xenophobia; secondly, a belief that foreigners cannot understand Japanese, a preference for those whose Japanese is not proficient and a feeling of discomfort and distrust toward those whose Japanese is fluent. He suggests three causes: one is that Japan has not had contact with foreign countries historically, geographically or ethnoculturally; secondly, Japanese people have little day-to-day direct communication with people of other countries; and thirdly, Japanese view language as inherently belonging to a particular people. I will discuss these comments later. Let us before that, however, mention another article related to this study.

Nida (1971) considers the issue of language contact from the point of view of second-language learning. He points out that some persons fail to learn a foreign language, despite continued and excellent exposure, and that such exposure does not prevent a leveling off in the process of language-learning at a level far below fluency. He examines these problems from the viewpoint of the learners and of the people surrounding them, and he provides interesting observations relating motivation toward learning to the learner's bias in terms of the language being learned. According to Nida, two reasons why one may not acquire skill in a foreign language are that one may be able to maintain a more prestigious status by not being able to communicate directly to the native speakers of a language or that one may be resentful of the society where the language is spoken. We will consider Nida's claims more in the discussion and conclusion of this study.

3.0. DATA FROM THE STUDY
In this section, I present the results of the project I undertook in making this study, which was primarily a questionnaire distributed to members of the American Chamber of Commerce in Japan, followed by interviews with some of the respondents to the questionnaire, and tape-recordings of a telephone conversation and of five ACCJ meetings. The interviews, which I conducted with five of the respondents, were intended to inquire further into the role of the Japanese language and of the Japanese words that were interspersed in the English used by the respondents. Information and impressions gleaned from the interviews will form part of the discussion in section 4 below.

3.1. Methodology of the Questionnaire
I chose to focus the study on businessmen, as distinct from students and visiting scholars, journalists, missionaries, military personnel or diplomats. This was because the experience of businessmen seems more typical of the situation of Americans in Japan than that of the other groups, who either have come to Japan as a result of a special interest in that country, or who live entirely separately from the Japanese people. As I mentioned earlier, I was fortunate in obtaining from the ACCJ a list of their members. According to the Tokyo Office, the ACCJ had, as of November 1978, 970 individual members in the Kanto district (centered on Tokyo), 99 in the Kansai district (centered on Osaka) and 393 corporate members.

To make the survey as uniform as possible, I restricted the sample to representatives of American-capital companies who either work or live in Tokyo and who are male. There are approximately 700 businessmen from about 300 companies who fall under the description given above. This number almost coincides with the total number of foreigners in Tokyo classified as 'executives' in the publication Statistics on Resident Aliens that was mentioned earlier. From the 700 eligible businessmen, 400 were chosen (by a systematic sampling) and were asked to fill in and return the questionnaire anonymously. The questionnaire was accompanied by a letter from the head of ACCJ requesting their cooperation. The analysis was based on the 157 responses received within two weeks of the original mailing date, completed by American nationals, and containing fewer than eight unanswered questions. The speed and thoroughness of the responses are good indications of interest in the subject of the study.

Since this was the first survey that has been conducted on this question, the questionnaires were exploratory rather than detailed. To encourage response, the number of questions was limited to thirty. The questions can be grouped into three categories: questions on the respondent's background, linguistic behavior, and the influence of Japanese on the respondent's English. In the first of these categories were questions on the length of the respondent's stay in Japan, his position in his company, and the native language of his wife. In the second category were questions on his and others' proficiency in Japanese, on the frequency and domain of his use of Japanese, on his command of Japanese prior to arrival, and on his estimation of the usefulness of Japanese for business in Japan and in America. In the final category were such questions as whether the respondent's English had been changed under the influence of the Japanese language, and which Japanese expressions were used in the English of long-time American residents of Japan.

3.2 Results of the Questionnaire
3.2.1 Responses on background and linguistic behavior
A. Background of respondents
The responses indicated a mean length of stay in Japan of 6.49 years; there was a large standard deviation (7.18 years), and the numbers were skewed to the right (the median being less than four years). Almost all respondents were at senior management level in their companies (41.3% being at Vice President or higher level). 13.4% were married to native speakers of Japanese.

B. Linguistic Behavior
First, as to the level of proficiency in Japanese of American businessmen in Japan, the questionnaire asked how many Japanese-speaking American businessmen the respondent had encountered.

(1) Japanese-speaking Americans encountered:
   Very many...1.3%, fairly many...5.7%, not too many...21.7%,
   very few...70.7%, none...0.6%

The responses in table (1) indicate that few American businessmen are considered by their fellows to be speakers of Japanese. In evaluating their own proficiency, respondents rated their speaking ability in Japanese as shown in table (2).

(2) Respondents' proficiency in spoken Japanese:
   Excellent...7.6%, good...10.8%, fair... 21.0%, poor...45.9%, none...14.7%

Although almost 20% rate their proficiency as 'good' or better, the figures show the general level to be fairly low. It is therefore perhaps surprising that many of the respondents had attended Japanese language classes (table 3).

(3) Attendance at Japanese-language classes:
         Have attended classes...73.3%, have not...26.1%, NR...0.6%

In terms of the usefulness of a knowledge of Japanese, some indications are provided by the data in tables (4) and (5).

(4) Language(s) used in the work-place:
         English only...19.7%, Japanese only...3.2%, both...77.1%

(5) Language(s) used in executive meetings:
         Eng. only..50.3%, Japanese only..7.6%, both..41.4%, NR..0.6%

The responses show that, in the great majority of companies in which the American businessmen work, some Japanese is used, although for executive meetings, where matters of greater importance are discussed, English predominates. The businessmen's perception of the usefulness of Japanese can be seen from the responses tabulated in (6) and (7).

(6) Is knowledge of Japanese helpful for business in Japan:
         Yes...73.9%, No...22.3%, NR...3.8%

(7) Is knowledge of Japanese useful for your work in the U.S.:
         Yes...17.2%, No...80.3%, NR...2.5%

As we see from the responses, businessmen tend to consider Japanese helpful only while they are in Japan. Moreover, as we will see below, those who consider Japanese as useful for their work in the U.S. tend to be on the high end of the proficiency scale.

Further indications on the businessmen's experience with the Japanese language are given by their responses detailing how often and with whom they use Japanese (tables (8) and (9)).

(8) How often do you use Japanese in everyday life:
         Often...38.9%, sometimes...18.5%, seldom...35.6%, never...7%

These results show a peak around two groups: those who often use Japanese and those who use it only seldom. The figure of 7% representing those who never use Japanese at all is also worth remarking, not least because it proves the possibility of living in Japan without using a word of the language. As we see in table (9), the respondents tend to use Japanese to Japanese people with whom they do not have regular close contact and to those who might not speak English. With Japanese business associates, English is considerably more often used.

(9) What language do you commonly use with the following persons: Wife, children, maids, Japanese friends, Japanese associates, sales clerks, Japanese in general?

Addressee\Lges.	Eng.	Jp.	Eng+Jp.	Others	NR
Wife	81.5(%)	2.5	6.4	0.6	8.9
Children	70.1(%)	0.6	3.8	0.6	24.8
Maids	35.0(%)	21.0	12.7	0.6	30.6

Addressee\Lges.	Eng.	Jp.	Eng+Jp.	Interp.	NR
Jp. associates	50.3(%)	8.9	30.6	8.3	1.9
Jp. friends	48.4(%)	16.6	29.9	0.6	4.5
Jp. in general	21.7(%)	42.0	26.1	3.2	7.0
Sales clerks	17.8(%)	52.2	24.8	1.3	3.8

This tendency is consistent with the number of English speaking Japanese encountered (tables (10) and (11)).

(10)   How many English-speaking Japanese businessmen have you met? Very many...31.2%, fairly many...43.3%, not too many...21.0% very few... 4.5%, none...0%

(11)   How many English-speaking Japanese have you met outside business and personal associates? Very many...12.1%, fairly many...33.1%, not too many...36.9% very few...15.3%, none...2.5%

The proportion of English-speaking Japanese seems higher among the associates of the American businessmen than in the general population, though even there they are not uncommon (table (12)).

(12)   Were you encouraged to speak Japanese by your Japanese business associates? Yes...44.0%, no...55.4%, NR...0.6%

Here what is at issue is the attitudes of Japanese people as perceived by the respondents. It is apparent from the results above that more than half of the respondents do not feel encouraged by their Japanese associates to speak Japanese. Combined with the relatively large number of English speakers among their

Japanese colleagues, this points to a surprisingly weak pressure on businessmen stationed in Japan to learn the language of the country.

3.2.2. Proficiency and related factors

Let us now turn to the relation between the respondents' proficiency in Japanese and factors that may affect their command of the language.

My preliminary hypothesis was that the more contact one has with the Japanese culture and language, the more frequently and better one employs the language. In tabulating the results, I divided the respondents into five groups depending on whether their stay was less than one year, between one and four years, between four and seven, between seven and ten, or at least ten years. The percentages in each group and the median level of proficiency for that group can be found in table (13).

(13)   Median level of proficiency grouped by length of stay:
       ($t < 1$ year: 3.2%)...none, ($1 \leq t < 4$: 47.8%)...poor,
       ($4 \leq t < 7$: 21.0%)...poor, ($7 \leq t < 10$: 7.0%)...fair,
       ($t \geq 10$ years: 21.0%)...good.

These results do show an increase in the average proficiency with length of stay, but it should be remarked that 27.3% of those whose stay in Japan was ten years or more still reported their speaking ability as 'poor' or 'none'.

It is not uncommon for an American businessman to marry a Japanese woman; indeed, more than 14% of the married respondents in this survey were married to native speakers of Japanese. It is reasonable to suppose that respondents married to Japanese women have more than average access to the culture and language of Japan, and more than average motivation to learn the language. Table (14) describes the relation between proficiency in spoken Japanese and the native language of the respondent's wife.

(14)   Proficiency according to whether wife is native speaker of Japanese:
       a) Proficiency of those married to native speaker of Japanese (13.4% of respondents):
       excellent...23.8%, good...23.8%, fair...19.0%, poor...28.6%, none...4.8%

b)   Proficiency of those not married to native speaker of Japanese (86.6% of respondents):
       excellent...5.1%, good...8.8%, fair...21.3%, poor...48.5%, none...16.2%

This table shows some relation between speaking ability in Japanese and the wife's native language. The modal level of proficiency for each group, however, is 'poor'. Moreover, as we shall see below, stronger relations can be found between proficiency and other factors surveyed.

If we tabulate speaking proficiency in Japanese according to whether the respondent had studied the language prior to arrival in Japan (table (15)), then we find considerably higher levels of proficiency among those who had prior study.

(15)   Prior study of Japanese/ speaking proficiency:
         a) Proficiency of those who had studied Japanese prior to arrival (19.1% of the respondents)
         excellent...23.3%, good...23.3%, fair...40.0%, poor...13.3%, none...0%

         b) Proficiency of those who had not studied Japanese prior to arrival (80.9% of the respondents)
         excellent...3.9%, good...7.9%, fair...16.5%, poor...53.5%, none...18.1%.

The strong contrast in speaking ability between those who had studied Japanese prior to arrival in Japan and those who had not is evident both in the higher median level of proficiency ('fair' for those who had prior study, 'poor' for those who had no prior study) and in the difference in the percentages of those whose speaking ability was 'poor' or 'none' (13.3% of the former group, but 71.6% of the latter). It is also worth remarking that there were virtually no differences in proficiency, aside from a slightly smaller number giving their proficiency as 'none', between the group of those who studied Japanese only after arrival and those who had never studied the language.

It is America, not Japan, that is the home country for the companies of a great preponderance of the respondents. Usefulness of Japanese in their home company would be a motivation for businessmen to learn the language. Table (16) illustrates the relation between speaking ability and the assessment of usefulness of a knowledge of Japanese at the respondent's home company in the U.S.

(16)   Proficiency/ assessment of usefulness of Japanese in the U.S.:

	Useful (17.2%)	Not useful (80.3%)	NR (2.5%)
Proficiency			
excellent:	29.6%	2.4%	25.0%
good:	25.9%	7.9%	0.0%
fair:	29.6%	19.8%	0.0%
poor:	14.8%	52.4%	50.0%
none:	0.0%	17.5%	25.0%

As table (16) shows, the relation between the respondent's assessment of Japanese as useful for business in the U.S. and his proficiency in Japanese is quite strong.

It is particularly remarkable that the median level of proficiency among those who regard Japanese as useful in the U.S. is 'good', while the median among the remainder of the population is only 'poor'. A comparison with tables (13) - (15) reveals that, for the factors that we have considered, the only other group whose median level of proficiency was 'good' were those who had lived at least ten years in Japan; moreover, for that group, fully 27.3% still classed their ability as 'poor' or 'none', in contrast to the only 14.8% of those who judged Japanese as useful for business in the U.S.

To summarize the above discussion on factors that influence proficiency, the degree of contact with Japanese culture, measured in years, or marriage with a native speaker of Japanese, do appear to be associated with a greater speaking ability in Japanese. Prior study of the language, or the judgment that a knowledge of Japanese will be useful even in the U.S., however, seem to be even more strongly associated with greater proficiency.

3.2.3. Influence of Japanese on the respondents' English
The respondents were asked whether their English had changed in any way under the influence of Japanese. Of the 43.3% who reported some change, only about one-fifth mentioned changes in grammar or pronunciation due to the influence of the Japanese language. More commonly-reported were accommodations to speaking with interlocutors who are not fluent in English; changes such as enunciating more clearly, speaking slower, or avoiding difficult sentence structures.

The questionnaire invited the respondents to list Japanese words and phrases commonly used in the English spoken by long-time American residents of Japan when talking among themselves. 34.4% of the respondents (54 people) filled in some words, while 4.5% (7) declared that there was no such thing as a Japanese expression used in English.

Vocabulary and expressions given in the questionnaires are cited below. There may be more actually used; yet the responses provide a good example of the most common expressions. The vocabulary and expressions are cited in alphabetical order. The symbol * is prefixed to any citation given by more than 10 respondents. The responses are divided into categories that are based on a revised version of those in Higa (1976) to describe borrowings in Hawaiian Japanese.

Japanese culture (things, matters, people)
  donburi (rice or noodle bowl) / futon / geta (clogs) / hibachi / kimono / sake / sanyaku (the three highest ranks below yokozuna in sumo wrestling) / soba (buckwheat noodle) / sushi / tansu (drawers) / tatami / tempura / tofu / zori (sandals)/ banzai / giri (a moral obligation)/ matsuri (festival)/

saru shibai (cheap theatrics, play-acting)/ seppuku (ceremonial suicide)/ yakuza (hooligan, gangster)

Loan words (except business terms)

apaato (apartment building)/ biiru (beer)/ depaato (department store)/ hotto-doggu (hot-dog)/ puresento (present)

Railways, place-names, etc.

eki (station)/ densha (train)/ kokutetsu sen (National Railways)/ shinkansen (bullet train)/ Tokyo doori (street)/ ku (ward)/ koban (police box)/ kooen (park)

Business and social life

beesu-appu (wage raise)/ buchoo (general manager)/ gyosee sidoo (administrative guidance)/ habatsu (faction)/ kumiai (union)/ kachoo (manager)/ kabushiki gaisha (corporation)/ Nihon shisha (Japanese branch)/ sarariman (salaried worker)/ shain (company employee)/ shosha (trade company)/ Gaimushoo (Ministry of Foreign Affairs)/ Kooseishoo (Ministry of Health and Welfare)/ Okurashoo (Ministry of Finance)/ yakusho (government office)/ enkai (banquet)/ kampai (cheers!)/ mama-san (female owner of bar)/ mizu-wari (whisky and soda)

Terms related to persons

*gaijin (foreigner)/ henna gaijin (strange foreigner)/ baka (fool)/ kanri-nin (apartment manager)/ kimi (you)/ okusan (someone's wife)

Quantity

chiisai (small)/ chotto (a little)/ moosukoshi (a little more)/ ookii (large)/ sukoshi (a little)/ takusan (a lot)

Others

migi (right)/ mizu (water)/ mondai (problem)/ shinbun (newspaper)

Expressions connected with interpersonal relations

konbanwa (good evening) / *konnichiwa,(goodday, hello) ohayoo, ohayoo gozaimasu (good morning, in polite form)/ oyasuminasai (good-night) oyasumi/ *sayoonara (good-bye) *arigatoo (thank you)/ doomo arigatoo (thank you)/ *doomo (thanks) / *doozo (please) / daijyoobu (O.K.) / gomennasai (I'm sorry) / gokuroo (Thanks for your effort)/ gochisoo sama (thank you for the meal) / genki (fine) genkide (keep well!) genki-desuka? (How are you?)/ kiotsukete (take care)/ onegaishimasu (please) / *sumimasen (excuse me) / ya (hi!) *hai (yes) / iie (no)/ hontoo (really) / naruhodo (indeed) / soodesu (that's right) soodesune, soodesuka (is that so?) soone, asoodesuka, soo ka / ano ne (um) / chotto matte (wait a minute), chotto matte kudasai (in polite form)/ ikimashoo (let's go), ikimashooka (shall we go?) / mooshi-mooshi (hello- on the telephone)/ sate (well)/ tonikaku (anyway)/ doko (where?)/ nani (what?)/ nanji (what time?)/ atode (later)/ hayaku (early, quickly)/ tokidoki (sometimes)

Expressions of evaluation, degree, etc.

chigau (different) / dame (no good) / ichiban (the first) ii (good) / kirei (beautiful)/ muri (impossible)/ muzukashii (difficult)/ omoshiroi (interesting)/ shibui (astringent)/ shikataganai (it can't be helped) / shinpainai (nothing to worry about)/ shooganai (it can't be helped)/ sugoi (terrible) / taihen (that's tough)/ takai (expensive, high)/ warui (bad) / yasui (cheap) / zannen (regrettable)/ narubeku (as much as possible)/ choodo (exactly)/ zen-zen (not at all)

Sentence-endings, suffixes

-desu (copula, polite)/ -kudasai (please do-)/ ne, nee?, ne, (acts as tag question)/ san (usual title- Mr., Ms.,etc)

Other expressions

abunai desu ne (it's dangerous, isn't it?) / arimasu(sen), (yes, there is; no there isn't)/ kondeimasu ne (it's crowded, isn't it?)/ machigai desu ne (that's a mistake, isn't it?)/ wakarimasen (I don't understand), wakarimasuka? (do you understand?)

A further question asked what, if any, special (Japanese or English) words, phrases, and expressions were used exclusively with Japanese associates. This question was asked in order to elicit expressions that are commonly used among American and Japanese businessmen on business-related occasions. 19.8% of the 157 respondents answered that there were such expressions, while 17.8% replied that there were not. The rest (except for three respondents who said that they did not understand the question) did not respond at all. The following are the responses given.

Business

base-up (wage raise)/ habatsu (faction)/doru (dollar)/roon (loan)/maruku (Deustchmark)/ salary man (salaried worker)/ shukkoo (temporary employee transfer)

Other words

gaikokujin (foreigner)/ jyugyoo (class at school)/ kazoku (family) / yasumi (rest, holiday)

Amount

sukoshi (a little)

Expressions of evaluation
atarimae (matter of course)/ dame (no good)/ shigataganai (it can't be helped)/ shooganai (it can't be helped)

Expressions connected with interpersonal relations
gokigenyo (good-bye)/ hajimemashite (delighted to meet you)/ konnichiwa (hello, good-day) / ohayoo gozaimasu, ohayoo (good morning)/ itte irrashai (a salutation said to one departing)/ itte kimasu (a salutation said by one departing)/ ki otsukete kudasai (please take care)/ tadaima (I'm back!)/ kampai (cheers!)/ a soodesuka (is that so?)/ hai (yes)/ hontoo (really)/ arigatoo (thank you) doomo arigatoo gozaimasu / desuka (isn't it?) / doomo (thanks)/ doozo (please)/ gambatte kudasai (good luck!)/ genki (how are you?) ogenkidesuka / gomen(nasai) (I'm sorry) / hajimemashooka? (shall we begin?)/ ja, mata (see you later)/ moo ichido onegaishimasu (once more, please) / moosukoshi yukkuri hanashite kudasai (please speak a little slower) / shinjinarimasen (I don't believe it)/ shitsumon arimasu (I have a question)/ shosho omachikudasai (please hold on a second)/ sumimasen (excuse me, thank you)/ wakarimasen (I don't understand)/ wakatta (understood)/ yoroshiku, doozo yoroshiku (nice to meet you)/zehi (certainly)/ itsu (when?)/ nani (what?)/ doshite (why?)

The data elicited in these responses will be discussed below in section 4.

3.3. Data from Tape Recordings
I had the opportunity of listening to recordings of ACCJ meetings and to a telephone conversation of one of the respondents to the questionnaire whom I interviewed. These additional materials provide real-life data on how and when Japanese expressions are used and on the kinds of Japanese words that occur in foreign businessmen's English. The Japanese expressions obtained from the tapes (with English translations in parentheses) are cited below following a general description of the content of each recording.

1. Meeting of the Board of Directors of the ACCJ
[General reports, farewell announcement by a member returning to the States, etc.]
'This is, I guess, in one sense, sayonara ("good-bye") and I'm going to Honolulu on November 1.'
'The Kansai ("Western region") group...'

2. Committee of the Asia-Pacific Congress of American Chambers of Commerce (APCAC)
[Plans for a trip to Kyoto, and a decision on who to invite as the speaker for their meeting]
'All in favor of Nakane-san ("Mr. Nakane")...'
'In your registration form, they ask you to fill out whether you are a small,

medium, or large for <u>kimonos</u> and <u>yukatas</u> ("a casual cotton kimono"), whatever they are..'
'And <u>Nagata-san</u> ("Mr. Nagata") has agreed to, I think...' '<u>Kansai</u> ("Western region") member'

3. Breakfast briefings for ACCJ members: Study group on U.S.Japan trade. (ACCJ)
[Discussion on international trade with the intention of further study]
'...though provision director in the <u>Gaimushoo</u> ("Ministry of Foreign Affairs") ...'
'...this includes <u>getas</u> ("clogs") and rubber <u>zooris</u> ("Japanese sandals")...'
'...the fear of retribution isn't so much at the higher levels, but it's at the <u>kachoo</u> ("manager") level.' (One of two instances)
'We could at least get a feeling through our channels of communication -- that would be MITI and <u>Keidanaren</u> ("the Federation of Economic Organizations") -- to get some kind of feed-back...'
'The Japanese government permitted 250 p.p.m. of this same product in, ah, <u>kamaboko</u> ("fish cake").'

It is noticeable that more Japanese business-related terms are used in this last tape than in others, probably because the participants are specialists on U.S.-Japan trade. The Japanese expressions were pronounced with an American accent (e.g. <u>kamaboko</u> pronounced [kam bouku] instead of [kamaboko]).

4. Talk and question & answer session (ACCJ)
[Technical discussion on joint-ventures and anti-trust legislation]
'...<u>kankoku</u> ("governmental   recommendation"),   which   is   a recommendation...' (Four instances including compounds such as <u>kankoku procedure</u>.)
'As a result of trying to avoid the reputation of the pre-war <u>zaibatsu</u> ("conglomerate, cartel").'

5. Talk by a professor of sociology
[A talk on labor relations in Japan]
Technical terms such as <u>doomei</u> ('labor federation'), <u>kyoogisei</u> ('consultation system') (Five instances)

6. Personal conversation between one of the interviewees and a British 'old-timer'.
[A phone call was received during the interview. The caller was a British businessman who was born and grew up in Japan. Recorded is, of course, only my interviewee's voice.]
'Hello. Yes. Oh, what do you know? Hah ha. <u>Shibaraku ne</u> ("It's been long, hasn't it?"). How are you?'
'<u>Aa soo</u> ("Ah so"), so, what's new with him?'

'100, you couldn't buy anything. And now 300; you can bring back some omiyage ("souvenir") or something.'
'Oh, Monday, oh, really ne ("right?").'
'Going down to Kobe and come back and you probably have your meeting Monday, and he goes...'
'Aa soo, soo, soone, taihen ne ("It's tough, isn't it?").'
'Soo, soo. Yeah, I know, I know.'
'Un ("Yeah"), un. Soo, sooyo ("that's right"). Sooyuu mondesu yo ("That's the way it goes"). It's true. It's exactly the same case...'
'Soo. Yessir. Un ("Yeah").'

The Japanese expressions were pronounced as a native-speaker would and very naturally inserted into the English-based conversation.

4.0. DISCUSSION AND CONCLUSION

This study has examined, primarily through a questionnaire answered by American businessmen in Tokyo, the linguistic aspect of the life of Americans who are separated from their normal social and linguistic environment and who are living in Japan and, thus, in everyday contact with the Japanese language.

The first question that was asked is whether or not American businessmen in Tokyo speak Japanese. A short answer to that question is 'not much.' In the questionnaire, the most common evaluation by the respondents of their proficiency in the spoken language was 'poor' (in the written language it was 'none.') Furthermore, more than 70% of the respondents replied that American businessmen who can speak Japanese are 'very few.' All these strongly suggest that, both in business and in their personal lives, the usual language of Americans in Japan is English.

This, however, is not to say that Americans in Japan do not attempt to learn Japanese. Although the proportion of people who had already started studying Japanese before coming to Japan is quite small, the number who take courses at language schools in Japan exceeds 70% of the population, a figure that Japanese people in general would find surprising. Even some of the respondents who claimed to know no Japanese at all filled in Japanese words in response to the question asking for Japanese expressions used by old-timers in Japan. It seems then that, if we adopt the broadest definition of the term 'bilingual' as discussed in section 2, the proportion of American businessmen in Tokyo who are at least minimally bilingual is quite high.

As we saw from the results of the questionnaire, there is a wide range of proficiency in Japanese among American businessmen in Tokyo, and we cannot treat this social group as a single class as far as linguistic ability is concerned. In seeking to explain the breadth of the range of ability in Japanese among

Americans, my initial hypothesis was that the use of Japanese would be directly proportional to the degree of contact with the Japanese language and culture. This was not, however, borne out by the data, which did not indicate a clear relation between contact with the culture and proficiency in the language. Rather, it was those who had experience with the language prior to arrival in Japan, and those who considered Japanese to be useful even after their return to their home country, whose evaluation of their proficiency was highest. Motivation comes, it seems, from quite practical considerations rather than from, say, breathing the air of Japan.

We may wonder about the reasons for the paucity of Americans who are fluent in Japanese. This has deep economic implications, and can perhaps be traced to the unprecedented global political and economic influence of the United States after the Second World War. Our interest, however, is in understanding the lack of motivation on the part of the individual businessman. The data from the questionnaire suggest three reasons why American businessmen do not learn Japanese: (1) their native language, English, is perceived as a universal language; (2) their position in Japan does not oblige them to attempt to assimilate to the Japanese-speaking society; and (3) whatever the possible business advantages accruing from a knowledge of Japanese may be, businessmen do not find Japanese to be indispensable.

In passing, we may speculate on another possible reason for an American businessman not to learn Japanese, which is that the prospect of becoming uniquely valuable at the Japanese office, and thus acquiring a permanent or frequently recurring station away from his home country, is not always welcome.

Nida (1971), as mentioned in section 2, discusses the reason why second language performance levels off, or even declines, and why one may totally fail to learn in the first place despite continued exposure to a second language. He discusses three elements that are involved in the leveling-off process: '(a) intellectual fatigue (...being mentally lazy); (b) no feeling for the need of greater identification with the surrounding community, and (c) the conviction that further effort will not produce compensatory results.' (p.63.) These are very similar to the three reasons which I postulated above for the low ability of American businessmen in Japanese.

My focus, up to this point, has been on the attitude of Americans toward language acquisition; for a fuller explanation of why so few Americans learn Japanese, we must also consider the attitude of the Japanese in the surrounding community. Nida lists three motivations for people in the surrounding community to adjust to foreigners' not speaking the language of that surrounding community. These are: '(1) the loss of hope that the learner is likely to improve, (2) the greater ease in adjusting to the learner's lower level than in attempting to teach him to advance, and (3) the advantage of keeping such a person relatively isolated and thus in a position where he can be more readily controlled. (p.63.)'

Observations (1) and (2) are also found in <u>Tozasareta gengo: Nihongo no sekai</u> (The closed language: The world of Japanese) (Suzuki, 1975).   (3) is also plausible, especially in the world of business where Japanese negotiating with Americans may feel more comfortable if they think the Americans are not too well-informed about the local situation.

One comment I have sometimes heard from those who do attempt to learn Japanese is that all attempts on their part to converse in Japanese are met with replies in English. It is as if their Japanese colleagues are uncomfortable with the prospect of Westerners who are fluent in their language.   Some Japanese who write on such issues (see, for instance, Suzuki, 1975) have taken their countrymen to task on account of such complaints and have criticized them as exclusionists. Many Westerners who consider themselves Japanophiles can become perplexed, if not embittered, when their efforts at learning the language fall victim in this way to the effects of what in <u>The Japanese Language</u> (Miller, 1967) is referred to as Preble's Law[4]:   the supposition that Japanese have greater facility at learning the language of foreigners than do foreigners at learning Japanese. In view of our questionnaire, what are we to make of such complaints?

One of the findings of the questionnaire was that 44% of the respondents said that they had the experience of being encouraged by Japanese to learn the Japanese language, while 55.4% of them said that they did not.   Those who had never received such encouragement were, thus, more numerous but only slightly so than those who had.   In fact, the percentage of those who felt encouragement was higher among those with a greater degree of proficiency in the language.   These data hardly support the image of the Japanese as fanatical exclusionists. Rather, there seems to be a certain critical point of proficiency below which one will find that it is simply more convenient for his Japanese colleagues to converse with him in English.   Once past this point, there is no resistance on the part of Japanese to conversing in Japanese.   This interpretation is confirmed by the experiences of the Americans I spoke with whose Japanese is fluent.   Preble's Law, I claim, represents the current imbalance in the degree of knowledge of each other language between Japanese and Americans, rather than the result of a predilection on the part of Japanese for keeping foreigners at arm's length.

Let us now turn to another point of interest, namely, the possible influence of the Japanese language on the English spoken by Americans in Japan. The literature on interactions between the Japanese and English languages is quite scarce.   As I mentioned in section 2, there are studies of 'Hawaiian Japanese' by Higa (1976)[5]. There and also some references in Miller (1967) to the 'ports lingo' of late 19th century Japan and of the incipient pidgin English that arose during the American occupation after WW II.   The influence of the Japanese language on English-speaking residents of Japan is also addressed in the article 'Linguistic fraternization' by Jorden (1977). The papers cited above will be useful in the discussion mainly to provide contrasts with what I believe to be the influence of the Japanese language on the English of Americans currently resident in Japan.

In his analysis of 'Hawaiian Japanese' -- a language based on Japanese, containing many borrowings from English and widely spoken in the community of immigrants of Japanese ancestry in Hawaii -- Higa claims that the language functions to create a bond, or group consciousness among its speakers. This group-consciousness excludes not only those of non-Japanese ancestry, but also Japanese who are not immigrants[6]. The differences in the situations of Japanese immigrants in Hawaii and of Americans temporarily resident in Japan are manifold: Americans in Japan have not cut their ties with their homeland, nor are they struggling for admission and advancement in an alien society where their native language is unknown. In Hawaii, to speak English is simply a necessity for any but the most cloistered existence; the American in Japan, however, can proceed with complete disregard for the language of the country surrounding him without risk of being either deprived or despised.

The situations in the 19th century and just after the war that are described by Miller reflect a time when there were many Japanese who had dealings with Americans and who needed some sort of pidgin English to communicate. That is far from the present situation between American and Japanese businessmen.

All of the facts we have considered notwithstanding, we must admit that there do exist English utterances containing loan words from Japanese that are used and understood only by current or former residents of Japan. This type of English I will refer to as 'Japanese-interspersed English.'

As I mentioned in section 2, Jorden (1977) treats Japanese-interspersed English as evidence of an in-group feeling among foreigners who feel themselves to be outsiders in Japan. Certainly, interspersing Japanese expressions in English may indicate some sort of peer feeling, but not simply the feeling of being excluded from the community of Japanese. An in-group feeling caused by a sense of being the out-group in Japan could be adequately expressed by speaking ordinary English. Indeed, if there are any who feel excluded by the use of Japanese words in English, it is the Americans who are newly arrived in Japan. There must be some other reasons for the introduction of Japanese expressions into English. One more clue to the function of Japanese-interspersed English is provided by the types of words that become loan words. Whereas in Hawaiian Japanese, the words borrowed from English include kinship terms and words indicating time and quantity, in Japanese-interspersed English, we obtain no such basic terms. Rather, we find expressions related to transportation and geography (probably treated almost as proper nouns), English loanwords in Japanese used in their Japanized pronunciation and form (e.g. apaato. an abbreviation from apartment), and words related to the social life that attends business transactions in Japan. The words related to the businessman's social life reflect also the conditions on use of Japanese-interspersed English which are, according to the interviews, usually in casual situations when speaking on topics that are not too important. In fact, we can summarize the conditions on the use of Japanese-interspersed English with the diagram in Figure 1.

The dashed lines indicate choices that are almost unanimously taken, whereas the dotted lines indicate choices that are merely likely. It is, for instance, perfectly possible for English to be used even in circumstances where the topic is unimportant and the situation is informal.

How, in the light of the foregoing discussion, should we summarize the role of Japanese-interspersed English? The conditions for use and the type of vocabulary lead me to the conclusion that Japanese-interspersed English functions to provide a sort of business slang -- an assortment of 'vogue' words and expressions -- which serves to fill the gap created by the businessmen's removal from the center of the greater English-speaking community. Lacking immediate contact with the most current business jargon and vogue words, Americans in Japan supplement their English with Japanese words that become, at least for them, 'vogue' words. It is, then, as a supplement to English rather than as dialect or a pidgin that I would describe the Japanese-interspersed language we have seen.

Figure 1   Choice of language with Japanese addressee[7]

```
            decision to speak
                   |
             addressee an
             English speaker
               /       .
      Yes    /          .  No
           /              .
        topic              .
     important              .
        /     .              .
 Yes  /        .  No          .
     /          .              .
situation        .              .
```

```
            formal          .              .
              /    .              .              .
  Yes  /        . No              .              .
     /              .              .         .
```

English   Japanese/Japanese-   Japanese
                     interspersed English

I wish to conclude by mentioning some topics that may be of interest to future researchers. One is to make a more thorough study of what prevents people from learning Japanese, and to make a comparison with the general situation of second-language learning as described by Nida. It may well be that the problems apparent from this study are not unique to Japan and its language. It would also be fruitful to conduct more detailed interviews on the actual use of Japanese and of loan expressions. In particular, there may be a difference in use and proficiency among businessmen temporarily transferred from America, people who have set up their own business in Japan, and Americans employed by a Japanese company. A survey of Japanese employees in American companies would highlight another aspect of bilingualism. Furthermore, it would be quite interesting to compare the linguistic behavior of Japanese businessmen overseas with that of Americans in Japan. Linguistic studies along the lines of this present paper have been all too infrequent, even though international contacts between businessmen are always increasing. This points to the need for continuing research in the future.

NOTES

1. An extensive account of the research can be found in Matsumoto (1979).

2. N.Y. Times Forum, December 9, 1990.

3. Personal communication with Osamu Mizutani of the Institute.

4. Named after Lt. Preble, who was a member of Commodore Perry's second expedition to Japan in 1854. This "law" is also mentioned in "Our far-flung correspondents -- Preble's law and other matters" (Frankel, 1963)

5. Descriptions of Hawaiian Japanese hereafter are also from Higa (1976).

6. Higa found that speakers of Hawaiian Japanese would speak Japanese (not Hawaiian Japanese) with visitors from Japan.

7. I have also consulted Sankoff (1972) in making this chart.

140   Second Language Acquisition and Development

REFERENCES

Bloomfield, L. 1933. Language. London: George Allen & Unwin Ltd.

Diebold, A. R., Jr. 1964. 'Incipient bilingualism,' Language in culture and society. D. Hymes (ed.). New York: Harper & Row. 495-508.

Frankel, C. 1963. 'Our far-flung correspondents: Preble's law and other matters,' The New Yorker 39:14.103. May 25. 74-109.

Haugen. E. 1953. The Norwegian language in America: a study in bilingual behavior. Philadelphia: University of Pennsylvania Press.

Higa, M. 1974. 'Hawai no nihongo (Hawaiian Japanese),' Gendai no esupuri: Kotoba to shinri 85 (Modern esprit: Language and psychology). Tokyo: Shibundoo. 178-197.

_____. 1975. 'The use of loanwords in Hawaiian Japanese,' Language in Japanese society. F.C.C.Peng (ed.). Tokyo: University of Tokyo Press. 71-89.

_____. 1976. 'Nihongo to Nihonjin shakai (The Japanese language and society), 'Iwanami kooza Nihongo 1: Nihongo to Nihongogaku (Iwanami lectures on the Japanese language 1: The Japanese language and linguistics). S.Oono and T.Shibata (eds.). Tokyo: Iwanami shoten. 99-138.

Hoomushoo nyuukokukanrikyoku (Immigration bureau of the Ministry of Justice). 1974. Zairyuu gaikokujin tookei (Statistics on resident aliens).

Jorden, E. H. 1977. 'Linguistic fraternization: A guide for the gaijin,' Proceedings of the symposium on Japanese sociolinguistics. The University of Hawaii. 103-124.

Kato, S. 1969. 'Amerika, Kyodaina kotoo: Amerika, 1962 (America, giant island-world: America 1962),' Nihon no uchi to soto (Inside & outside of Japan). Tokyo: Bungeishunjuu sha. 279-321.

Miller, R. A. The Japanese language. The University of Chicago Press.

Nida, E. A. 1971. 'Sociopsychological problems in language mastery and retention,' The psychology of second language learning, P. Pimsleur and T. Quinn (eds.). Cambridge University Press. 59-65.

Sankoff, G. 1971. 'Language use in multilingual societies: some alternative approaches,' Sociolinguistics, Preide & Holmes (eds.). 33-51.

Suzuki. 1975. Tozasareta gengo: Nihongo no sekai (The closed language: the world of Japanese). Tokyo: Tsuushoosangkyooshoo sangyooseisaku kyoku (Ministry of International Trade and Industry, Industrial Policy Bureau). 1978. 'Shoowa 53 nen ban gaishi-kei kigyoo no dookoo (Trends in companies supported by foreign capital).' Tokyo.

SECTION THREE:
ISSUES IN INTERLANGUAGE DEVELOPMENT

ABRUPT RESTRUCTURING VERSUS GRADUAL ACQUISITION

Hanna Pishwa
Technical University of Berlin

1.0. INTRODUCTION

There is always restructuring in the process of language-acquisition as learners build up a linguistic system of their own. This system is constantly compared with the target language or some approximation of it, depending on the learning conditions. Thus some restructuring is always necessary to adjust the present system to the next phase. These adjustments can vary from minimal or gradual changes to abrupt changes with a total switch-over from the old system. There is also radical restructuring of the surface form without any real change in the underlying learner system. In the following, I will investigate different forms of abrupt restructuring in the development of the German subject-verb agreement rule, as well as relate the restructuring[1] to gradual progress.

The reason for strong variation in the acquisition of rules has generally been alleged to be due to different learner types, learning situations, or methods of data collection. Because of this assumption, there has been no systematic investigation concerning the question whether restructuring occurs in all phases of acquisition and in all areas of grammar.

The subject-verb agreement rule is well suited for a detailed investigation of the scope of restructuring, as its development reflects progress in all other grammatical components: the lexicon, semantics, pragmatics, syntax, and phonomorphology. This is confirmed in many typological studies. Even the rather simple rule of case-marking implies the involvement of pragmatic and semantic principles (Clahsen 1984). Thus, the present study can reveal mechanisms in the process of acquisition and shed light on the interrelationship of grammatical areas, which has been quite a neglected area.

In order to reveal many subtle principles and details in the acquisition of a morphological rule, one has to consider the kind of data, the method of analysis, and the framework. To this end, longitudinal studies on several individuals must serve as a basis for ascertaining both individual developments and overall development. The data have to be analyzed in different contexts, as the rule to be acquired expands gradually, not suddenly. Variation and developmental theory advocated by C. -J. Bailey (1982, 1984, forthcoming) has proved to be a suitable theoretical framework for analysis dealing with change and variation. Developmental analysis is time-based: Explanation and prediction--the two goals of the theory--depend on an understanding of how things have developed into what they are. Time differences create implicational structures. Except for lexical items, the temporal sequencing depends on language universals. The temporal sequencing also reveals the markedness of items in ways specified by developmental theory. The developmentalist distinction between connatural changes (bioneurologically caused), and abnatural changes (are sociolinguistically caused)--they often change in different directions and do not play a significant role in the present study.

Detailed investigation of mechanisms of interlanguages seems to be very important despite abundant research of the interrelation of symbol and meaning: Many studies still rely on counting the correct and the faulty forms. These methodological problems are mainly due to the fact that results from language acquisition are based either on longitudinal studies with single learners or on cross-sectional studies showing no individual development.

In this paper, we will look at results from a longitudinal study of fifteen young Swedish school children learning German. The object of the study was the German SUBJECT-VERB AGREEMENT rule with both individuals and groups. I will use data from individuals to find answers to questions about restructuring vs. gradual acquisition of rules, which have implications for our understanding of different learner types, mechanisms in interlanguage, and discussion about methodology in second language research.

2.0. THE STUDY
The data stem from fifteen informants, aged seven to twelve years, recorded during three school terms in 1982-1983, in grades one through five. The children investigated attended Swedish classes at the German School in Stockholm and were to acquire both a bilingual and bicultural education. The instruction in German consisted of three hours per week in the first grade, but was increased year by year so that the Swedish and the German classes could be merged in grade seven.

At the beginning of the project, three children each were selected from the first and second grades, and six from the third. Three Swedish girls were selected from the German fourth class to serve as a sort of control group. There were eight data-gathering situations: five of them were interviews, and three were play situations. The analysis of the data was thus based on individual and group development (see further Pishwa 1989). There were eight data-gathering situations, five interviews and three play situations. The analysis of the data was thus based on individual and group development (see further Pishwa 1989).

3.0. GENERAL DEVELOPMENT
The three verb categories, the copula, non-modal main verbs, and modal verbs

were separated because of paradigmatic and semantic differences. The development of the agreement rule was investigated in detail only in the present tense. The whole phenomenon was new to our learners as modern Swedish does not exhibit any subject-verb agreement rule. The target endings are shown in Table 1:

Table 1. German subject-verb agreement rule in the present tense

person	copula	main verbs	modal verbs
1s	bin	-e	o
2s	bist	-st	-st
3s	ist	-t	o
1p	sind	-en	-en
3p	sind	-en	-en

2p ist left out because of few occurrences
s = singular, p = plural

The copula is suppletive and has to be acquired in terms of separate lexical entries. Main and modal verbs differ only in the 1s and 3s as far as suffixes are concerned; the paradigm of modal verbs is not transparent, because the same form is used for the 1s and 3s. In all categories, the first and the third person plurals are formally identical, although they represent different person constellations. The first person plural is not a genuine plural of 'I' , but includes 'me' and others--perhaps 'you' as well.[2] Regular main verbs exhibit no change in the stem vowel, whereas irregular main verbs and modal verbs do, though in different ways.[3]

The personal forms developed in the copular and main verbs in the sequence 3s > 1s > 2s > 1p > 3p; in the initial phases of acquisition, the 3s ending was used as a kind of base suffix for all persons and numbers in complex contexts. Number was in fact acquired later than the person categories. With modal verbs it was not possible, because 1s = 3s--to point out any constant development. But 1s remained invariant in acquisition, while 3s and 2s exhibited greater variation; number was, as said, acquired last.

Before the target forms had been acquired, the learners used a base form, which was usually that of the 3s. This form was interpreted as person categories not yet formally acquired, as well as for contexts to which the rule had not yet been extended. Sometimes the ending used could be the lexical form used in all person categories and contexts, like the irregular verb essen (eat).

The agreement rule was not acquired in all contexts in a person category simultaneously, but was progressively expanded from one context to another.

Factors considered for the definition of a context were different for the kinds of three verbs. In the following, we will discuss u-contexts (unmarked), m-contexts (marked), and M-contexts (overmarked), which constitute a scale of markedness.

For the copula, the u-contexts involved the SV and (X)VS (inversion)[4] word orders with a definite subject, with no new entities being introduced into discourse. New entities were introduced in m-contexts, where the subject was adjacent (on both sides) to the verb; it could include numerals and had to be indefinite. In M-contexts, the subject and the copula were not adjacent: in German subordinate clauses the verb is in a sentence-final position.

Or the subject could be prothetic *es/das* (hence das-context), which does not agree with the verb; instead, the logical subject or theme agrees with the verb, unlike English:

(1)   It/That's two boys. (English)
(2)   Es/Das sind zwei Jungen. (German)
       That   are two   boys.
       "There are two boys."

For the copula, word order (linear order and distance between the relevant items) and the definiteness of the subject constituted the main factors. The modal verbs were even simpler, as definiteness was not relevant there: They always appeared in definite contexts. Inversion ((X)VS) constituted the m-context here, and subordinate clauses with verb-final position constituted the M-context. With main verbs all of these factors were relevant; and additionally redundancy, which means subjects modified by all kinds of quantifiers and co-ordinate subjects, constituted a factor. For semantic reasons, this factor was not relevant for the copula and modal verbs (see Pishwa 1989). Markedness degrees were as follows for main verbs: u-contexts included all structures with definite subjects adjacent to the verb (before or after); m-contexts included cases where the relevant items were non-adjacent, these included co-ordinate verbs (*He comes and goes*), where the second verb is distant from the subject, M-contexts comprised all redundant indefinite contexts, including the prothetic das-context. Increased semantic information resulted in an accumulation of redundancy, thus creating added markedness. Hence, redundancy cannot be regarded as a learning strategy.

Despite the factors mentioned, there were many others, some of which were relevant to this paper. The most important one was the telic[5] character (Dahl 1981), especially transitivity of verbs (cf. Hopper & Thompson 1980). In these structures, the verb no longer agreed with the subject in the present data (cf. Clahsen 1986), instead, it appeared in its base or lexical form. The influence of transitivity was common in the phase of sentence expansion, i.e. before the agreement rule was applied in subordinate clauses.

On the whole, the development started with (1) the construction of sentences, i.e. with the assessment of subject and verb. After this phase, (2) the sentence was extended, and it was not until after this phase that (3) the fine differentiation of semantics at the sentence level was made. The very last phase was (4) pragmatic (see Pishwa 1990b). The development of the agreement rule parallelled this development.

4.0. RESTRUCTURING
We will investigate three kinds of abrupt restructuring:

(1)   restructuring as a result of internal change of the
       rule itself (extension or restriction);
(2)   restructuring brought about by a change in another
       (sub-)area of grammar;
(3)   restructuring due to a selection of an uncommon
       base form.

In the following, the three kinds of abrupt restructuring will be compared with gradual acquisition. I should point out that these three types cannot always be separated; they can also develop jointly. We will start out with the most common kind of restructuring and end with the least common form.

4.1. Restructuring as a result of internal change of the rule itself
This kind of restructuring occurs in every learner language when a learner expands the scope of the rule or restricts it (cf. Bowerman 1982). Without this, we could not even talk about a learner. But it is not my principal aim to describe the normal kind of restructuring that constitutes gradual progress in the interlanguage. I would like to compare two rather different types of rule acquisition. The learners were two boys from the same grade (the third, at the beginning of data collection). One of them made use of relatively complex syntactic and semantic structures and exhibited abundant variation; the agreement rule developed gradually from one context to the other with the other learner, who never attempted structures which he had not learned yet.

Robert and Ragnar
Tables 2 and 3 show the development of both boys in the three verb categories. The Roman numerals indicate the occasions of data collection.

Table 2: Robert: 3p

Main Verbs	Copula	Modal Verbs

	u	m	M	u	m	M	u	m	M
I	t	t	t	i	i	i	en*		
II	en			i	i	i			
III	en#	t#		s		i	O	O	
IV	en			s	s				
V	t	t				en			
VI	x	t				en			
VII	en	t#				i	x		
VII	x	x		s	i	x	O		O

Table 3. Ragnar: 3p

	Main Verbs			Copula			Modal Verbs		
	u	m	M	u	m	M	u	m	M
I	en	x				i	O		O
II	en	x	t			i	en	en	
III	en	x		s		i	x		
IV	en	x			s		x	en	O
V	en	en		s		i	en	en	
VI	en	en	t				i	en	
VII	en	en						en	
VIII	en								

i = *ist*, s = *sind*
* = uninflected; # = markedness according to telic-atelic
u = atelic/intransitive
m = telic/transitive
x = variable

The two learners were clearly different: The plural rule of main verbs was variable with Robert, who exhibited two separate starts (I and V) ending in a variable phase (VIII); Ragnar showed gradual development in all three verb categories. With the exception of the last occasion where Robert relapsed into the use of singular forms for plurals, the agreement rule with the copula and the modal verbs developed in much the same way with both boys.

On the fifth occasion (V), when Robert seemed to relapse into the use of - t, he produced many transitive constructions. It may have been this complexity that caused him to regress[6] But Robert also generally used more transitive constructions (28.5 %) than Ragnar did (21.1%). Robert seemed to be especially sensitive to the immediate context of the verb, constituted by the telic nature of a verb (object and locative constituents).

Ragnar was sensitive to transitivity--more marked cases--in the third interview, where he produced the t-encoding in transitive verbs in subordinate clauses in the ls (ex. 3) and 3p and also in 3p in one transitive verb whose object was a clause (ex. 4). At this time, the agreement rule was difficult for him in subordinate clauses.

(3)   Wenn ich zu viel ans TV guckt, dann kriege ich so ...
         When I too much TV watch+3s, then get I so ...

(4)   Das ist nur so böse Jungen, sie macht was man nicht machen soll.
         That is only such bad guys, they do+3s what one not do should.

After the third occasion, complexity was created by other syntactic structures for Ragnar: *das*-context, co-ordinate verbs.

Another difference among the learners was their reaction to the complexity of their final task--the story of Hansel and Gretel--due to temporal and causal relations as well as lexical difficulties. Ragnar was not influenced by the complexity, while Robert's output varied in all verb categories. Here, he was quite sensitive to the immediate context; i.e. he would carry over a singular form from a preceding sentence or encode the verb according to some other item close to it. Ragnar used mostly the past and the perfect forms and thus produced only a few verbs in the present. All forms were correct The big difference between Robert and Ragnar, then, was their reaction to the markedness of structures and the complexity of discourse.

On the whole, Ragnar behaved more strategically in reducing complexity whenever it did not affect the intelligibility and correctness of his message. He almost never used indefinite subjects; instead, everything was taken for granted in his speech. When introducing new items, he adopted the attitude that the interviewer knew what was being talked about, whereas most other children would use typical structures *Da kommt ein Mann. Er . . .* (There comes a man. He . . .). It was such existential structures that caused so many problems in the application of the agreement rule. On the other hand, Ragnar was the only informant who knew how to use the passive. But it will be shown below that gradualness was not necessarily a characteristic of his development.

We have seen two different learners. The one restructured his plural rule, the other one exhibited gradual progress and thus less radical restructuring. As restructuring caused by internal change in the rule itself is the most frequent phenomenon in language acquisition and has been described in detail in Pishwa (1989; see also Pishwa 1990a, 1990b), we need not look at further examples.

4.2. Restructuring due to another rule

Another frequent phenomenon was the sudden change of a rule effected by a change in some other rule, which either got introduced, expanded, or restricted. The most common case was overextension of the agreement rule to other grammatical categories, which were by no means arbitrarily selected by the learners, but were always semantically or syntactically related categories: The introduction of -en into the 3p was often heard in 3s (see Table 7), which shares the person category (the third), but not the number with the 3p, whereas it never appeared for this reason in the first or second persons, which share neither of the features with 3p (cf. Bybee 1980). Here I will show in which domains a girl was influenced by indefiniteness of subject and how tenses can effect each other.

Sissi: Influence of an Indefinite Subject

Sissi, who was in grade three at the beginning of the data collection, acquired the plural rule for main verbs on the very first occasion of data collection and extended it even to complex 3s contexts. The plural rule gradually reached most contexts in the 3p. Sissi was very sensitive to indefiniteness in the subject; sometimes she would produce utterances like the following:

(5)   Dann kommt zwei Jungen. (correct- kommen)
         Then come+3s two boys.

Even though the indefinite, quantified subject in the inverted-order context was the most marked context for all learners in main verbs, Sissi was able to use the plural rule in this context on occasion five. At this time, plural agreement for the copula was found only if the subject preceded the verb and was definite. On the sixth occasion, there was no instance for the copula in the plural.

In VII, Sissi applied the plural rule in all environments of the copula:

(6)   Die sind da. (u-context)
         They are there.

(7)   Und da sind zwei, die ... (m-context)
         And there are two, who...

(8)   Es sind viele Leute...   (M-context)
         That are many people...

(9)   Es sind drei Männer... (M-context)
         That are three men...

At the same time, she neutralized the plural rule for the main verbs in the context of an indefinite subject altogether:

(10)   Eine Junge und eine Frau sitzt... (correct: sitzen)
        A boy and a woman sit+3s (m-context)

(11)   Und es kommt eine Junge und eine Mutti. (correct: kommen)
        And it come+3s a boy and a mother. (M-context)

(12)   Es steht zwei Leute. (correct stehen)
        It stand+3s two people. (M-context)

(13)   In eine Fenster steht es zwei Männer. (correct: stehen)
        In a window stand+3s it two men. (M-context)

In some of the above examples, we have the most marked case for the agreement rule: the formal and the real subject competing with each other. The formal subject prevails, since its number is a less-marked category, although it is the logical subject that agrees with the verb in German. Note that this was not the case with the copula (ex. 6-9).

In the last situation, Sissi restored singular marking of the copula in marked contexts of the 3p. She had made several attempts to apply the plural rule in the das-context during the investigation, probably because the teacher had recognized this as a source of mistakes. But Sissi always reverted to the use of *ist* in this complex context. The seventh occasion was her most successful try; previous attempts had only brought about a couple of correct forms. The fact that she reduced the scope of the plural rule of main verbs demonstrates the great complexity of indefinite structures, especially in the das-context.

Unfortunately, it is impossible to state whether Sissi used the plural rule with the main verbs in the last situation in indefinite contexts, as there were no such contexts. Her plural rule was also revived with only a few exceptions.

Except for the restructuring described, Sissi's sensitiveness to indefinite subjects had implications for the acquisition order of the plural rule in the three verb categories: she learned the agreement rule for plurals of the modal verbs better and earlier than for the copula, which was the reversed order--something that can be explained by the function of the verb categories: The copula was mostly used to introduce new entities into discourse. Certain structures with main verbs served the same function, but the subject of the modal verbs was almost categorically definite--old information. As indefinite, new-information structures constituted a difficult context for Sissi, she applied the plural rule in verbs with definite subjects--modal verbs--first.

I have shown how two verb categories were simultaneously governed by the same pragmatic principle with Sissi: The plural rule of the copula was extended to context with an indefinite subject, and the plural rule of main verbs was neutralized in indefinite contexts.

Gunnar: Influence of Tense
Even the extensive use of another tense than the present impeded a proper agreement rule in the present tense. This happened to a gradual learner, Gunnar, who had been applying the agreement rule in 3p in the present tense for some time. On the last occasion, Gunnar told the story of Hansel and Gretel in the perfect tense, using the agreement rule there, but disregarding it in the present and the true past tense in all verb categories:

Table 4. Gunnar: Encoding of 3p tenses in VIII

	Main Verbs	Copula	Modal verbs
Present	5s	---	---
Past	13s/1p	3s	5s
Perfect	9p/1s	---	----

Numerals = Instances of occurrences
s = singular form
p = plural form

Note that the reduction of the agreement rule took place only
in 3p; the 1p with the same suffix was perfectly target-like in all tenses.

General Tendencies
This kind of restructuring--viz. due to change of another rule--was typical, but was not found with every learner. The crucial trigger could be located in any area of grammar: semantics, syntax, or pragmatics. But the principle was that restructuring occurred only in a related area.

It was never the case that the introduction or expansion of an agreement rule with modal verbs affected the same rule with the copula or the main verbs, whereas the plural rule was sometimes introduced into these verb categories at the same time, although this was not very common; modal verbs were the last verb category to be acquired. They were treated as a separate category in all respects, except for some semantic features (see below).

A frequent case was the acceptance by the learner of a patient/experiencer as the subject to be agreed with across non-modal and modal verbs categories: In the early phases, only agents served as subjects to be agreed with. After a patient and an experiencer began acting as subject to a main verb, the agreement rule was also extended to subject-external (Bouma 1973) or extra subjective (Bech 1951) modal verbs, which have subjects similar to a patient; an example would be *müssen* (have to), where the subject's intentions are subject to some external force. A study of this type of restructuring can reveal much about the interdependence and independence of domains of language.

4.3. Restructuring due to an uncommon base form
This is the most interesting kind of restructuring in that the researcher can, with the right tools, discover high systemization in seemingly chaotic data. This kind of restructuring was also the most apparent one, though not so frequent as restructuring due to internal change of the rule itself and restructuring due to another rule. It occurred when a learner used an uncommon base suffix or form to start with. Base means the initial form used for all categories not acquired yet and not the target form. According to markedness theory, this is the most unmarked form, if iconic, it is likewise the least of "markering"[7]. As already mentioned, the least marked form is generally that of the third person singular (for grounds see Mayerthaler 1981, Bybee 1985). Thus, learners would say *Die Kinder ist da* (The children is there) instead of *Die Kinder sind da* (The children are there). Sometimes the learner would select another form, e.g. the most markered form, starting out with the more markering forms as the unmarked use.

Hans and Anna
Let us first look at an instance of the copula from a boy in the second grade---Hans. This development will be compared with the gradual development of the rule with a girl-- Anna--from the same grade. In order to show that restructuring was not typical of this boy, we will look at his main verbs, too.

Our informant, Hans, selected sind (3p) as a base form for some reason. It is unclear why, since other students selected ist[8]. Sind is the most marked form; it represents the two features of person and number. As this form is rarer than the singular form and is a markered form, he got mixed up with the unmarked ist and so continued to restructure his output.

Table 5. Copula Usage, Hans

	3s		3p	
	ist	sind	**sind**	ist
I	9	19	5	
II	6	9	11	1
III		19	9	
IV	19	1	1	

V	29		1	4
VI	11		5	3
VII	23	10	3	
VIII	6	9	6	1

The encoding of the copula in the third persons by Hans can be summarized as follows:

I-III: base encoding *sind*, 3s = 3p; *ist* in M-context.

IV-V: base encoding *ist*, 3s = 3p; use of *sind* in M-context in 3p.

VI-VII: number first differentiated: *ist* in 3s, *sind* in 3p in unmarked contexts; the reverse in M-contexts.

VIII: reversion to the use of *sind* even in 3s; M-context differentiated in both persons.

On occasion I, Hans used sind in the 3s and 3p in equational sentences (ex. 14, 15); *ist*, in other cases, especially when introducing new entities (ex. 16). On the second occasion, the same principle was maintained for the singular; in the plural, *sind* was also used in the context of indefinite subjects; *ist* was used in the marked environment of *das* in the 3s and 3p (ex. 4).

(14)   Er sind klein. (correct: ist)
          He are small.

(15)   Die sind glücklich.
          They are happy.

(16)   Ein Ei ist das und dann ist eine Vogel.
          An egg is that and then is a bird.

(17)   Das ist zwei Strasse. (correct: sind)
          That is two streets.

In III, *sind* was used categorically in both persons and contexts. The fourth occasion exhibited a total reversal to *ist* in 3s and *sind* in 3p (only one instance)! The differentiation of these two personal categories was maintained on occasion V through *das*-context: *sind* in 3p, *ist* in 3s; but simultaneously *ist* was the dominant form in all other contexts in both 3s and 3p. This means that the original base form *sind* remained in the most marked context--*das*-context---in the most marked person category--3p.

It was not until the sixth occasion that Hans acquired the proper personal forms: 3s *ist* and 3p *sind* in unmarked contexts and *ist* in overmarked (viz. das-) contexts. It was at this time that Hans' output was exactly the same as that of the other childrens' (see below). But already on occasion VII, he introduced new environments with new entities in the 3s, where he used an incorrect *sind* (instead of *ist*). Among the other children this usually happened in the 3p: After having acquired *sind* as the plural form, they could still use *ist* in new marked environments. Because of the complexity of the story of Hansel and Gretel with temporal and causal relations on the last occasion, Hans reverted to an increased use of *sind* in both numbers, but the marked *das*-context retained a differentiation of 3s and 3p.

It is easy to see that Han's development was reversed by the wrong symbol: He first differentiated the persons in the overmarked *das*-context. A similar case was a boy--Jonas--from the first grade who began with -en (the plural encoding of the target language) instead of - t in all contexts in both the 3s and 3p and acquired the first and second person after the third person plural. This order was unique. The uncommon selection by Jonas occurred only with main verbs---something that disconfirms the assumption that the different approaches are due to different learner types.

Both cases--Hans and Jonas--prove that learners create a balanced system of their own. If it does not follow the general markedness principles (for morphology, see Mayerthaler 1981), it becomes system-dependent (Wurzel 1984, 1987) and the order expected is possibly changed.

In contrast to Han's development is the development the copula by a young girl also from the second grade--Anna. During the whole period of the study she produced the correct *ist* in the 3s; *sind* appeared only once--on the third occasion. Therefore, only 3p is taken notice of here:

Table 6. Encoding of 3p copula, contexts of Anna

	u	m	M
I	ist	ist	
II	(sind)	ist	ist
III	(sind)		ist
IV			ist
V	ist	ist	ist
VI	sind	ist	
VII		sind	
VII	sind	sind	

The mode of this development was gradual, the plural rule being applied first in unmarked contexts and subsequently in marked contexts. The two instances of *sind* in II and III were repetitions of the input and thus need not be regarded as deviations in the development.

We can see that the development of the agreement rule in the third person was basically the same with both Hans and Anna, even with respect to the time of the acquisition of number. Hans even seemed to be sensitive to the markedness of the context caused by indefiniteness and das-context earlier than his mate.

The main verbs were variant with Hans, but there was no multiple restructuring:

Table 7. Hans: Main Verbs

	3s		3p		
	-t	-en	-e	-en	$-t^9$
I	33	3		2	4
II	10		1	4	3
III	37		1	1	22
IV	26	5		7	6
V	19	1		1	13
VI	13	7		10	
VII	12	3		13	5
VIII	37	1		12	17

At level I, the encoding of both personal categories was -t; the en-suffixes appeared in certain irregular verbs: *essen* (eat), *sprechen* (speak). On the second occasion, Hans seemed to copy forms from the other children he played with. He also repeated the same verb: *geht* (goes) (S out of 10) in 3s and *spielen* (play) with two different suffixes (-t and -en) (3 out of 7) in 3p. The latter suffix, -en, was used with co-ordinate verbs:

(18)   Die spielt und spielen Fussball. (correct: spielen)
        They play+3s and play-en football.

The third occasion was even more t-dominant; the only -en suffix in 3p appeared in a syntactically marked context, which means that it was no plural but an indicator for markedness:

(19)   ... und sprecht.[10] was diese machen.

...and talk+3s what these do-en.

At level IV, a play situation, the encoding was more variable, but 3s was not wholly restructured to -en; there was only an increase of en-suffixes, found with irregular verbs used in co-ordinate structures (see example 18). In the 3p, no regularity could be found in the variation. In the next interview, V, -t was still dominant. The only en-suffix in 3s was transferred from the preceding context, and in 3p it was caused by an indirect question (see ex. 19).

At VI, Hans used only -en in the 3p. This was the result of the fact that almost all contexts were unmarked: 90 % were SV, the subject being frequently a pronoun *sie* (they). At the same time, some plural forms were carried over to the singular.

At VII, there was no new development except that some t-suffixes appeared again in the 3p. Two instances were caused by a new irregular verb (*Ablaut*): *liest* (reads) instead of *lesen*. One t-suffix was due to a transfer from the context. And finally, there was a marked case: a telic verb and an indefinite subject:

(20)   Kinder geht zum Garten. (correct: gehen)
        Children go+3s to the garden.

These two factors influenced verb encoding with most of our learners in the early syntactic phase. In the singular, gehen (plural in German) appeared instead of geht in a telic verb. Additionally, there was a case of Ablaut with the impersonal or generalizing subject *man* (one). Note that this kind of irregular verb was heard with -t in the 3p:

(21)   Man sehen in die Schule. (correct: sieht)
        One see+3p into the school.

On the last occasion--VIII---3s remained stable (with -t, there was only one deviation), whereas the 3p exhibited an increased number of t-encodings. The en-suffix in the 3s occurred in a marked context with a telic verb in a subordinate clause. In the 3p Hans used -t in all subordinate temporal clauses. Furthermore, -t appeared in co-ordinate verbs (see ex. 18) and also generally after co-ordinate subjects. The task on this eighth and last occasion was the generally difficult story of Hansel and Gretel, which caused relapses among a lot of the learners. The form of the paradigm played an important role even here: For irregular verbs with the *Umlaut* (a becomes ä in 2s, 3s) now appeared with the *Umlaut* and -t in 3p, contrary to the target language. Previously, Hans had used either the infinitive form or a t-suffix without Umlaut. Now that he had learned the formation rule for this kind of paradigm, he forgot the use of the en-form. The development in short:

I   3s = 3p: -t; -en due to irregular paradigm (<u>Ablaut</u>)

II   3s = 3p: - t; - en in m-contexts (syntactic)

III   3s = 3p: -t; -en in m-contexts (syntactic)

IV   3s: -t; -en for irregular verbs in m-contexts
         3p: variant

V   3s = 3p: -t; -en in m-contexts in 3p

VI   3s: mainly -t; -en overgeneralized from 3p
         3p: -en

VII   3s: -t; -en for telic and irregular verbs
         3p: -en; -t in m-contexts and irregular verbs

VIII   3s: - t

We have seen that Hans was really no special sort of learner--one that restructured everything. His acquisition of the copula varied because of his selection of sind instead of *ist* as the base form. Main verbs also exhibited variation, but this was due to the syntactic and pragmatic markedness of contexts as well as to formal criteria.

Ranar

I will show now that Ragnar was not such a gradual learner as he might have seemed to be. He, in fact, switched back and forth between *haben* (have) and *sein* (be)---which are used as auxiliaries in the perfect tense in German--in his compound tenses: Where German uses sein for verbs of movement and those which imply a change of the state, e.g. *einschlafen* (fall asleep), Ragnar used both *haben* and *sein*. *Sein* is also used with the copula in German. For all other verbs, *haben* is used in the target language; Ragnar used mostly *sein*.

Table 8. Ragnar: Auxiliaries in the perfect tense

	haben	*sein*
I		3s:(3)
II	3s:**3**; 2s:**3**; 1p:**2**	1s:(1)*; 3s(1)#
		1s:**2**,(1); 3S:**6**, (6)
IV	1s:**28**, (1); 2s:**1**; 3s:**17**,(3)	1s:**3**, (5); 3s:**3**; 3p:**1**
	1p:**7**	1p:**4**, (1)
V	1s:**1**; 3s:**7**, (3)	3s:(1)

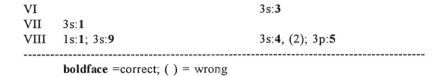

VI		3s:3
VII	3s:1	
VIII	1s:1; 3s:9	3s:4, (2); 3p:5

boldface =correct; ( ) = wrong

At I, there were only incorrect instances of *sein*, replacing correct *haben*. At II, *haben* mostly occurred. This in turn changed in III: All auxiliaries were *sein* again. On the fourth occasion, both auxiliaries were used, but only partly in a target-like way. It is difficult to find much of a system in their use[11]. The tendency seems to be an overuse of *sein* for the 1s:

(22)   Ich bin mich versteckt. (correct: habe)
       I am (have) hidden myself.

(23)   Ich bin sie gelernt. (correct: habe)
       I am (have) learnt them.

(24)   ich bin nur gehammert. (correct: habe)
       I am (have) only hammered.

(25)   Da habe ich auf einen Baum gegangen. (correct: bin)
       Then I have gone on a tree.

In 3s, Ragnar made use of the structure *Da hat* ... (Then has...) without any regard for the semantics of the verb--the cause of the overuse of *haben* in this personal category. On the fifth occasion, he increased the use of *Da hat....* It is difficult to make any statements concerning the next two occasions because of the few instances--which were all correct. In the last (play) situation, the distribution of these two auxiliaries was correct except for two cases, where Ragnar used *ist* instead of *hat*.

The use of perfect auxiliaries proves that Ragnar's development was not gradual in all areas: The fact that he chose sein as a general auxiliary caused him to restructure his system a couple of times, though he learned all other domains gradually. *Sein* was also usually overused by Ragnar. Otherwise it was *haben*, which was the first auxiliary learned by the others. *Haben* is more frequent and has fewer restrictions than *sein*.

5.0. CONCLUDING REMARKS
Abrupt restructuring of a rule was the most common case in the present data and gave an excellent opportunity for testing markedness values. This type of restructuring is also usual, even necessary, in all developing languages; e.g. pidgins and creoles (cf. Mühlhäusler 1980, 1985, 1990), where changes are highly

dependent on the naturalness of the linguistic system.

All of my subjects restructure their linguistic systems several times; the reason is that the agreement rule overlaps so many grammatical (sub)areas. The further the learners are advanced in their development, the less restructuring was observed. After the acquisition of the agreement rule in the overmarked context--actually already before that---there was hardly any restructuring of the agreement rule. This means that restructuring took place up until the moment when the parts of the sentence had been internalized. Restructuring always accorded with the sequence in which grammatical features were acquired (see the section on **General Development**).

The only difference between learners was (I) the quantity of restructuring and (2) individual preferences or weak points. There was not a learner that exhibited any restructuring whatsoever, but there were quantitative differences, as we have seen. Ragnar (Table 3) was the learner with the least restructuring and Robert (Table 2) was one of the learners with the most. The amount of restructuring was partly dependent also upon individual sensitivities, as shown in data from Robert, Sissi, and Ragnar data. Robert's susceptible point was the influence of the immediate context; Sissi's, indefiniteness--a pragmatic phenomenon; and Ragnar's, the non-adjacency of subject and verb. But I would like to stress that the learners were influenced by all of these factors--to different degrees.

The same principles were valid for restructuring of another rule. As indicated by the cases shown in this paper, the two rules--the effecting and the effected rule-- must be governed by, or share the same principle or feature. Huebner (1983), whose study exhibited restructuring to a high degree, raised the question as to whether a change in one area of grammar always has to effect others. The answer is no. Huebner's study included the acquisition of three grammatical features that were earlier governed by pragmatics and later by syntax. This order is predictable (Givon 1979, 1985, Pishwa 1990b) in language development because communicative competence develops first, and there was probably no interaction between the separate features. It is possible that some other area not investigated by Huebner was also acquired gradually, independently of these three domains.

The third form of restructuring, which was caused by the selection of an uncommon base form, always started in initial phases of the acquisition of the agreement rule. It was quite hard for each learner to adapt her/his system to the target system until s/he had gone through the whole development of restructurings. It is not possible to say what grammatical areas this could happen in. But there was no individual restructuring of modal verbs, except for *sollen*, which deviates from the general paradigm of the modals exhibiting no change of the stem vowel in the singular. Also, its meaning was a transfer from Swedish. It is also difficult to tell exactly what kind of learners were entrapped in this kind of restructuring.

It was learners who were not very much worried about the output (Jonas and Hans) and the monitoring type (Krashen 1981) who had probably noticed that there were two auxiliaries but were unable to get the distribution correct (Ragnar).

5.1. Learner Types
I have not been able to single out any real restructurer in the present study; all learners did restructure in one domain and acquired the phenomena of another domain gradually. Restructuring could therefore hardly be ascribed to introverted or extraverted personalities (Vogel 1990, Fillmore 1979). But it appears with the more-sensitive and more-monitoring learners, an observation that again leaves us with the problem of changes in these attributes--which were by no means permanent.

The learner type (Krashen 1981, Ellis 1985) was rather determined after the right utilization of learning capacity. To this capacity belongs a sense for the complexity of structures, as seen with Ragnar and Robert. Even if Ragnar was the most successful learner orally, he was poor in writing, according to his mother; whereas his twin brother--Gunnar--who neutralized the plural forms in the present and past tense in favor of the perfect tense, lagged far behind him in oral ability, but was a lot better at writing. The role of capacity was also seen with one of the girls in the control group--a hopeless case for the teachers because of her many mistakes. She was always compared with another girl, also a member of the control group, who never made mistakes. After a detailed investigation of the oral production of these two it was clear to me that what caused the hopelessness, in comparison with the other girl, was that her grammar and language were very complex (cf. Bowerman 1982). Also Hahn (1982) shows how students of English relapsed if the teacher expected structures that were too advanced.

None of the learners were genuine "chunk-learners" (Hatch 1983), either; most of them occasionally made use of prefabricated structures (e.g. Ragnar: Da hat...), especially the younger students. But as it is not possible to learn a language by repetition, rule-application has to be introduced. Repetition of a special phrase or a word, even where not appropriate, is not only typical of learner languages; it is also a frequent phenomenon in everyday speech of native-speakers.

5.2. Implications for Methodology
Linguistic results are dependent on length of the study (longitudinal or cross-sectional), on the data (spontaneous or elicited), and on the method of analysis. As these issues have been discussed over and over again (e.g. Ellis 1985, Berko Gleason 1985, Preston 1989), I will only concentrate on the points for which the present study has implications.

None of the important details gained through the longitudinal study of the fifteen children would have been revealed by a cross-sectional study, because such studies do not show individual development. The greatest defect would have been the failure to capture the amazing systematicity behind seemingly chaotic data, individual similarities and differences, as well as the interrelationship and overlapping of grammatical domains in the different acquisition phases. General development can be revealed by means of cross-sectional studies if an analysis is done correctly (see below).

The language produced in the five interviews and the three play situations in the present study did not exhibit any difference other than that some learners would imitate others in play situations. In the interviews, I avoided giving the children any input except when I wanted to test whether a form would be transferred or not. But language is influenced by how one collects his/her data. For example, Bean & Gergen (1990) found that data from the same informants were different depending on whether one used a test, an interview, or free oral production (cf. Clahsen et. al. 1990). Tests are necessary, but they should be based on longitudinal research that considers many factors (see Pienemann et. al. 1988).

A proper analysis is at least as important as good data. It has been shown in this paper that learners make up a system of their own. Without taking this fact into consideration, a totally reversed analysis can result. If one should desire to investigate the proficiency or the order of acquisition of the agreement rule in the plural (3p) with some of the informants and if one of the advanced informants happened to use only overmarked contexts while one of the beginners were Hans in his initial use of the copula at the time one carried out the investigation, the results would show poor proficiency for the advanced learner and high for Hans. Also, the order of acquisition would turn out to be wrong. We have seen enough in this paper to be able to imagine how all cases of restructuring would influence the final results.

In a proper analysis, markedness of a phenomenon itself and its contexts has to be considered--i.e. simple and complex contexts have to be separated. Related domains or features must be considered. The framework to be used for such analyses has to include everything if it is to be adapted to the needs of the study: It has to be dynamic, i.e developmental and flexible.

A simple list of unrelated phenomena as the order of acquisition can scarcely accomplish much for explanation or prediction. Researchers of second languages ought to first begin with universal linguistic phenomena, e.g. typological differences or pidgins and creoles from a range of fields and then think out the methodological implications of different approaches. It is not even possible to analyze everyday speech without considering context. And language-acquisition is so much more complex, including cognitive and social factors. One might be tempted to use a simple analysis because of the delusively simple-looking appearance of second language data.

5.3. Conclusions for the Interlanguage

The cases of abrupt restructuring that we have been confronted with in this paper have exhibited a good deal of variation, some of it was apparently almost chaotic. Yet there is a high systematicity behind the diversity of outputs. The systematicity involves degrees of markedness of contexts, in one of which the agreement rule gradually emerges. Also the symbolizing of the rule is essential for the system. For the learner to maintain this system in extremely complex cases, the usual order of acquisition of the person categories could get reversed; this means that the semantic and pragmatic principles of the construction of the sentence are stronger than the semantic and pragmatic principles underlying personal categories. Even degrees of markedness of diverse structures can be reversed to maintain system in the interlanguage.

The use of the dynamic framework has made the finding possible: There are no abrupt restructurers among the learner types; all informants acquired the agreement rule gradually, despite different outputs.

NOTES

I would like to thank C.-J. N. Bailey for extensive comments, especially stylistic ones.

1. Hence, when talking about "restructuring", abrupt restructuring is meant unless otherwise specified.

2. In Tok Pisin, *yumi* is a basic category (Mühlhäusler 1990).

3. In irregular main verbs, it is the 2s and 3s that change the stem vowel; in modal verbs, the whole singular (1s, 2s, 3s).

4. In German, VS-inversion is used in questions and wherever the clause begins with anything other than the subject.

5. "Telic" verbs include verbs of movement with a goal and transitive verbs with an orientation of the activity.

6. He also applied the agreement rule to modal verbs with plural subjects on this occasion. But it is difficult to determine whether this could have triggered his relapses to main verbs, as there were only two instances of modal verbs on this occasion the analogical influence of modal verbs on non-modal verbs was not general (see below).

7. Markering (*Merkmalhaftigkeit*) refers to the ways in which items of differing degrees of markedness are symbolized. The iconic ideal is for less marked categories to be symbolized less and more marked ones more; e.g. the singular, being usually a less marked category, is almost always symbolized by less inflection, etc. than the plural: "book" vs. "books".

8. As Hans was a very sensitive boy this behavior may have been caused by teachers' corrections.

9. Infinitives of main verbs were influence by the dominating suffixes: in III, -t; in IV, -en; in V, -t.

10. On the first occasion, Hans used *sprechen* as 3sp.

11. All instances indicate that result as well as progressive activity were marked by *sein* and other kinds of activities by *haben*.

REFERENCES

Bailey, Charles-James N. 1982. On the yin and yang nature of language. Ann Arbor: Karoma Publishers, Inc.
_____. 1984. Markedness-reversal and the pragmatic principle of reading between the lines in the presence of marked usages . Papiere zur Linguistik 31.43-100.
_____. Forthcoming. Essays on time-based linguistic analysis. Oxford University Press.
Bean, Martha, and Constance Gergen. 1990. Individual variation in fossilized interlanguage performance. Variability in second language acquisition. Proceedings of the tenth meeting of the Second Language Research Forum, Vol. 1. 205-220.
Bech, Gunnar. 1951. Grundzüge der semantischen Entwicklungsgeschichte der deutschen Modalverba. Historisk-filosofiske Meddelelser 32/6 von Det Kongelige Danske Videnskabernes Selskab. 1-28.
Berko Gleason, Jean. 1985. Studying language development. The development of language, ed. by Jean Berko Gleason. Columbus: Merrill Publishing Company.
Bouma, Lowell. 1973. The semantics of the modal auxiliaries in contemporary German. The Hague: Mouton & Co.
Bowerman, Melissa. 1982. Reorganizational processes in lexical and syntactic development. Language acquisition, ed. by Eric Wanner & Lila Gleitman. Cambridge: Cambridge University Press.
Bybee, Joan. 1980. Child morphology and morphophonemic change. Historical morphology, ed. by J. Fisiak. Amsterdam: Benjamins.
_____. 1985. Morphology. A study of the relation between meaning and form. Amsterdam: Benjamins.
Clahsen, Harald. 1984. Der Erwerb von Kasusmarkierungen in der deutschen Kindersprache. Linguistische Berichte.
_____. 1986. Verb inflections in German child language. Acquisition of agreement markings and the functions they encode. Linguistics 24.79-121.
_____. 1990. Lexikalische Ebnen und morphologische Entwicklung: Eine Untersuchung zum Erwerb des deutschen Pluralsystems im Rahmen des Lexikalischen Morphologie. MS.
Dahl, Osten. 1981. On the definition of the telic-atelic (bounded-non-bounded) distinction. Syntax and semantics, vol. 14. Academic Press.
Ellis, Rod. 1985. Understanding second language acquisition. Oxford: Oxford University Press.
Fillmore, Lily Wong. 1979. Individual differences in second language acquisition. Individual differences in language ability and language behavior, ed. by Charles Fillmore, Daniel Kempler & William Wang. New York: Academic Press. 203-228.
Givon, Talmy. 1979. On understanding grammar. New York: Academic Press.
_____. 1985. Syntax. A functional-typological introduction. Volume I. Amsterdam: Benjamins.
Hahn, Angela. 1982. Fremdsprachenunterricht und Spracherwerb. Dissertation, Passau.
Hatch, Evelyn. 1983. Psycholinguistics. Rowley: Newbury House.
Hopper, Paul, and Sandra Thompson. 1980. Transitivity in grammar and discourse. Lg. 56.251-299.
Huebner, Thom. 1983. A longitudinal analysis of the acquisition of English. Ann Arbor: Karoma.
Krashen, Steven. 1981. Second language acquisition and second language learning. Oxford: Pergamon Press.
Mayerthaler, Willi. 1981. Morphologische Natürlichkeit. Wiesbaden:Athenaion.
Mühlhäusler, Peter. 1980. Structural expansion and the process of creolization. Theoretical orientations in creole studies, ed. by A. Valdman and A. Highfield. New York: Academic Press.
_____. 1985. Patterns of contact, mixture, creation and nativization: their contribution to a general theory of language. Developmental mechanisms of language, ed. by Charles-James

N. Bailey and Roy Harris. Oxford: Pergamon Press. 51-87.

_____. 1990. Towards an implicational analysis of pronoun development. Development and diversity, ed. by Jerold Edmondson, Crawford Feagin, and Peter Muhlhausler. Arlington: SIL.351-370.

Pienemann, Manfred, Malcolm Johnston, and Geoff Brindley. 1988. Constructing an acquisition-based procedure for second language assessment. SSLA 10.217-243.

Pishwa, Hanna. 1989. Erwerb der deutschen Kongruenzregel. Technical University of Berlin dissertaion. Arbeitspapiere zur Linguistik 23. TU Berlin.

_____1990a. Markedness reversals in the acquisition of morphology. See Muhlhausler 1990. 529-546.

_____1990b. Phases in the acquisition of the agreement rule in German. See Bean & Gergen. 595-608.

Preston, Dennis. 1989. Sociolinguistics and second language acquisition. Oxford: Blackwell.

Vogel, Klaus. 1990. Lernersprache. Linguistische und psycho-linguistische Grundfragen zu ihrer Erforschung. Tübingen: Gunter Narr.

Wurzel, Wolfgang. 1984. Flexionsmorphologie und Natürlichkeit. Berlin: Akademie-Verlag.

_____. 1987. System-dependent morphological naturalness in inflection. Leitmotifs in natural morphology, ed. by Wolfgang Dressler, Willi Mayerthaler, Oswald Panagl, and Wolfgang Wurzel. Amsterdam: Benjamins.

VARIABILITY IN GRAMMATICAL ANALYSIS: ON RECOGNIZING VERBAL MARKERS IN FOREIGN WORKERS' GERMAN

Carol A. Blackshire-Belay
Temple University

1.0. INTRODUCTION AND OVERVIEW

In a relatively short period of time Germany[1] has become a multilingual society. In comparison to many of its European neighbors this situation is a young and new experience. As result of the Second World War the country's physical boundaries and constitutional status were largely decided upon by foreign powers. Also since that time the native population has been struggling to come to terms with its past, as well as with the problem of finding a new identity for itself. Unified Germany represents one of the places in the world that presents the researcher with almost laboratory conditions to study and explore contact between languages or language varieties in a truly established multilingual and multicultural society.

The social and linguistic problems faced by foreign workers in Germany[2] have raised new questions of educational policy within the country itself. Furthermore, this new situation has created a unique opportunity for scientists to study how languages develop, as well as how individuals acquire knowledge of a language. The present situation in Germany vividly illustrates, that human migration brings with it certain consequences. Germany is now much more ethnically, linguistically, religiously, and culturally diverse than ever before in its history.

The rise of multilingualism in Germany began earlier than one might have anticipated, and large-scale immigration of foreign workers into the country is not exactly a new phenomenon. In the time of rapid industrial expansion and growth between the unification of Germany in 1871 and the beginning of World War I, many thousands of people came from neighboring countries to the south and east in search of employment. In the first years of World War II thousands were forcibly imported as slave labor. The most recent wave of immigration of workers began in response to a campaign of recruitment initiated by the government of the prior Federal Republic in the 1950s. Its purpose was to solve the shortages in the work force that became apparent in the country. The recruitment of the so-called *Gastarbeiter*[3] 'guest workers' enabled Germany to bring workers to the country mostly from southern Europe, and especially from the Mediterranean countries. This process was stopped in 1973. This consequently led to stricter immigration laws which were introduced following the economic decline in the early 1970s.

By this time the foreign workers living in the country totalled over 4 million people.

Although the number of foreign workers declined over the following decade, the relatively high birthrate and the continued right of family members to join their relatives meant that the overall number of the workers continued to increase. By 1982 the total number of workers and their families living in the country totalled almost 4.7 million (7.6 per cent of the population). After unification of the former East and West Germany there has been an increase in the number of foreigners in the country. This is due to the foreign workers that had been employed in the eastern part, and now they too must be brought into the foreign worker discussion.[4]

Generally speaking, the adult foreign workers have had no exposure to the German language before arrival in the country. More often than not, no instruction was received once they were fully employed in a factory. The workers ultimately acquired a form of German for use among themselves and with the native population. With little exposure to the target language and no formal instruction in the language, the workers learned German based on the people with whom they came in contact. This situation provided the initial motivation for academic interest in the speech of the workers.

It has been argued that in order to provide the adult workers with an adequate knowledge of German to enable them to function adequately and be accepted in German society, more needed to be known about both their actual communication needs and the process by which their knowledge of the German language had been acquired. Some studies maintained this objective and led to practical attempts to improve the provision of appropriate language teaching programs for adults.[5] Other researchers focused their attention more strongly on the linguistic system itself. Still others regarded the speech of the foreign workers and the workers themselves as "social" problems urgently demanding social solutions, which ultimately developed into a hot topic for sociolinguistic discussion and debate.

2. 0. THEORETICAL BACKGROUND
There have been numerous attempts to go beyond mere observation and discussion of the German of foreign workers (henceforth "(F)oreign (W)orkers' (G)erman)". From earlier studies concerned with providing the adult foreign workers with an adequate knowledge of German, studies moved on to the linguistic system itself and to other questions concerning the acquisition of a second language in general. In particular, it has been indicated by Clahsen et al. (1983), Keim (1984), Klein and Dittmar (1979), Hinnenkamp (1982), Meisel (1980), Blackshire-Belay (1989;1990;1991) that the act of classification is essential to linguistic inquiry at all levels of analysis.

Anyone confronted with a new language for the first time would likely have difficulty in learning and distinguishing between the grammatical forms and the meanings that they carry. The task is even greater when no formal instruction is received. Quite often it is assumed from the outset that the speakers of an inflecting language would have little difficulty recognizing, categorizing and successfully producing the "new" forms. Speakers of an isolating or an agglutinative language would be faced with more difficulties. The factor that makes the foreign worker situation so interesting to the researcher is that many languages involved in the foreign worker community in Germany (Turkish, Arabic, Greek, Serbo-Croatian, Spanish, Italian, Azerbaijan and Portuguese) are typologically different from each other and from German.

Researchers have focused a great deal of attention on the linguistic behavior of these adult learners of different first languages. Clyne (1968) and Bodemann and Ostow (1975) studied the speech of various nationalities, such as Turkish, Spanish, Greek, and Serbo-Croatian workers. The Heidelberger Forschungsprojekt: Pidgin Deutsch (1975;1978) and Dittmar (1978;1979;1980) observed the German of Spanish and Italian workers. Keim (1978) observed the speech of Turkish adult males, of Greek and Turkish workers (1982), and of Turkish workers (1984). Orlovic-Schwarzwald (1978) observed the German of Serbo-Croatian speakers. The studies conducted in Wuppertal (the ZISA project) by Meisel (1975;1977;1980), Clahsen (1980) and Pienemann (1978;1980) were done with Spanish and Italian workers.

Morphological, syntactic, and semantic aspects of FWG have been discussed in the literature. FWG features such as the omission of obligatory elements that would not occur in any other variety of German have been the topic of discussion. Such features as the omission of the definite and indefinite article, preposition, subject, verb, auxiliary verb have been studied. In addition, other features such as the negator *nicht* (or *nix*) preceding rather than following the finite verb in the main clause, retaining subject-verb word order instead of inversion in question formation. Other observations include some of the following: reducing the three genders to all feminine, omission of articles to signal case, lack of inflection of nouns to indicate singular versus plural, apparent use of infinitive form instead of inflected verb forms, as well as semantic reductions and paraphrasing.

It has been clearly shown that speakers of Romance languages (Castilian Spanish, Portuguese, Italian), Slavonic languages (Serbo-Croatian, Slovene, Macedonia), and Turkish and Greek are remarkably similar in their production of FWG. Furthermore results also indicate that despite the considerable variation between individual speakers of FWG, these differences are less remarkable than the large number of features that seem to be common to most FWG-speakers, regardless of their first language. Thus the speech varieties that have independently arisen among the foreign workers have enough in common to justify their inclusion under the single heading FWG.

Despite the fact that considerable variation can be observed among and between the speakers of FWG, these differences are less in number to the number of similarities found in the German of foreign workers, regardless of their first language. In an attempt to account for uniformity and variation in the German of the foreign workers researchers have discussed "the process of acquisition"[6], the "transfer hypothesis"[7], the "pidgin hypothesis"[8], the "foreigner-talk hypothesis"[9], and the "universal simplification hypothesis"[10]. This author finds the most interesting and intriguing aspect of all concerning FWG is that there appears to be a remarkable similarity in FWG by speakers of different first languages, and none of the above theories have sufficiently accounted for this observable fact.

The purpose of this chapter is to investigate some of the features that are common to most FWG speakers. Its primary focus is on the use of German verb markers in the speech of adult speakers of different first languages.

With specific focus on the regular, irregular, and modal verbs, Blackshire-Belay (1991) described the verb morphology in the speech of seven Serbo-Croatian speakers, six Greek speakers, and three Turkish speakers. The individuals involved in the study arrived in Germany after the age of 20 and had been living there for at least 10 years. In addition, the speakers were selected who exhibited a predominance of features which prior researchers had shown to be characteristic of FWG.

Her analysis showed that the speakers were remarkably similar in their usage, regardless of the first language. This allowed Blackshire-Belay to characterize the FWG verbal system as follows:

> 1. There was frequent use of verb forms that represent the present indicative in the target language in all tense environments: VØ, Ven, Vst, V(e)t.
>
> 2. The majority of speakers demonstrated the use of verbal markers that were reserved for the past tense only.
>
> 3. Because of the irregularity in the verb paradigm of *sein, haben, werden* and *wissen*, as well as the modal auxiliaries, it was strongly believed that the speakers had realized these forms as separate lexical items.
>
> 4. There was variation in the speech of a given individual, as well as variation from one speaker to the next, but the selected speakers used features that were common to all of them regardless of how close a

speaker was to the target in his/her production.

5. A number of "admixtures" or invented forms were produced by all of
the speakers.

This chapter attempts to expand on the characteristics of the verbal markers in
FWG by exploring the regular verbs in more detail by close examination of the
weak and strong verbs. The analysis will concentrate on the person-number and
tense markers.

3.0. SELECTION OF SPEAKERS
This study analyzes data from sixteen speakers. The choice of the speakers was
based on the following criteria:

1.   All the speakers were non-native speakers of German.
2.   They all had either only minimal or no formal instruction in
     German.
3.   They had been living in Germany for at least ten years.[11]
4.   All individuals knew the interviewer prsonally, and a trusting
     relationship had been established prior to the recording session.

Table 1: Summary Background Information for Selected Speakers

SPEAKER	COUNTRY	AGE	YEARS IN GERMANY	FIRSTLANGUAGE
Marija	Yugoslavia-Bosnia	43	13	Serbo-Croatian
Vladimir	Yugoslavia-Bosnia	41	14	Serbo-Croatian
Jovanka	Yugoslavia-Serbia	37	15	Serbo-Croatian
Hasan	Turkey-Anatolia	50	21	Azerbaijan/Turkish
Dmitris	Greece-Valos	45	22	Modern Greek
Thanassis	Greece-Athens	63	27	Modern Greek
Maja	Yugoslavia-Herzegowina	36	15	Serbo-Croatian
Kimon	Greece-Valos	42	20	Modern Greek
Kostas	Greece-Tanagra	36	18	Modern Greek
Ephemia	Greece-Thessaloniki	39	20	Modern Greek
Stefanos	Greece-Thessaloniki	45	14	Modern Greek
Nilüser	Turkey-Izmir	35	13	Turkish
Slobodan	Yugoslavia-Titov Vales	32	12	Serbo-Croatian
Dragica	Yugoslavia-Bosnia	43	15	Serbo-Croatian
Nadiye	Turkey-Trabzon	40	14	Turkish
Jelenka	Yugoslavia-Serbia	34	17	Serbo-Croatian

The corpus of data consisted of approximately 280 utterances from each speaker.

4.0. DATA ANALYSIS FOR PERSON-NUMBER MARKERS

In this paper the author has restricted herself to the following groups of verbs: the weak and the strong verbs.[12] Before preceding to the verbal markers in FWG, the author believes it is worthwhile to examine the target forms as a basis of comparison in FWG. This will be briefly discussed in the following.

4.1. Person-Number Markers

For **The Weak Verb Morphemes** in modern German the infinitive adds the following endings to the verb stem:

-en:	sag-en, lach-en, arbeit-en[13]
-n:[14]	klingel-n, änder-n

The following endings are added to the verb stem in the present tense:

1sg	-e	ich	sag-e
2sg	-st	du	sag-st
3sg	-t	es[15]	sag-t
1pl	-en	wir	sag-en
2pl	-t	ihr	sag-t
3pl	-en	sie	sag-en[16]

For **The Strong Verb Morphemes** the infinitive of strong verbs always has the ending -en.

komm-en	nehm-en	biet-en

The ending pattern for the present tense of strong verbs follows the same basic rules as the weak verbs. Stong verbs with the stem vowels -e-, -a-, and -au- (and one with the vowel -o-) change their stem vowel[17] in the 2nd and 3rd person singular: the vowel -e- changes to -i- or -ie-(geben: *du gibst, es gibt* or sehen: *du siehst, es sieht*), -a- to -ä-[18] (fahren: *du fährst, es fährt*), and -au- to -äu- (laufen: *du läufst, es läuft*). All plural forms follow the pattern of weak verbs.

Based on thorough examination of various aspects of the verb morphology in German of foreign workers, it has been determined that the speakers use a series of different word-forms and word-form combinations. It has been observed that an enormous amount of variation exists in a given speaker's repertoire, and that variation exists from one speaker to the next.

In the group of regular verbs, the author was able to group the speakers in four different groups ranging from the least targetlike to the most targetlike based on the person-number markers in the usage of each speaker. This information is provided in Table 2 below:

Table 2: Person-Number Markers for Regular Verbs

Least Targetlike <---------------------------> Most Targetlike

GROUP 1	GROUP 2	GROUP 3	GROUP 4
No person-number opposition	Second Person Singular Inflection	First and Third Person Singular	First, Second, and Third Person

4.1.1. Group 1

In this group, morphological markers for person-number are basically lacking. Two speakers are grouped here: Thanassis (G), and Stefanos (G). These two speakers use a series of word-forms in expressing the different persons and numbers. There is not a single word-form that has been reserved for any meaning in particular, as the following examples illustrate

1st person sg:	ich sitze	(= VERB: sit)
	ich verdien∅	(= VERB: earn)
	ich anfangen	(= VERB: begin)
	ich zusammenlebt	(= VERB: live together with)
2nd person sg:	verstehst du	(= VERB: understand)
	du bezahlen	(= VERB: pay)
3rd person sg:	es kostet	(= VERB: cost)
	meine Frau anrufen	(= VERB: telephone)
	wie heiß∅ **Name**	(= VERB: call, the name of)
	komme die Frage	(= VERB: arise)
3rd person pl:	meine Kinda bleiben	(= VERB: stay)
	sie (pl) arbeit∅	(= VERB: work)
	Deutsche verheirate	(= VERB: marry)

The verb forms **Ven** and **V∅** are more frequently used by these speakers than any other forms, and these remain unmarked for all inflectional categories. An occasional targetlike marker may occur, such as **Ve** for 1st person singular, or **Vt** for 3rd person singular, but this seems to be more at random for both speakers.

As has been indicated above, for the second and third person singular of the strong verbs, the stem vowels almost always change. Among the two speakers in Group 1, the author made the following observations: Thanassis (G) produced several inflected second or third person singular forms, but they were all weak verbs, as in: klopft, kostet, verstehst du, zusammenlebt. Stefanos' usage was quite similar: bleibt, bringt, guckt, kassiert, kommt, (strong verb, but there is no vowel change in the target), kostet, sagt, kommst du, and wohnst du.

4.1.2. Group 2

Marija (Y) and Kostas (G) have been placed in this group demonstrating a second person singular inflectional marker. These two speakers indicate a clear second person singular opposition by using the verb form Vst + du, it is definitely a target marker in form, but not always in meaning. For example, the verb form Vst occurs in the corpus in command, but this stands in contrast to the target:

> gehst   du   diesen
> go/2SG PRO   OBJECT
> 'go   you   fetch'
>
> bringst   du   meine Lotto   auch
> bring/2SG PRO   POSS NOUN/3SG   ADVERB
> 'bring/take you my   lotto   too'

Occasionally it is also used in question formation:

> hörst   du   zu
> hear/2SG PRO   PREFIX
> 'listen   you   to'

Or in statements:

> nachher   gehst   du
> ADVERB   go/2SG PRO
> 'after that   go   you'

An interesting development is that when the subject precedes the verb, the verbal marker is changed from Vst to Ven, as in:

> du gehen 'you go'
> du sagen 'you say'

As in Group 2, all verb forms remain unmarked for tense. For the second and third person singular inflected forms, both speakers produced only weak verb forms. For example, Marija (Y) produced the verb forms: bringst du, gehst du (no vowel change in the target), hörst du, and geht. Kostas (G) produced heiratet and kommt.

4.1.3. Group 3

Four speakers can be found in this group: Kimon (G), Nilüser (T), Ephemia (G), and Nadiye (T). For all of the speakers in this group Ve and VØ (which occur regularly in the spoken form of the target), are used only in the first person singular. Several examples of their usage of this form is provided in the following:

vielleicht bleibe   noch   fünf Jahre
ADVERB   stay/1SG ADVERB NUM   NOUN/3PL
'perhaps stay   yet   five years'

Beispiel für die   Arbeit   ich frage   Deutschland
NOUN   PREP ARTICLE NOUN/3SG PRO ask/1SG   NOUN/3SG
'example for   the   work   I ask (for)   Germany'

For the third person singular these speakers use the verb form **Vt** or **Vet** (for verbal stems ending in a dental):

aber schwer fällt   mit die Kinder zwei Schule gehen
CONJ ADJ   occur/3SG PREP ART NOUN/PL NUM
                                      NOUN/PL go/3PL
'but difficult   for the children two schools go'

weiß   nix genau erstemal wie geht mit   arbeit
know/1SG NEG ADJ ADV ADV go/3SG PREP
                                     NOUN/3SG
'know not exactly at first how goes with work'

As in the previous two groups, all verb forms remain unmarked for tense. In terms of the second and third person singular weak versus strong verb inflection, sporadically several strong verb forms were produced. For example, Kimon (G) produced *gibt*, third person singular from *geben*, and *läuft* from the verb *laufen*. Ephemia (G) uses *fällt* from the verb *fallen*, Nilüser (T) produces *gibt* from *geben*, und *gefällt* from *gefallen*, while Nadiye (T) produces the verb form *gibt* from *geben*.

4.1.4. Group 4
Eight speakers showed a clear first, second and third person singular opposition: Vladimir (Y), Dmitris (G), Hasan (T), Maja (Y), Dragica (Y), Jelenka (Y), Jovanka (Y), and Slobodan (Y). In this group as well, the verb forms **Ven** and **VØ** are still used as general unmarked verb forms. However, there is greater development of the **Ve** for first person, **Vst** for second person, and **V(e)t** for third person singular. Less clear is the number distinction.

Where the inflection for the second and third person singular weak versus strong verb inflection, most of the speakers in group 4 produced more of these forms: Hasan (T) uses *sieht* from *sehen*, Vladimir (Y) *nimmst du* from *nehmen*, and *siehst du* from *sehen*, Dmitris (G) produces *gibt* and *gibst* from *geben*, *nimmt* from *nehmen*, *laufst du* from *laufen* (which is an interesting form here because the target form is umlauted: *läufst du*), and *siehst* from *sehen*. Jovanka (Y) and Dragica (Y) both produced *gibt* from *geben*.

5.0. DATA ANALYSIS FOR TENSE MARKERS
The simple past and the compund past tenses were considered in the analysis.

5.1.1. Preterite, Imperfect Tenses
In the past tense (Preterite, Imperfect), weak verbs add the past tense indicator -**te** to the stem (similar to English -**ed**).[19] The following endings are provided in the following:

1sg	-**te**	ich	sag-**te**
2sg	-**te-st**	du	sag-**te-st**
3sg	-**te**	es	sag-**te**
lpl	-**te-n**	wir	sag-**te-n**
2pl	-**te-t**	ihr	sag-**te-t**
3pl	-**te-n**	sie	sag-**te-n**

The strong verbs, on the other hand, change their stem in the past tense (Preterite, Imperfect) and add the following endings[20]:

Endings	*kommen*		*fahren*	*gehen*
Ø	ich	kam	ich fuhr	ich g**ing**
-st	du	kam-st	du fuhr-st	du g**ing**-st
---	es	kam	er fuhr	er g**ing**
-en	wir	kam-en	wir fuhr-en	wir g**ing**-en
-t	ihr	kam-t	ihr fuhr-t	ihr g**ing**-t
-en	sie	kam-en	sie fuhr-en	sie g**ing**-en

Among the sixteen speakers only seven of them produced this type of form for the verb types under observation in this study: Hasan (T), Thanassis (G), Stefanos (Y), Nadiye (T), Dragica (Y), Ephemia (G), and Jovanka (Y). Although the forms were relatively few in number, both weak and strong verb forms were produced. The following preterite-like verb forms occurred in the corpus of data by these speakers: Thanassis (G) *verstand* from *verstehen*, Stefanos (G) *gang* from *gehen* (target form is *ging*), Ephemia (G) *kam raus* from the verb *rauskommen*, *stand* from *stehen*, *gab's* from *geben*, Nadiye (T) *dachte* from *denken*, and *sagte* from *sagen*, Hasan (T) *sprach* from *sprechen*, Jovanka (Y) *dachte* from *denken*, *klappte* from *klappen*, *kam* from *kommen*, *merkte* from *merken* und Dragica *liebten* from *lieben*.

Although the verb forms are targetlike in appearance, in closer observation that might not be the case at all. For example, one speaker, Hasan (T) uses one preterite-like form, but semantically it represents a present tense construction:

er geht   nach Kneipe   trink   seine Schnaps oder Bier PRO go/3SG
PREP NOUN/3SG   drink/3SG POSS NOUN/3SG CONJ
                                          NOUN
'he go   to bar   drinks   his Schnaps or beer

und   sprach   sprach   sprach   bis morgen früh
CONJ   talk/3SG talk/3SG talk/3SG PREP ADV   ADV
and   talk   talk   talk   until morgen early'

Thanassis (G) used the preterite-like form *verstand* from the verb *verstehen* 'to understand' which occurred in both present and past tense environments and *verlor* from the verb *verlieren* 'to loose' occurs once in a past tense environment. Ephemia (G) used the verb forms *gabs, kam, stand*. In the target these word-forms would occur with a singular subject only (and notice there is no person-number marker for singular subjects). For all the preterite-like verb forms mentioned above, the speakers used them with plural subjects. Three additional speakers used various verb form types as well, but their situation is less clear. Dragica (Y) uses V(t)en once in the corpus and it is accompanied by a plural subject, which corresponds to the target. More evidence is needed in this regard. Nadiye (T), on the other hand, uses the verb form type V(mod)te, as in *ich dachte, ich sagte*. These forms corresponds to the target forms, but these are the only word-forms of this type occurring in the corpus. Jovanka (Y) uses the verb form type V(mod)Ø on seven different occasions in the lexeme *kommen*, expressed by the word-form *kam*. Again this is a target form, but it appears to be restricted only to this one lexeme.

5.2. Past Participle Usage
The past participle of weak verbs[1] is formed by placing the prefix **ge-** before the stem and adding the **-t** or **-et**.

sagen   **ge-sag-t**
antworten   **ge-antwort-et**

In comparison, the past participle of strong verbs is formed with the prefix **ge-** before the stem and the ending **-en** after it. As for the past tense, strong verbs change the stem vowel for the past participle. The resulting vowel may be the same as that of the past tense, that of the infinitive, or a different vowel.

INFINITIVE	PAST TENSE	PAST PARTICIPLE
schreiben	schrieb	geschrieben
biegen	bog	gebogen

fahren	fuhr	gefahren
kommen	kam	gekommen
werfen	warf	geworfen
singen	sang	gesungen

The speakers attempted to produce both types of verbs, but without the use of an auxiliary verb. This is a verb form type that does not occur in the target, nor in any of its other varieties or dialects. This type of verb form in FWG will be discussed in the following section.

5.3. Past Participle-Like or Ge-Forms

These are interesting word-forms because they are not target forms, and all of the sixteen speakers use them. It is also unmarked for person-number, but almost always occurs in past tense environments. It also occurs alone (without an auxiliary verb) in positions where other one part word-forms are used. This word-form type can take one of the following combinations:

ge-Vt	ge-VØ	ge-Ven	ge-V(mod)en/t
gesagt	gearbeit	gekaufen	geboren
gekommt	gekrieg	gegeben	gegangen
gemacht	gekomm	geschlagen	gebracht

All sixteen speakers share this feature, regardless of whether they mark person-number for the other verb forms or not. Some examples of this type of verb form utterances are provided in the following:

ich von   zweiundsiebzig Berlin gekommt
PRO PREP ADV   ADV   come/past
'I from seventy-two   Berlin came'

deutsche Leute   meine Mutti   gefragt
ADJ   NOUN/3PL POSS   NOUN/3SG ask/past
'German people my   mother   asked'

aber meine Tochter   vier Kilo halb wann geboren
CONJ POSS NOUN/3SG NUM   NOUN ADJ CONJ born/past
'but my   daughter four kilos half when born'

und meine kleine Buch Deutsch/Serbo-Kroatisch gekauft
CONJ POSS ADJ   NOUN ADJ   ADJ   buy/past
'and my   small book German/Serbo-Croatian bought'

All of the sixteen speakers use verb forms that are unmarked for tense. Whenever these verb forms occur, the listener may rely on distinguishing between the present, past or future by adverbial markers, context or some other non-linguistic indicator. In addition, these same speakers have a way of marking the past. In reference to the inflectional category of tense, three groups may be observed. In Group 1 only the past participle-like or ge-forms were used with reference to the past. Marija (Y) was the only speaker that restricted herself to just this one type. In Group 2 four speakers are represented: Maja (Y), Kostas (G), Stefanos (G), Thanassis (G). In this group alongside the verb forms unmarked for tense, the ge-forms were used, as well as verb form combinations that were invented by the speakers.

5.4. Auxiliary plus Past Participle

The majority of speakers used the compound verb forms of the auxiliary verb plus the past participle to express the past tense. An interesting feature was that to a larger degree, person-number was marked more often than observed in the other verb forms. This might be explained due to the irregularity of the auxiliary verbs of *haben* and *sein* in the target language. But often the speakers used *sein* instead of *haben*, and *haben* instead of *sein*, as in:

FWG FORMS	TARGET FORMS
hat geblieben	ist geblieben
hat gewesen	ist gewesen
war gemacht	hat gemacht
war gearbeitet	hat gearbeitet

In addition because of the difference between the inflection of the weak versus strong verbs in the target, it has also been observed that the speakers produced nontargetlike forms, as seen below:

FWG FORMS	TARGET FORMS
bin gegang	bin gegangen
bin gekomm	bin gekommen
habe gefundet	habe gefunden
ist gelernen	hat gelernt
hat gekost	hat gekostet

6.0. CONCLUDING REMARKS

What emerges from this discussion is that the first language plays but a minor role in the verbal markers of person-number, and tense in the German of speakers of three different first languages. Furthermore, the claim in the literature that the FWG speakers almost always use the infinitive form of the verb is not supported in this study or previous ones conducted by this author.

Contrary to what we would assume, that is that the first language determines to a large degree what the structure of the second language is, is not supported by the evidence provided in this study. In addition, from other observations that this author has made involving other linguistic aspects of FWG, the same holds true.

The evidence from this study clearly demonstrates that there are two different types of word-forms that the FWG speakers have at their disposal:

1. <u>Word-forms without reference to tense</u>
These types of word-forms occurred in the usage of all of the speakers regardless of how targetlike they were in their usage. The following forms occurred:

VØ, Ven, Ve, Vst + du, Vt, Vet

The examination of all the verb forms that occurred in the usage of each individual speaker shows that unlike the target, where these forms represent present indicative forms, these forms occur in the usage of <u>all</u> speakers in all tense environments. The foreign workers do not consistently mark tense by morphological means. Another point of interest is that in the usage of some of the speakers, some forms were marked for person, not number; or number was marked, but not person. But even the speakers whose usage was closer to the target make use of the unmarked verb forms as well. These forms were generally Ven and VØ.

2. <u>Word-Forms with reference to tense</u>
In the corpus most of the speakers also used word-forms to express tense (generally the past) in several different ways. These word-forms could only be found in contexts with reference to past time.

Finally, there remains still some very interesting questions that demand further investigation:

> 1.Why are there so few inflected strong verb forms in the corpus of data?
> 2.Of the inflected strong verb forms that do occur, how best can be determined if the speakers have internalized the infinitive form of the verb and its inflected forms, or have these speakers learned them inflected forms as lexical entities themselves?
> 3.Or can we see this as a beginning of the inflectional system?

The author has concluded that based on the evidence in the corpus of data pertaining to the weak and strong verbs, the FWG speakers can thus be categorized along a continuum from the least to the most targetlike based on the features in their verbal morphology.

One interesting aspect worthwhile pursuing would be to explore the hypothesis that <u>all</u> native speakers possess the ability to acquire language and regardless of the first language to be acquired, the structure will be the same. In other words, FWG speakers are implementing quasi-universal strategies of linguistic simplification. This poses interesting and intriguing insights into an area of study worthy of further investigation.

NOTES

1. Germany is used here to refer to the former German Democratic Republic which represented East Germany and the former Federal Republic of Germany which represented West Germany.

2. Although the circumstances that contributed to the recruitment of foreign workers in both the former East and West Germany differ, the result has been the same in terms of the linguistic and social conditions of all groups.

3. The German term *Gastarbeiter* is used to indicated the temporary basis on which the workers were brought to the country. The initial idea was that of rotation, that is, that the workers would come to the country for relatively short periods of employment, and then return home to allow the next workers to come to Germany. This idea was not realized by either side due to the great interest of both parties: Germany needed the workers for the country's economic growth, and the foreign workers needed the work to support him-/herself, as well as family members, friends and relatives.

4. This explains clearly why the term *Gastarbeiter* can no longer be used in reference to the workers. In fact, this term has become very derogatory in meaning and attempts have been made to replace it with more acceptable terms. For example, such terms as *ausländische Arbeitnehmer* 'foreign employee' or *ausländische Mitburger* 'foreign fellow citizen' have been suggested. The term *Immigrant* 'immigrant' is unacceptable because Germany still does not consider itself a country of immigration. For the lack of a better term I would therefore like to suggest that researchers use the more appropriate term of "foreign workers" in reference to this population group.

5. Please see e.g. Barkowski et. al, 1979.

6. See Clahsen et al. 1983, and the *Heidelberger Forschungsprojekt* 1975.

7. See Keim 1984.

8. See Mühlhäusler 1986; Holm 1988-89; *Heidelberger Forschungsprojekt 1975*; Blackshire-Belay 1990-91, among others.

9. See Bodemann, Ostow 1977; Tekinay 1984.

10. See Meisel 1980; Hinnenkamp 1982.

11. Data provided by other researchers have not used this as a major criteria. The author of this paper strongly believes that this requirement allows the researcher to assume that the German of these speakers has achieved its maximum state of development or slowed down sufficiently to be considered fossilized.

12. Compound verbs (those verbs that are combined with other words or syllables or prefixes) have been included in the corpus as well, such as the verbs:

fangen	anfangen	auffangen	verfangen
kommen	bekommen	unterkommen	vorwärtskommen
bleiben	verbleiben	stehenbleiben	unterbleiben
gehen	fortgehen	untergehen	entlanggehen

In conjugated verb forms, the SYLLABIC PREFIX (inseparable prefix, bound morpheme) is always connected with the verb stem, whereas the VERB COMPLEMENT (separable prefix, free morpheme) may also occupy a different position in the sentence. The conjugated forms of compound verbs follow the conjugational pattern of the verb stem.

13. If the stem of the verb ends in -d or -t, or if it ends in -m or -n preceded by another consonant (except -l- or -r-), a linking -e- is inserted before the ending of the second and third person singular and the second person plural, for the sake of ease of pronunciation.

14. The omission of the -e- in the infinitive after an -h- occurs only in poetic or in nonstandard colloquial usage: gehn, ziehn, ruhn, etc.

15. For the sake of simplicity, all verb paradigms list only the neuter es for the third person singular. The same ending pattern, to be sure, also applies to the feminine sie (singular) and the neuter es: sie sag-t, es sag-t.

16. The polite (formal, conventional) form of address Sie (used for both singular and plural) always follows the ending pattern of the third person plural: Sie sag-en.

17. The verb *nehmen* also changes the consonants (*nehm-* --> *nimm-*), as in: du *nimmst* and er, sie, es *nimmt*.

18. By analogy, an -ä also sometimes appears on weak verbs: *er frägt*. This, however, is <u>not</u> accepted as standard German.

19. The following verbs CHANGE THEIR STEM, but use the endings of the weak conjugation: brennen (brannte, gebrannt) kennen (kannte, gekannt), nennen (nannte, genannt), rennen (rannte, gerannt), senden (sandte, gesandt), wenden (wandte, gewandt), bringen (brachte, gebracht), denken (dachte, gedacht).

20. The vowels change according to definite patterns, the so-called *A blaut* classes. The consonants at the end of the stem change according to Verner's Law (*Grammatischer Wechsel*) regarding the unvoicing or transformation of final consonants, e.g. **d > tt**: leiden, litt; **h > g**: ziehen, zog; **s > r**: erkiesen, erkor. The doubling of consonants, loss of a double consonant, and a change from **tz** to **ß** are among some of the other consonant changes found in the class of strong verbs.

21. The present perfect and the past perfect tenses are formed with the auxiliary verbs *haben* or *sein*. These are called compound tenses.

184   Second Language Acquisition and Development

REFERENCES

Barkowski, H., U. Harnisch and S. Kumm. 1979. Sprachlernen mit Arbeitsmigranten im Wohnbezirk. Deutsch Lernen 1/79:5-16.

Blackshire-Belay, C. 1991. Language Contact: Verb Morphology in German of Foreign Workers. Tübingen: Gunter Narr Verlag.

Blackshire-Belay, C. 1990. "The Role of the Subject NP in Foreign Workers' German," Proceedings of the 10th Second Language Research Forum, (eds. Hartmut Burmeister, Patricia L. Rounds), The University of Oregon Press, pp. 221-232.

Blackshire-Belay, C. 1989. Sociolinguistic Problems of Foreign Workers in the Federal Republic and West Berlin. University of Pennsylvania Review of Linguistics 13, 47-58.

Bodemann, Y. and R. Ostow. 1975. Lingua Franca und Pseudo-Pidgin in der Bundesrepublik: Fremdarbeiter und Einheimischer im Sprachzusammenhang. Sprache Ausländischer Arbeiter. Zeitschrift für Literaturwissenschaft und Linguistik 18: 122-46.

Borris, M. 1973. Ausländische Arbeiter in einer Großstadt. Eine empirische Untersuchung am Beispiel Frankfurt. Frankfurt: Europäische Verlagsanstalt.

Clahsen, H. 1980. Psycholinguistic aspects of L2 acquisition: Word order phenomena in foreign workers' interlanguage. Second Language Development, ed. by S. Felix, 57-79. Tübingen: Gunter Narr.

Clyne, M. 1968. Zum Pidgin-Deutsch der Gastarbeiter. Zeitschrift für Mundartforschung 35: 130-9.

Decamp, D. 1977. The development of pidgin and creole studies. Pidgin and Creole Linguistics, ed. by A. Valdman, 3-20. Bloomington: Indiana University Press.

Dittmar, N. and W. Klein. 1979. Developing grammars: The acquisition of German syntax by foreign workers. Berlin/Heidelberg: Springer-Verlag.

Felix, S. (ed.) 1980. Second Language Development. Tübingen: Narr.

Felix, S.W. 1977. Interference, interlanguage and related issues. Deutsch im Kontakt mit anderen Sprachen/German in contact with other languages, ed. by C. Molony, H. Zobl, and W. Stölting, 184-212. Kronberg/Ts.: Scriptor Verlag.

Ferguson, C. and C. DeBose. 1977. Simplified registers, broken language and pidginization. Pidgin and Creole Linguistics, ed. by A. Valdman, 99-125. Bloomington: Indiana University Press.

Fox, J. 1977. Implications of the jargon/pidgin dichotomy for social and linguistic analysis of the Gastarbeiter pidgin German speech community. Deutsch im Kontakt mit anderen Sprachen/German in contact with other languages, ed. by C. Molony et. al, 40-6. Kronberg/Ts.: Scripton Verlag.

Gilbert, G.G. 1978. Review of Klein (ed.) Sprache ausländischer Arbeiter. Language 54: 983-7.

Hall, R.A. 1966. Pidgin and creole languages. Ithaca: Cornell University Press.

Grimshaw, Allan D. 1971. Some social forces and some social functions of pidgin and creole languages.Pidginization and Creolization of Language, ed. by D. Hymes, 427-446. Cambridge: Cambridge University Press.

Heidelberger Forschungsprojekt: Pidgin Deutsch. 1975. Sprache und Kommunikation ausländischer Arbeiter. Kronberg/Ts.: Scriptor Verlag.

Heidelberger Forschungsprojekt: Pidgin Deutsch 1977. Aspekte der ungesteuerten Erlernung des Deutschen durch ausländische Arbeiter. Deutsch im Kontakt mit anderen Sprachen/German in contact with other languages, ed. by C. Molony et. al., 147-183. Kronberg/Ts.: Scriptor Verlag.

Hinnenkamp, V. 1982. Foreigner Talk und Tarzanisch. Hamburg: Buske.

Holm, J. 1988-89. Pidgins and Creoles. Vol. 1: Theory and Structure; Vol. 2: Reference Survey. Cambridge: Cambridge University Press.

Keim, I. 1978. Gastarbeiter Deutsch. Untersuchungen zum sprachlichen Verhalten türkischer Gastarbeiter. Tübingen: Gunter Narr Verlag.

Keim, I. 1982. Kommunkikation ausländischer Arbeiter. Studie zum deutschsprachigen Interaktionsverhalten von griechischen und türkischen Arbeitern. Tübingen: Gunter Narr Verlag.

Keim, I. 1984. Untersuchungen zum Deutsch türkischer Arbeite. Tübingen: Gunter Narr Verlag.

Klein, W. 1974. Variation in der Sprache. Kronberg/Ts.: Scriptor.

Meisel, J. 1980. 'Linguistic simplification', in Felix 1980: 13-46.

Meisel, J., H., Clahsen and M. Pienemann. 1979. On determining the developmental stages in natural second-language acquisition. Wuppertaler Arbeitspapier zur Sprachwissenschaft, No. 2: 1-53.

Meisel, J. 1975. Ausländerdeutsch und Deutsch ausländischer Arbeiter. Zur möglichen Entstehung eines Pidgins in der B.R.D. Sprache ausländischer Arbeiter. Zeitschrift für Literaturwissenschaft und Linguistik 18: 9-53.

Mühlhäusler, P. 1986. Pidgin and Creole Linguistics. Oxford: Blackwell.

Orlovic-Schwarzwald, M. 1978. Zum Gastarbeiterdeutsch jugoslawischer Arbeiter im Rhein-Main-Gebiet. Eine empirische Untersuchungen zur Morphologie und zum ungesteuerten Erwerb des Deutschen durch Erwachsene. Wiesbaden: Steiner.

Pienemann, M. 1978. Überlegungen zur Steuerung des Zweitspracherwerbs ausländischer Arbeiterkinder. Wuppertaler Arbeitspapiere zur Sprachwissenschaft No. I:38-61.

Stölting, W. 1975. Wie die Ausländer sprechen: Eine jugoslawische Familie. Sprache ausländische Arbeiter. Zeitschrift für Literaturwissenschaft und Linguistik 18. ed. by H. Kreuzer, 54-67.

Tekinay, A. 1984. 'Wie eine "Mischsprache" entsteht', Muttersprache, No. 5-6, pp. 396-403.

Weinrich, U. 1953. Languages in contact. Findings and problems. The Hague: Mouton.

Whinnom, K. 1971. Linguistic hybridization and the special case of pidgins and creoles. Pidginization and creolization of language, ed. by D. Hymes, 91-115. Cambridge: Cambridge University Press.

Zweitspracherwerb italienischer und spanischer Arbeiter 1983. Deutsch als Zweitsprache. Der Spracherwerb ausländischer Arbeiter. Tübingen: Gunter Narr Verlag.

SKETCH OF AN INTERLANGUAGE RULE SYSTEM: ADVANCED NONNATIVE GERMAN GENDER ASSIGNMENT[1]

Joe Salmons
Purdue University

1.0. INTRODUCTION

In this chapter, I compare evidence on the gender assignment rules of a group of native speakers of German with the parallel rule system of a group of advanced but nonnative German speakers with substantial formal instruction in the language. Advanced nonnative speakers need functioning rule systems to assign gender to German nouns they do not know, but these rules will be shown to differ significantly and systematically from those of native speakers. That is, the nonnative speakers discussed here will be shown to have developed interlanguage rule systems for assigning gender to German nouns. My goals are first to present data on gender assignment to foreign words by nonnatives, an issue which has never really been treated in the literature, and second to outline some parts of the interlanguage system(s) found in these data.

The problem of gender assignment for the speaker of German is no small one. German gender assignment rules are, in fact, so complex and so obscure that a variety of linguists in recent years have denied that the entire matter constitutes rule-governed behavior. Maratsos (1979: 235), for example, describes German gender assignment as "arbitrary" and declares that "no underlying rationale can be guessed at". de Bleser & Bayer (1988: 51) label gender "...idiosyncratic in German. Thus it must be encoded in each gender-bearing lexical element." Lapointe (1988: 83) does not deny rhyme or reason to gender assignment, but says that "in many languages, certainly in the familiar European ones, any semantic relations underlying gender distinctions seem hopelessly obscure." Heath (1985: 105) warns against searching for the "meaning" of noun classes, dismissing as "academic" the question of "...whether or not there is any synchronic motivation for the assignment of" a particular word to a particular class. These statements reflect two somewhat different views of German gender assignment: (1) that no rules exist and (2) that if any rules do exist, they are unimportant. Both set of claims might be taken to violate perhaps the single most important assumption that linguists make, sometimes implicitly and sometimes explicitly, namely that language constitutes rule-governed behavior. Language acquisition must then be seen as the learning of a system of rules which are language-particular but follow certain universal constraints. If the rules are--in this case, the rules for German gender assignment--are so unclear to linguists, then it is hardly surprising that natives find the matter baffling and that nonnatives despair.

There is a long and extensive tradition of research on how native speakers assign gender to loanwords and other lexical innovations, and on the workings of gender assignment rules within the lexicon (see Corbett 1986 for a detailed bibliography). This research indicates that German gender assignment is definitely rule-governed, although it shows numerous exceptions as is common with lexical phenomena. Moreover, German gender assignment cannot in any way be seen as peripheral to the grammar of German: every noun in the German lexicon must be associated with a gender, and gender assignment is productive in regular ways for the steady stream of new lexical items being constantly added to German.[2] Still, relatively little has been written on how nonnative speakers deal with this complex problem (but see Rogers (1987)) and virtually nothing about how advanced learners deal with it.

One fairly common view of the acquisition of a second language (henceforth L2) is that L2 acquirers develop an interlanguage, i.e. rule systems close (and ever closer) to those of the target language but not identical to the target. I will adopt this interlanguage hypothesis as a framework for investigating nonnative gender assignment in German in this study. The interlanguage hypothesis, originally proposed by Selinker (1972) and greatly developed since, generally invokes a number of principles to account for these intermediate grammars, including interference, simplification and (over-) generalization.[3] English grammar does not organize nouns into classes in the manner that German gender does[4], so that English speakers learning German therefore have no general parallel to German gender--the role of gender in English grammar is trivial by comparison. This difference would seem to exclude direct interference and would then leave simplification and generalization as the two governing principles for English speakers learning German.[5]

The situation here is somewhat more complex than for many other interlanguage rule systems, since L2 learners and native speakers of German alike often tend to believe that no rule system for gender assignment exists. This holds at least for the lexicon beyond a few basic patterns such as natural gender and certain derivational suffixes categorically associated with a particular gender. Textbooks and most pedagogical grammars seldom present any rules at all for gender assignment beyond natural gender.[6] Thus, acquisition of this rule system is per force unconscious. With no even approximate model from their native language and no substantial explicit instruction on how gender assignment works, native English speakers--like speakers of other languages without grammatical gender--must formulate gender assignment strategies for themselves based purely on data, namely the German nouns they know the gender for.[7] Put another way, if we think of L2 acquisition in terms of acquiring rules (in traditional terms) or developing patterns, the question here becomes which of several possible types of rules or patterns are invoked by the learner.[8]

This paper represents a small step along this barely explored road. After a brief overview of gender assignment in German and the data and data collection, I will turn to a comparison of gender assignment among native and nonnative speakers, organized by various rule types, phonetic/phonological, morphological and semantic. The data show that few of the advanced nonnatives in my study have acquired more than a handful of the most salient rules for gender assignment to loanwords. For example, many of the nonnatives studied here lack some firmly established morphological rules found among natives and the semantic rules they do appeal to function quite differently than for the natives.

2.0. OVERVIEW OF GERMAN GENDER ASSIGNMENT

What is gender assignment in German and how do natives assign gender? Modern German has three grammatical genders, traditionally referred to as masculine, feminine and neuter or by the appropriate nominative form of the definite article, *der, die, das*, respectively. As illustrated in (1), these are not marked directly on the noun itself, but rather are marked primarily on determiners.[9] These genders are marked only in the singular; no surface distinction whatsoever is made based on gender in the plural. Nominal inflection in German is organized around gender, i.e. paradigms--at least in the singular--are based on gender and the four cases of Standard German (nominative, accusative, dative and genitive):

(1)	Masculine	Feminine	Neuter	Plural (all genders)
Nom	*der* gute Mann	*die* gute Frau	*das* gute Kind	*die* guten Kinder
Acc	*den* guten Mann	*die* gute Frau	*das* gute Kind	*die* guten Kinder
Dat	*dem* guten Mann	*der* guten Frau	*dem* guten Kind	*den* guten Kindern
Gen	*des* guten Mannes	*der* guten Frau	*des* guten Kindes	*der* guten Kinder
	'the good man'	'the good woman'	'the good child'	'the good children'

The many and often complex criteria used to describe gender assignment can be broken down as follows: 1) rules operating within the lexicon (including both phonetic and semantic rules) and 2) derivational rules (e.g., that a compound takes the gender of its head, the rightmost element). These criteria will be discussed at more length later, but a few examples of semantic and phonetic-phonological criteria may make the following discussion easier to follow.[10]

First, natural gender tends to stipulate grammatical gender; that is, masculine beings tend to be *der* (*der Vater* 'the father', *der Bruder* 'the brother') and feminine beings tend to be *die* (*die Mutter* 'the mother', *die Schwester* 'the sister'). Still, there are a few well-known and often-cited exceptions, often derogatory, such as:

> 2) das Weib   'broad bitch'
>   das Mensch   'slut'
>   die Wache   'guard (military), watchperson'

and among loanwords:

das Girl
der Girlfriend
der Stripper.

Second, words which are superordinates (terms denoting classes or groups of items) tend, although somewhat less powerfully than natural gender assignments, to be neuter, an issue treated at length by Zubin & Küpcke (1986 and elsewhere). They have established a number of other, somewhat more tenuous categories:

3)   power/strength --> feminine die Kraft, Macht, Gewalt
                                     all meaning 'power' or 'force'

        games   --> neuter   das Poker 'poker'

        waste   --> masculine   der Dreck 'muck, shit'

        Gestalt: line --> masculine der Stock 'stick'

        pointed objects--> feminine die Spitze, Klinge, Nadel
                                     'point, blade, needle'

Phonetic and phonological rules are not categorical. Nouns ending in a high front unrounded vowel (orthographic -ie, -y, -i, etc.) are overwhelmingly feminine (as in the first half of 4), below), except for -i suffixes indicating humans, where a rule usually described as a natural gender rule generally overrides the phonetic tendency, as in the second half of 4).[11] -i words for humans generally show up as masculine while words referring specifically to women can be assigned feminine.

4) die Apathie   'apathy'
   die Theorie   'theory'
   die Batterie   'battery', etc.

But:

   der Hirni   'dummy, idiot'
   der Alki   'drunk, alkie'
   die Tussi   'girl, girlfriend'

Monosyllabics ending in nasal plus consonant are largely masculine (*der Sand* 'sand'), while monosyllabics in /ft/, /çt/, /xt/ tend to be feminine:[12]

5) die Luft   'air'
   die Schicht   'shift'
   die Schlacht   'battle', etc.

This tendency is, however, overridden by the *Ge-* prefix, which usually invokes fronting or umlaut of the stem vowel as well. Note that this occurs in many cases with superordinates (which tend to be neuter), as in 6). This is particularly important as an example of a semantic tendency overriding a phonological tendency.

6) das Getränk   'drink, beverage'
   das Gehöft   'farm, farmstead'

Other phonetic or phonological tendencies include word-final schwa (i.e., orthographic *-e*) --> feminine (*die Erde* 'the earth', *die Pflanze* 'the plant'), monosyllabics beginning with *kn-* --> masculine (*der Knall* 'the bang', *der Knast* 'the slammer, joint') and so forth. Until the relatively recent work by for instance Zubin & Küpcke and Mills, little attention had been devoted to the interaction among these various sets of rules. Traditionally, the attempt has been made to distinguish between rules and their domains rather than looking at the overlap between or among rules. Several gender assignment rules or tendencies reflect the convergence of two or three criteria, such as the overlap between superordinates and *Ge-* derivatives. Note that a tendency toward such redundancy of criteria would reflect an economical organization of the lexicon.[13]

This interaction is relatively complex, in that certain segments of the vocabulary may be more or less sensitive to particular tendencies. For instance, well-established loanwords can tend to follow semantic rules even where relatively strong phonetic/phonological rules exist, a point I have treated elsewhere (Salmons in press) and one to which we will return briefly below. That is, semantic rules may be more likely to override phonetic/phonological rules for loanwords than is the case in native vocabulary.

3. 0. DATA AND DATA COLLECTION
To gather data on the rule systems of advanced L2 learners of German, a questionnaire was used consisting of almost 100 English words, which might be borrowed into German or used as nonce borrowings in German spoken in the United States (see appendix). As will be treated in more depth below, only a few of the words from this list have actually been loaned, i.e. are included in standard lexica, and these are generally not widely used nor even known as loans among nonnatives, judging from among other things their gender assignment. The rationale for using English words was to ensure that all speakers tested associated meaning with the items, so that semantic considerations could be incorporated in addition to phonological and morphological characteristics.

Informants were asked to fill in a definite article for each of the nouns listed. They were specifically asked for quick, intuitive responses. In addition to the gender assignment itself, nonnatives were asked the following biographical questions: (1) whether they speak more English, more German, or about half of each in their daily lives at the time they filled out the questionnaire; (2) how many years they had spent in German-speaking countries; (3) the age at which they started learning German. Such biographical information might be relevant to the acquisition of the rules in question, but they clearly cannot be understood as an indicator of proficiency in German, which was controlled only by the subjects' faculty or graduate student status in the three German departments surveyed. While the biographical information will not be dealt with at length here, I should note that preliminary analysis does not indicate any powerful (perhaps not even significant) correlation of any of these factors with differences in gender assignment rules.

Data came from 35 native speakers of German (who all knew and used English, albeit with a wide range of proficiency) and 38 nonnatives, 36 of those native speakers of English.[14] Informants came from among the faculty, staff and graduate students from three large German departments in the United States: University of Texas at Austin, Indiana University-Bloomington, and Purdue University-West Lafayette. Natives and nonnatives were asked if they would be willing to fill out a brief questionnaire assigning German gender to some English nouns. This study does not, then, reflect the speech of a single speech community--beyond an extremely broad sense of that term: Germanists in large departments in the United States--but rather the speech of three parallel academic communities. The majority of informants were specialists in or students of literature, pedagogy, or philology.[15]

Note that this population is radically different from those acquiring German in informal settings in German-speaking situations. Such work would no doubt find substantially different mechanisms for gender assignment. For example, my fieldwork among third to sixth generation German-American bilinguals in small towns in Texas and Indiana has found a propensity to avoid use of gender marking, particularly in prepositional phrases with loaned or native German nouns. Carol Blackshire-Belay (personal communication) reports similar phenomena among foreign workers in Germany, particularly with loanwords from their native languages.

4.0. GENDER ASSIGNMENT: NATIVE VERSUS NONNATIVE SPEAKERS
In this section, I turn to the question of what native rules or patterns this group of nonnatives has acquired, including examples from the rule types noted in section 2. I have divided this section according to those types: 1) phonetic/phonological, 2) morphological, and 3) semantic, in addition to a fourth brief section on loanword gender as seen in the questionnaire data.

4.1. Phonetic/phonological tendencies

Predictably, the patterns or rules most widely acquired by members of this group are the more common ones. Let us begin with a phonetic/phonological rule: -*i*: - -> feminine. This rule is among the best known and most powerful of the rules for native and thoroughly nativized items. It applies for usually more than 90% of the native speakers. In these cases the closest semantic equivalent is generally also feminine, for example the English word from the list *Bakery* (97.1% feminine) has a cognate which is its closest semantic equivalent, namely *die Bäckerei*.[16] Two exceptions to this tendency appear where the equivalent is not feminine, and both of these show up as neuter for native speakers in the questionnaire data: Country (88.6% neuter) = *das Land and Valley* (88.6% neuter) = *das Tal*.

Nonnatives agree on the majority of items showing both -*i*: and a closest semantic equivalent with feminine gender: *Bakery* (92.1% feminine), *Dairy* (92.1% feminine) = *die Molkerei*, etc., including one established loanword: *Prairie* (natives 100% feminine, nonnatives 92.1%). However, for those cases where the closest semantic equivalent is not feminine--and natives assigned gender based on semantic grounds rather than on the basis of the final vowel-nonnatives are split largely between feminine and neuter:

7)	der	die	das
Country	13.2	39.5	47.4
Valley	16.2	45.9	37.8

This could indicate either of two related situations, first that the semantic criterion here overrides the phonetic one. Second, the phonetic tendency, while common throughout the lexicon, might not be productive. Either way, many of the nonnative speakers have overgeneralized the native rule.

Let us turn now to another phonetic/phonological rule tested in the questionnaire which proves substantially more problematic, and which brings to the fore differences between gender assignment for loanwords versus native vocabulary. This is the tendency for words ending in the affricate /č/ (sometimes transcribed in German linguistics as /tš/) to be overwhelmingly masculine within the native vocabulary. I have observed elsewhere (Salmons ms.) that established nineteenth and twentieth century loanwords from English ending in /č/, in contrast, show only a vague tendency toward masculine, while many appear instead to follow semantic tendencies. The questionnaire data support this as a general tendency for new loans and potential loans. In fact this set of items showed some of the greatest variation found in the entire questionnaire among native speakers, as seen in 8):[17]

8)	Native			Nonnative		
	der	die	das	der	die	das
Beach	40	60	0	68.4	15.8	15.8
Peach	47.1	50	2.9	42.1	31.6	26.3

Beach might be explained as the result of conflicting semantic equivalents: *der Strand* and *die Küste*. I have no idea why Peach would show equally great variability among native speakers.

Given the neutralization of voicing distinction in word final position in German, this tendency might be extended to items with original final /ʒ/, such as *Language and Garbage* (discussed in section 3.3 below). However, both of these follow semantic criteria clearly, the former being assigned feminine gender by 100% of the natives and by 94.7% of the nonnatives, while the latter was 68.6% masculine among natives and showed no clear trends among nonnatives. Note that Gregor (1983: 92-95) connects this suffix with the French *-age* /a: ʒ(ə)/ suffix. Gregor sees the English-derived suffix as having no gender-assigning power, based on two examples where assignment was based on semantic features, *Advantage* (*der*) and *Cottage* (*das*, from an original die at the time when the word had a French pronunciation in German).

4.2. Morphological tendencies
Among the morphological tendencies, specifically suffixal rules were tested. While German has some morphological tendencies related to prefixes such as *Ge-* --> neuter, *Ver-/Be-* --> masculine, these are not categorical as many of the suffixal rules are. Moreover, English shares few of these prefixes. For these reasons then, prefixes were not tested.

The simplest morphological tendency in the data is perhaps -šən-Extension, Education, Promotion-where native speakers and nonnative speakers alike consistently assigned feminine over 90% of the time. Note that this suffix is realized phonetically very differently in German, but given cognates, orthographic parallels, etc., the population tested would be expected to identify these suffixes with one another.

Almost as clear were items ending in *-er--Counter, Hanger, Pencil sharpener, Drawer*--all of which showed from around 90 up to 100% masculine among native speakers. Among nonnative speakers, the trend was the same for most items, although Drawer showed only 60.5% masculine and 28.9% feminine, presumably by comparison to German *die Lade* (or perhaps more commonly *Schublade*)[18] The fact that the *-er* terms all appear as masculine without any straightforward semantic motivation would support the contention that, at least for loanwords, *-er* has some weight as a productive morphological tendency.

The suffix -ən(t)s (with some variation in the unstressed vowel) found in Insurance, Preference, etc. is generally rendered feminine in the corpus, over 90% for natives and around 80% for nonnatives. Gregor (1983: 98-99) argues that this is based on close similarities in form and meaning to the German -enz suffix. However, one significant exception occurs: Ambulance shows a very direct semantic equivalent assigned masculine gender, namely der Krankenwagen. The semantic equivalent overriding the suffix is the most promising explanation for this.[19]

The cases treated thus far in this section show a close match between German and English in phonetic shape and/or morphemes. The pattern can be extended to somewhat less precise matches. -ship [šɪþ] matches German -schaft in general form and in meaning as well. Partnership and Relationship both showed a clear tendency toward feminine among native speakers (77.1% and 85.7% respectively) with similar although somewhat lower numbers for nonnative speakers. Sponsorship showed ca. 63% feminine for natives and nonnatives alike with a notable minority choosing neuter.

Moving now to morphological rules which differ more significantly between natives and nonnatives, let us look at two examples, the suffixes -ment and -ing. First, the suffix -ment shows generally 90-100% neuter for natives and often somewhat below 50% for nonnatives. That is, less than half of the nonnative speakers have acquired the native rule assigning -ment suffixes to neuter. Among the rest of the nonnatives, there appears to be some tendency toward using the gender of the closest German equivalent (i.e. a semantic criterion), as seen in the examples presented in 9) with the most likely German equivalents.

9)	Native			Nonnative			
	der	_die_	_das_	_der_	_die_	_das_	
Advertisement	2.9	2.9	94.3	26.3	34.2	39.5	(die Werbung, Reklame)
Basement	5.7	0	94.3	42.1	10.5	47.4	(der Keller)
Department	0	0	100	15.8	31.6	52.6	(die Abteilung)
Treatment	2.9	5.7	91.4	27	40.5	32.4	(die Behandlung)

Second, -ing shows a similar pattern of divergence between the two groups, as in 10).

10)		Native			Nonnative		
		der	die	das	der	die	das
Roofing	6.1	0	93.9	21.1	36.8	42.1	(die -ung)
Air Conditioning	8.6	25.7	65.	77.9	63.2	28.9	(die Klimaanlage)
Casing	3.0	6.1	90.9	28.9	44.8	26.3	(der Überzug, die Hülle)
Covering	17.6	8.8	73.5	13.2	52.6	34.2	(die Decke, die Hülle, etc.)
Meeting	2.9	0	97.1	7.9	36.8	44.7	(die Sitzung)

Native speakers clearly appear to treat -ing items as deverbatives-- derivation which leads categorically to neuter gender in German--rather than identifying them with -ung, a very productive abstract suffix (cf. Gregor 1983: 116-117).[20]

Only the most salient of the morphological tendencies then appear to have been acquired by the nonnatives sampled. Note also that the last two suffixes treated are represented by numerous well-established loanwords. These include -*ment* and -*ing* items such as *Advertisement* and *Treatment*, both included in the questionnaire (cf. also Gregor (1983: 126-127)) and Dressing, Marketing, Merchandising, and Meeting, the last of these also on the questionnaire (cf. Gregor (1983: 115-117)). Still, less than half of the nonnative sample had acquired these rules.

4.3. Semantic tendencies
The semantic tendencies tested by the questionnaire include two items for the relatively powerful tendency for words in the semantic field "waste" to be masculine. *Garbage* and *Trash* both showed substantially stronger tendencies toward masculine among native than among nonnatives:

11)	Native			Nonnative		
	der	die	das	der	die	das
Garbage	68.6	5.7	25.7	28.9	47.4	23.7
Trash	85.7	2.9	11.4	71.1	2.6	26.3

In the first item, a sound-based/morphological rule competes with the semantic one, namely the strong tendency for -age words (generally French loans) to be feminine. This had virtually no effect among native speakers, but presumably had a strong effect on the nonnative speakers, almost half of whom assigned feminine, presumably largely on this basis. Trash, on the other hand, is supported in its semantic tendency by phonetic/phonological factors pointing toward masculine: the *tr*-Anlaut, monosyllabicity, and possibly the final /š/.

The most problematic aspect of the corpus with respect to the native speaker data is probably the occasional case where semantic factors override sound-based or morphological tendencies. Predicting when such factors come into play remains problematic even in view of Zubin & Küpcke's work. Evidence on how closest semantic equivalents are accessed could prove useful here. Some words have more immediate equivalents in another language (words with a single translation, for example) than others (such as polysemous items), and the former might be more quickly accessed than the latter. For example, numerous nouns, especially those denoting concrete objects, have relatively close one-to-one correlations from English to German: *Basement* vs *Keller*, *Ambulance* vs *Krankenwagen*, etc. These English words have closer semantic equivalents in German than some others showing less consistent gender assignment. For instance, a word like Amount can be considered to have a less clear semantic equivalent because it carries meanings rendered by several distinct German items representing all three genders: *der Betrag, die Menge, die Summe, das Ausmaß*, among others depending on context. This might be the case for some other instances noted above, such as the inconsistent responses for Drawer. My impression is that the more quickly the equivalent can be found, the greater the likelihood that semantic tendencies will come into play, although this speculation reaches far beyond the goals of the present essay.

4.4. Loanwords
Finally, a word should be said about those words contained in the questionnaire which represent relatively established loanwords in contemporary Standard German, and words which are familiar to most native speakers. In general, few nonnatives had acquired these items, even though many are in widespread colloquial usage and some are directly relevant to everyday life or even to the specific academic environment in the United States. Only a few items showed more than half of nonnatives choosing the Standard German gender:

12)	Native	Nonnative
Prairie (die)	100	92.1
Business (das)	85.7	65.8
College (das)	97.1	55.3

A number of other common items showed far greater differences, such as:

13)		
Fairness (die)	91.4	29.7
Box (die)	94.3	28.9
Farm (die)	97.1	42.1
Happiness (die)	82.4	42.1

This evidence indicates that many advanced nonnatives have not acquired some very widely known and often used loanwords, items which one regularly encounters in reading the German press for instance. This extends to words central to the daily vocabulary of the academic environment in which all of these people work, such as *Department* (100% neuter among natives, just over half neuter among nonnatives) and *Meeting* (97.1% das among natives and only 44.7 das among nonnatives.)

5.0. CONCLUSIONS

A number of observations can be made based on this brief discussion of the character of the interlanguage systems of nonnative German speakers. Only highly salient and widely applied tendencies appear to have been learned by the nonnatives tested, e.g. the sound-based rule -*i* --> feminine. About half of the nonnative speakers are missing some well-established morphological rules, e.g. -*ment* --> neuter and -*ing* --> neuter are virtually categorical for native speakers but have not been learned by most nonnative speakers. In the absence of other rules, nonnatives often tend to use closest semantic equivalent, for example with words in -*ment*. The nonnatives also appear to have developed different rules from natives for some suffixes, e.g. the rule found among many nonnatives making -*ing* feminine, presumably motivated by the close similarity to categorical -*ung* --> feminine for natives. The German suffix is often rendered as [æä] in colloquial speech, close to the [Iŋ] of the English, which is sometimes also reduced.

The role of semantic equivalents is in some ways different for natives and nonnatives. Natives override other considerations fairly often to follow semantic tendencies. Although it cannot yet be easily predicted exactly when and how, the examples of this sort cited here would be consistent with the suggestion that more salient or closer semantic equivalents in German aid in overriding other gender assigning tendencies. At any rate, it is hardly surprising that nonnatives miss such cues, following instead other criteria for gender assignment.

Also striking among the group studied was the fact that frequent and well-established items had not been acquired, even when the nouns in question refer directly to aspects of the environment in which these speech communities exist, e.g. *Department* and *College*.

The interlanguage rule system sketched in broad outlines here is a particularly difficult one, given the complete absence of any even vague parallel in English and the near total lack of attention given to gender assignment rules (at this level of complexity) in the German pedagogical tradition. Working under these difficult circumstances, nonnative speakers of German appear unable to develop rules like those of native speakers, but do to an extent appear to develop a rule system.

NOTES

1. I am happy to be able to thank the following people for various comments on earlier versions of this manuscript and discussions on this topic: Carol A. Blackshire-Belay, Margie Berns, Greg Humpa, Monica Macaulay, and Dan Nützel. All mistakes of fact or interpretations are of course mine alone.

2. It should be noted that German speakers face very high numbers of lexical innovations and most natives coin items themselves. This is possible for several   reasons, most notably the great derivational flexibility, the common tendency toward compounding and the quick acceptance of loans from the numerous languages with which German has ongoing contacts.

3. See works such as Appel and Muysken (1988: 83-92), Hamers and Blanc (1989: 225-228), Preston (1989), and Ioup and Weinberger (1987) for additional discussion on the notion of interlanguage.

4. Because the data for this study come from such a language, I cannot deal here with gender assignment from the base language. Clearly, though this would be a central topic for those studying gender assignment by native speakers of Greek or French, for example.

5. Note here the crucial difference between the present project and much work on interlanguage, which explicitly aims to determine the role of transfer or L1 interference.

6. The *Duden Grammatik* is an exception here although it can hardly be counted as a pedagogical grammar, see Grebe et al (1973: 149-162).

7. Athough I cannot substantiate the claim, it is my very distinct impression that many nonnatives who have learned German in formal settings are disinclined to use loanwords or other lexical innovations, which is where the productivity of gender assignment becomes most apparent. Moreover, as Carol Blackshire-Belay has pointed out to me, many other nonnatives (who have more likely acquired German in informal settings) use loanwords, but without any determiner to mark gender assignment. This avoidance, if confirmed, could be the result of a combination of several factors such as the strong prescriptive tradition in American German studies, and the resultant feeling among nonnatives that they should strive to use "real" and "proper" German.

8. This use of "pattern" is loosely based on that found in Natural Morphology (e.g., Bybee 1988).

9. Gender is also marked on relative pronouns and on adjectives within the same NP (albeit not as distinctly on adjectives following a definite article), etc. but the most characteristic marking is that given in (1).

10. See also Mills (1986: 27-35), the various works of Zubin & Köpcke, as well as Augst (1973: 149-164). These sources are some of the most recent and sophisticated attempts to uncover the relevant rule system(s). Earlier studies reach back into the nineteenth century (see Wilson 1899-1900) and are overwhelmingly descriptive attempts, although a number of scholars, such as Lang (1976), have contributed substantially. For loanwords in particular, Gregor (1983) has been most useful, with additional reference to Schlick (1984, 1985). The closest project to the present one is perhaps Clyne (1969), which compared gender assignment for English items between Germans with and without knowledge of English.

11. -*i* suffixes are particularly common and productive in German youth language, where they tend to follow the same rules. See Moehle-Vieregge (1989: 160-168).

12. If we could add /st/ to this group, it would form an obvious natural class: voiceless fricatives plus /t/. /st/ however shows just over half of the approximately 50 items I checked as masculine, even leaving natural gender aside.

13. In touching on more basic theoretical issues surrounding gender assignment, it is perhaps important to note the distinction between the lexical-derivational domain of gender assignment clearly from the inflectional-syntactic function of gender. While assignment to a gender class rests on semantic and/or phonetic-phonological characteristics, once assigned, gender classes clearly "serve as syntactic devices permitting accurate cross-referencing and anaphora" (heath 1985: 104). The assignment to a class does not appear particularly relevant to the syntactic and inflectional uses of genders.

14. One of the two nonnative English speakers was Hungarian-American and the other a native speaker of Swedish who is near-native in English.

15. Naturally occurring conversational data might have been preferable especially for the nonnatives, who as a group show far greater variability in gender assignment. However, such data would be virtually impossible to collect, given the infrequency of loans in nonnative speech. Basically, the data treated here are much more like data used by linguists concerned with competence than that used by linguists concerned with performance, i.e. more like generative than sociolinguistic data.

16. The term "semantic equivalent" has been traditionally invoked in discussions of loanword gender. I use it here with the caveat, developed somewhat below, that such equivalency across languages must be understood along a continuum of more or less equivalent. This is of course parallel to problems with synonymity within a single language. Note also that capitalization of examples follows that used on the questionnaire.

17. Only a small group of monosyllabics showed greater variation-*Bag, Bid, Dish, Vote*-none of which showed even a majority choosing one gender. In several of these cases, conflicting tendencies exist, e.g. the two convenient semantic equivalents of *Bag, der Sack* and *die Tüte*.

18. Monica Macaulay (p.c.) suggests that the lack of transparency of -*er* as a suffix in Drawer might be at work here.

19. The fourth - nts example form the corpus, Sentence, showed some of the greatest variation among native speakers found in the entire project, with just over half masculine and the rest split evenly between feminine and neuter. This variation was paralleled by the results from the nonnatives.

20. Note that, as has been discussed elsewhere, German-American communities show a clear tendency to treat deverbal -*ing* suffixes as feminine (see the extended discussion in Salmons (in press)). That is, native speakers have shown the tendency found here among nonnatives, under different circumstances, most notably perhaps the absence of influence of the standard language.

Appendix: List of items tested

Advertisement, Agency, Agreement, Air Conditioning, Ambulance, Amount, Approach, Avenue, Axle, Bag, Bakery, BBQ, Basement, Beach, Bid, Box, Breakdown, Bulb, Bunch, Business, Car, Casing, College, Community, Counter, Country, Covering, Creek, Crowd, Curb, Dairy, Department, Dish, Drawer, Drink, Education, Engine, Excuse, Extension, Fairness, Fan, Farm, Fee, Fence, Front, Fuse, Garbage, Grade, Grease, Hanger, Happiness, Insurance, Jail, Kick, Language, Laundry, Legislature, Library, Meeting, Mistake, Mixture, Neighborhood, Office, Paint, Partnership, Pasture, Pavement, Peach, Pencil Sharpener, Prairie, Preference, Promotion, Receipt, Relationship, Road, Roofing, Score, Sentence, Service, Settlement, Sink, Speech, Sponsorship, Supply, Touchdown, Trash, Treatment, Trip, Valley, Vote, Yard.

REFERENCES

Appel, René and Pieter Muysken. 1987. Language Contact and Bilingualism. London: Arnold.

Augst, Gerhard. 1973. Duden Grammatik. Mannheim: Duden.

_____. 1975. Untersuchungen zum Morpheminventar der deutschen Gegenwartssprache. Tübingen: Gunter Narr.

de Bleser, Ria & Josef Bayer. 1988. On the role of inflectional morphology in agrammatism. M. Hammond & M. Noonan (eds), Theoretical Morphology: Approaches in Modern Linguistics. New York: Academic Press. 45-70.

Bybee, Joan. 1988. Morphology as lexical organization. M. Hammond & M. Noonan (eds), Theoretical Morphology: Approaches in Modern Linguistics. New York: Academic Press. 119-142.

Carstensen, Broder. 1980. Das Genus englischer Fremd- und Lehnwörter im Deutschen. Wolfgang Viereck (ed), Studien zum Einfluß der englischen Sprache auf das Deutsche. Tübingen: Niemeyer. 37-75.

Clyne, Michael. 1969. Inhalt, Klangassoziation und Genus in der deutschen Sprache bei Ein- und Zweisprachigen. Zeitschrift für Phonetik, Sprachwissenschaft und Kommunikation 22. 218-224.

Corbett, Greville G. 1986. Gender in German: A Bibliography. Linguistische Berichte 103. 820-286.

Fleischer, Wolfgang. 1975. Wortbildung der deutschen Gegenwartssprache. Tübingen: Niemeyer.

Grebe, Paul et al. 1973. Duden Grammatik der deutschen Gegenwartssprache. 3rd edition. Mannheim: Duden.

Gregor, Bernd. 1983. Genuszuordnung: Das Genus englischer Lehnwörter im Deutschen. Linguistische Arbeiten, 129. Niemeyer: Tübingen.

Hamers, Josiane F., and Michel H. A. Blanc. 1989. Bilinguality and Bilingualism. Cambridge: Cambridge University Press.

Heath, Jeffrey. 1985. Discourse in the field: clause structure in Ngandi. Johanna Nichols and Anthony C. Woodbury (eds), Grammar inside and outside the clause: some approaches to theory from the field. Cambridge: Cambridge University Press. 89-112.

Ioup, Georgette, and Steven H. Weinberger, eds. 1987. Interlanguage Phonology: The Acquisition of a Second Language Sound System. Cambridge, MA: Newbury House.

Köpcke, Klaus-Michael. 1982. Untersuchungen zum Genussystem der deutschen Gegenswartssprache. Tübingen: Niemeyer.

_____. 1989. Schemas in German plural formation. Lingua. 74. 303-335.

_____., & David Zubin. 1984. Sechs Prinzipien für die Genuszuweisung im Deutschen: Ein Beitrag zur natürlichen Klassifikation. Linguistische Berichte. 93. 26-50.

Lang, Adrianne. 1976. The semantic base of gender in German. Lingua. 40. 55-68.

Lapointe, Steven G. 1988. Toward a unified theory of agreement. Michael Barlow and Charles A. Ferguson (eds), Agreement in Natural Language: Approaches, Theories, Descriptions. Stanford, CA: CSLI. 67-87.

Maratsos, M.P 1979. Learning how and when to use pronouns and determiners. Language Acquisition: Studies in First Language Development, eds. P. Fletcher and M. Garman. Cambridge: Cambridge University Press. 225-240.

Mills, Anne E. 1986. The Acquisition of Gender: A study of English and German. Berlin: Springer.

Moehle-Vieregge, Linda. 1989. Jugendsprache 1979-1985: A definitive, descriptive and derivational analysis of a German sociolect. PhD dissertation, University of Texas at Austin.

Preston, Dennis R. 1989. Sociolinguistics and Second Language Acquisition. Oxford: Blackwell.

Rogers, Margaret. 1987. Learners' Difficulties with Grammatical Gender in German as a Foreign

Language. Applied Linguistics. 8 (1). 48-74.

Salmons, Joe. In press. Sources of Variation in German Gender Assignment. Current Issues in Germanic Linguistics, eds. J. Salmons & S. Hughes. Amsterdam: Benjamins.

_____. Manuscript. The Structure of the Lexicon: Evidence from German Gender Assignment.

Schlick, Werner. 1984. Die Kriterien für die deutsche Genuszuweisung bei substantivischen Anglizismen. The German Quarterly. 57(3). 402-431.

_____. 1985. Diese verflixte englische Geschlechtslosigkeit: Zur deutschen Genuszuweisung bei neueren Lehnsubstantiven aus dem Englischen. Muttersprache. 95 (3-4). 193-221.

Selinker, Larry. 1972. Interlanguage. International Review of Applied Linguistics. 10. 209-231.

Wilson, Charles Bundy. 1899-1900. The Grammatical Gender of English Words in German. Americana Germanica. 3. 265-233.

Zubin, David & Klaus-Michael Küpcke. 1984. Affect classification in the German gender system. Lingua. 63. 41-96.

_____. 1986. Gender and folk taxonomy: The indexical relation between grammatical and lexical categorization. Colette Craig (ed), Noun Classes and Categorization. Amsterdam: Benjamins. 139-180.

NOTES ON THE CONTRIBUTORS

Carol Aisha Blackshire-Belay is presently Research Associate Professor at Temple University in Philadelphia and is the Director of the International Afro-German Network. Widely recognized as one of the leading experts on minorities in contemporary German society, Dr. Blackshire-Belay has published in the *Journal of Black Studies, University of Pennsylvania Review of Linguistics, OSU Foreign Language Publications*, and *ERIC Resources In Education*. Included among her books are Language Contact: Verb Morphology in German of Foreign Workers, Foreign Workers' German: A Concise Glossary of Verbal Phrases, and Language and Literature in the African Imagination. Her major interests are cultural and linguistic diversity in society, in particular issues confronting Afro-Deutsche in Germany as well as on the continent of Africa, and the enormous impact of African culture on language and society. One of her major upcoming works is entitled The Germanic Mosaic: Cultural and Linguistic Diversity in Society.

Francis Byrne is currently Associate Professor of Linguistics at Shawnee State University in Portsmouth, Ohio. During his career, he has held positions at the Universidad de Oriente in Cumaná, Venezuela, and Howard University in Washington, D.C. Professor Byrne is currently the president of the Society for Pidgin and Creole Linguistics and the author of three books (Una Introducción a la lingüística general, Algunos aspectos del Saramacán, Grammatical relations in a radical creole), numerous articles in reputable journals, and has edited two volumes (Development and structures of creole language, The Atlantic meets the Pacific).

Elsa Lattey is presently a lecturer at the University of Tübingen in Germany where she specializes in second language acquisition, second language classroom research, and language teaching methodology. Dr. Lattey is one of the leading experts on theories and implications of first and second language acquisition research. German-English bilingual, Ph.D. in Linguistics at City University of New York in 1980. Dr. lattey has been concerned with the mating of languages and cultures since her childhood. She has been teaching linguistics and English in Tübingen since 1984, specializing in bilingualism and language contact, second language acquisition, sociolinguistics, as well as idiom usage and translation. Her publications include articles in the above fields, and two workbooks on English idioms (Hieke, A. E. & E. Lattey Using Idioms: Situations - bezogen Redensarten; and Lattey, E. & A. E. Hieke Using Idioms in Situational Contexts.

Yoshiko Matsumoto is currently Assistant Professor of Japanese Linguistics at Stanford University. Her research interests are in pragmatics and discourse analysis.

Terence Odlin is Associate Professor of English at The Ohio State University. His current research focuses on the influences of Gaelic on the English of Ireland and Scotland.

Hanna Pishwa is presently a research scholar at the Technical University in Berlin involved in an interdisciplinary project where she provides psychologists with linguistic devices for text interpretation as well as conduct research on mental verbs. Dr. Pishwa taught languages in Stockholm in grades 9 to 12 which stimulated her interest in more detailed knowledge about language acquisition. This resulted in a longitudinal study of the acquisition of German by fifteen Swedish school children. The topic of her dissertation was The Acquisition of the German Agreement Rule.

Robin Sabino is currently Assistant Professor of English at Auburn University. She has written articles and presented papers on the topic on phonological aspects of the Dutch creole.

Joe Salmons is Associate Professor of German and Linguistics at Purdue University. He has written numerous articles and chapters in books in both of these areas. Professor Salmons is the author of the book entitled German Like We Talk it Here: A Sociolinguistic History of German and German Speakers in Texas. Among his forthcoming books are The Glottalic Theory: Survey and Synthesis, and Accentual Change and Language Contact: comparative Survey and Case Study of Early Northern Europe.

Ulrich Steinmüller is Professor at the Institute of Didactics for German and Foreign Languages at the Technical University of Berlin. Dr. Steinmüller has published numerous articles and books on the subject of second language learning and bilingualism of the second generation of the foreign worker population in Germany.

Copyright © 1994 by
University Press of America®, Inc.
4720 Boston Way
Lanham, Maryland 20706

3 Henrietta Street
London WC2E 8LU England

Library of Congress Cataloging-in-Publication Data

Current issues in second language acquisition and development /
edited by Carol A. Blackshire-Belay.
p.   cm.
Includes bibliographical references.
1. Second language acquisition.   I. Blackshire-Belay, Carol.
P118.2.C86   1993   418—dc20   93–11718 CIP

ISBN 0–8191–9181–7 (cloth : alk. paper)
ISBN 0–8191–9182–5 (pbk. : alk. paper)

CURRENT ISSUES IN SECOND LANGUAGE ACQUISITION AND DEVELOPMENT

Edited by

Carol A. Blackshire-Belay

UNIVERSITY
PRESS OF
AMERICA

Lanham • New York • London